CHATEAU Monty

Monty Waldin

CHATEAU Monty

Monty Waldin

PORTICO

First published in the United Kingdom in 2008 by
Portico Books
10 Southcombe Street
London
W14 0RA

An imprint of Anova Books Company Ltd

ISBN 9781906032289

Illustrations by Lotte Oldfield (www.lotteoldfield.com)

A CIP catalogue record for this book is available from the British Library.

10 9 8 7 6 5 4 3 2 1

Printed and bound in the UK by CPI Mackays, Chatham, ME5 8TD

This book can be ordered direct from the publisher.
Contact the marketing department, but try your bookshop first.

www.anovabooks.com
www.tigeraspect.co.uk

AN IMG ENTERTAINMENT COMPANY

Mixed Sources
Product group from well-managed forests and other controlled sources
www.fsc.org Cert no. TT-COC-002341
© 1996 Forest Stewardship Council

To the villagers of St-Martin-de-Fenouillet
& Bill Baker (1954–2008)

MONTY'S

FRENCH RED

2007

BIODYNAMICALLY
GROWN

CERTIFIED ORGANIC

Vin de Pays des Côtes Catalanes

80% CARIGNAN + 20% SYRAH,
GRENACHE & MACCABEU GRAPES

VEGAN SUITABLE

Prologue

O N ANY NORMAL SUMMER DAY MY JOURNEY TO PERPIGNAN, CAPITAL city of France's Roussillon region, and home of a potential supplier of certified organic feed for my flock of laying hens and goslings, would have been an easy enough two-to-three hour round trip. I say 'easy enough'. Any road trip in these parts was potentially hazardous. The initial stretch of the journey to Perpignan between my rented house in the mountainous village of St-Martin-de-Fenouillet and the small town of St-Paul-de-Fenouillet, 20 minutes drive away on the valley floor, was a predictably narrow, winding and bumpily steep descent.

Then there was my vehicle, a 1976 Renault Estafette, described officially as a van but actually more of a small truck. Excess speed wasn't the main danger: the van had a pitifully slow top speed, downhill and with the proverbial following wind, of 60 km per hour. No, I was more worried about her creaking wheels, dodgy brakes and suspiciously flimsy suspension. They'd stand no chance against any of the large stones that continually found their way onto the road. These sharp lumps of granite, showing fewer obvious signs of weathering than the van despite being at least 500 million years older, would have been kicked there by the wild boar on their nocturnal slides across the dry-stone walls skirting the road. The walls, built originally to stop the forest from over-running the road, were in various states of boar-induced disrepair, and were likely to remain so in Roussillon, which was France's least wealthy agricultural region.

Reconstruction was too painstaking and costly in terms of labour, time and money for locals who were having enough trouble making ends meet as farmers or winegrowers (or both), with winegrowers especially hard hit. Even though more wine was being drunk worldwide than ever before there was a global wine glut and French wine exports were in meltdown, due to inconsistent quality, inflexible prices and confusingly elitist French-only labels. Even the French themselves were drinking less of their own wine than ever before, and their supermarkets had even started stocking Chilean and Australian wines.

The boar, however were thriving, and the forest was their preferred home, offering near-impenetrable cover from humans and other predators, and plenty of food in the form of acorns from the ever-present, evergreen Holm or Mediterranean oaks (*Quercus ilex*). At night or when acorns were in short supply the boar would tramp their brittle hooves through the forest, scrabble down the dry-stone walls and cross the road to reach the hay fields or vineyards, in search of roots, worms and, come autumn, ripening wine grapes. Was I worried about hitting a boar? The front of the van was high enough off the ground to mean that in any collision with a wild boar – most likely at dusk around full moon if the wind had dropped, boar being averse to high winds – the van was more likely to survive than the boar. Instead, the collision I feared most was with another vehicle, specifically the local taxis, which in rural France usually doubled up as ambulances and which speeded recklessly whether a healthy fare-paying passenger, an injured case for accident and emergency, or (most likely, this being demographically the oldest part of France) a dead body was aboard.

The Estafette was integral to my new life as a farmer-winegrower, despite its limitations and the self-imposed oath I had taken after selling my second car in 1993 that I'd never buy another one ('too many cars already in the world'). I just couldn't turn down the lure of the Estafette, if lure is the correct word for a barely roadworthy rust bucket.

The van had been used for years by the village's employee-come-handyman, Philippe, whose tasks included collecting and dumping household rubbish once a week, carrying a box-like water tank in summer to prevent flowers in the municipal pots and beds from wilting and keeping the village street lights, drains, ditches and other amenities in working order. New European Union rules governing insurance for municipal workers like Philippe had meant that it was more cost-effective for St-Martin's villagers to invest in a new van than risk a hefty pay-out in the event of an accident. A vote was taken by the mayoral committee to sell me the van for one symbolic euro, as a way of welcoming me to the village and getting a potential liability off their hands. I tried vainly to imagine the walnut-faced councillors of an English town in the Home Counties making such a generous, friendly and imaginative gesture to a young Frenchman starting say an organic pork pie and pickle business there.

The Estafette was particularly alluring because on the most basic level she was my passport to the relative civilization of St-Paul, which had all the things St-Martin lacked: a small supermarket, newsagent, several cafés, bakers and butchers, banks with hole-in-the-wall cash dispensers and a post office, albeit the slowest one in the northern hemisphere. True, the village of St-Martin did have its *auberge*, named after the local ruined Taïchac castle, with bar and restaurant, but there was no way I could afford to eat there every day, although its selection of locally produced beer and organic lemonade was proving expensively hard to resist. And yes, both a general supplies van and a bread van came at least once a week, hooting their horns furiously on the way in to draw many of St-Martin's forty inhabitants into its main square in a feeding frenzy not dissimilar to that created by the clang of my metal feed bucket at the door of the hen house each morning, my preferred form of avian reveille.

But, my (purposefully short) hours of work and (agreeably lengthy) breaks for siestas were so irregular and chaotic that I'd often miss both the supply vans and the set meal-times at the Auberge Taïchac. And anyway I wanted to make the odd trip to St-Paul because it had essentials like organic coffee and today's English newspaper (printed that very morning in France) that neither St-Martin's Auberge Taïchac nor its supply vans could provide.

The main reason for having the van, though, was purely practical: managing my newly rented, certified organic but biodynamically farmed vineyard would be impossible without it, in such isolated terrain and on such a limited budget. The van's main task was to get me and my vineyard kit up to and around my new vineyard, at around 500 metres it was one of the highest mountain vineyards in this part of France. The cream-coloured cab may have only held the driver and one passenger, making it useless for sightseeing trips with family and friends, but it was entirely suited to Harry, my Jack Russell terrier, whose tendency to dribble with excitement whenever we went for a drive posed no meaningful threat to the van's decaying interior upholstery. The back of the van, meanwhile, was low enough to the ground for easy loading. Items could be slid on since I'd removed the original fold-down back-door flap before it had slipped its rusted hinges. At over two-metres long and roofless the back of the van could take any amount of awkward or tall items like vine posts, grape-picking crates at harvest-time, or shovelfuls of organic compost in autumn.

When mayor André Foulquier signed the van over to me he was up-front enough to warn me she needed a bit of maintenance – bald tyres replacing, suspension checking, broken head lights mending – to get through France's biennial road-worthiness test, or *contrôle technique*. The mayor was kind enough to make sure Philippe gave me a crash course on its workings, too. Car engines have never been my thing – I failed to work out how to change even a spark plug during a 'motor maintenance' course I did at secondary school – and when I tried to launch myself into the Estafette's cab head rather than feet first Philippe must have wondered what on earth his mayoral boss was doing sending him such a mechanically inept foreigner as me. Luckily Philippe never saw my first run-out: I almost drove straight through the Auberge Taïchac, having got first and reverse gears muddled – easy to do on an old-style, back-to-front stick shift gearbox.

'She leaks a bit of oil, so check that at least once a week, or if you are going any kind of distance.'

'Like, how far?'

'Oh, more than 40 km I'd say…' That was about as far as Perpignan, one way.

'I've left you some engine oil in the cab, plus some liquid lead substitute for when you fill her up with unleaded – 95 octane is best – and you'd be crazy not to carry plenty of water around with you.'

'Right. In case I break down and it's hot.'

'What?'

'You know, if I get stuck and start to dehydrate.'

'Yes,' said Philippe, restraining himself. 'But I was thinking more of the engine. She gets through quite a bit of water anyway as she is old, even more so since there is a water leak, too, probably a washer somewhere behind the engine that needs tightening and that's impossible to get to. Unless you've the time and money to take her to bits. So keep her well topped up, otherwise she'll blow.'

'Blow?'

'Blow. As in blow up. Die. *La fin des haricots* ['the end of the beans']. But if you remember what I told you, don't thrash the engine over 60 km and keep her well juiced, you couldn't wish for a more perfect runner.' Albeit a runner with a marathon streak in terms of water intake rather than potential for distance covered.

Such mechanically challenging thoughts were entirely absent as I swivelled the van through the hairpin at the first mountain pass between St-Martin and St-Paul. This was the point where the road's black, blistered course doubled back on itself to surge down across 'mad man's bridge', sited over the Agly river in a fault-line in the mountain, a space like a decayed cavity in a mountain range shaped like a gum-shield. Turning into this hairpin in summer filled the van's airless cab with the heat of the Marin wind, sucked through gaps in the mountains at high speed by air rising off the Mediterranean, just 40 km to the east.

I tried freewheeling down here in neutral once when the van appeared to be almost out of fuel, but the wind effortlessly pushed the van's flat snout and Noddy-style headlamps back up the mountain so I had to put her in gear. The incomprehension on my face matched the despair on the faces of the tourists riding touring bicycles alongside me as they realised that on this particular mountain one had to pedal as hard down as up it.

The Agly flows into the Mediterranean just north of Perpignan, although you'd never know this in summer when both sea and city are usually concealed under a metallic cloak of pollution haze. You cross the Agly a second time at Estagel, less famed as a wine town than either Maury to the west, which makes port-style reds from Grenache grapes growing on imposing slabs of dark schist, or Rivesaltes to the east, which makes port-style whites from Muscat grapes grown on scrabbly, often chestnut-coloured pebbles. Perhaps it would be more accurate to say that Estagel is less 'infamous' than either Maury or Rivesaltes. Both historically made old-fashioned, high-alcohol (15.5% plus), high-sugar wines that fell out of favour with modern health- and diet-conscious drinkers, and were considered symbols of just how far off the pace Roussillon had become wine-wise. But, that's what had attracted me to the region: its potential for normal – or non-port style – wines was undervalued. Especially if you escaped the hot valley floor where the grapes ripened too quickly and with too much alcohol and headed instead to the mountains where cooling breezes allowed the grapes to ripen slowly enough to retain all the mineral flavours contained in some of Planet Wine's most geologically complex soils.

It wasn't just ripening grapes that needed to slow down in

Estagel, the cars did too – town buildings squeezed the main road to near single-file – but once I rejoined the open road again I knew my limited top speed meant that camper vans, overtaking me with a high-octane mixture of impatience and nervousness, their Dutch or north German number plates jittering in the cross-winds, bound for mid-summer breaks on the Costa Brava, Barcelona and points south, were more menacing than the police speed-traps, often ingeniously disguised in roadside groves of olives, juniper, cherry, or oak.

The last big obstacle into Perpignan for slow-motion Estafette drivers like me was the frantic, double-lane roundabout sandwiched between the Barcelona – Perpignan motorway on one side and the airport on the other. The short slice of dual carriageway that runs between the roundabout and the centre of Perpignan was inevitably clogged with traffic. The Estafette had one of those whirring engines that preferred working to idling, especially when the summer heat was already extreme enough to be re-melting the tar on the recently resurfaced road. I tried vainly to remember the last time I had followed Philippe's warning about replenishing the water seeping out of the Estafette's cooling system. By the time I had inched my way into the centre of Perpignan, the Estafette was steaming noisily and visibly enough for pedestrians to have begun waving at me to get out for my own safety.

I cursed my lackadaiscal attitude – it had probably been nearly a month since I had last topped up the Estafette. But, cursing myself simply augmented my stubbornness (a kind of impossible/self-perpetuating reverse logic), I was damned if I was going to abandon the van for three compelling reasons. Number one, I was English (with a large dose of Yorkshire) and

Englishmen simply just don't walk away from a crisis – we revel in them. Second, the line of traffic behind me was substantial and I was potentially blocking not only the main road linking Perpignan and the motorway but the road linking the railway station and the main shopping district. It was Friday afternoon rush hour, after all. Third, in the rear-view mirror I could see a police car.

It was about 50 metres back but in an adjacent lane controlled by a different set of lights to the ones I was prisoner to, and contained what I was sure were the same two officers who had stopped me in Perpignan about ten days before for failing to display a rear number plate. This was supposed to be attached to the rear door but wasn't because the rear door was no longer attached to the van. The Estafette had barely escaped being impounded on the spot. Having stopped me and checked the van was insured the policeman's first words were, 'Good afternoon, sir. I am sure you know it's against road-traffic laws to fail to display a rear number plate. This leaves you with two options. Option number one is a 90 euro on-the-spot fine and the car gets impounded until you get it fixed. Option number two is I caution you and let you go on your way.'

I made sure I looked like I was listening intently.

'Unfortunately, option number two isn't available today...'

In fact, he got his pocket book out immediately, asked me if I had money on me to pay the fine (I did, the cash originally destined for the chicken coop) and told me my car was going to be seized. I'd gambled that passive compliance was my best bet, allied to some time wasting. I made sure that I fumbled around as long as humanly possible with the paper part of my driving licence, offering to help him note down the long number as I held it higher than normal to make it flap uncontrollably in one of Perpignan's typically strong cross-winds. I had pleaded that I was making the journey to Perpignan purely on animal rights and environmental grounds – my chickens were arriving in two days time and were integral to the success of my organic vineyard (egg shells are a great anti-radioactive aid when added to soil compost), and that with no hen house to live in a fox-inspired massacre of biblical proportions was inevitable. I explained that I'd removed the rear door (and thus number plate) for good reason – it was about to fall off and cause a traffic accident (true). I forgot to mention that the prime reason was to make loading the chicken coop easier. I padded out my somewhat slim defence by saying that the number plate was due to be welded to the nearside rear bumper the very next morning first thing by a Monsieur da Silva at the Peugeot garage in St-Paul (also true), adding 'that his workshop is just up from the supermarket', thinking any splash of local colour could only augment the verisimilitude of the case I was building.

My final flourish to the uniformed jury of two was that as I had no mobile phone either of the policemen (my money was on 'Officer Nice' rather than 'Officer Nasty') could call da Silva's garage for themselves to see if my story stacked up without me first tipping the mechanic off to fake an appointment. I now realised that what had seemingly charmed the police – the contradiction of a smartly dressed (dress shirt, not T-shirt), well-travelled young man (speaking good enough French to crack an ice-breaking joke or two) driving a motorised scrapheap with no mobile phone – would now be grounds for a financial flogging should I abandon ship. Today, they could have me for driving a sub-standard vehicle: the brakes would never pass muster and I knew the 'I am getting them fixed' get-out-of-jail card had already been used for its only time. They could have me for the rear near-side brake light, broken two days previously by a neighbour reversing his ATV into it while on the way to feed his donkeys. They could have me for the rear number plate, safely welded to the rear bumper but illegally so because the little light needed to illuminate it for night driving was still in Mr da Silva's workshop. I hadn't let him finish the job because I had needed the van to get my newly housed chickens and geese some food. And, I was fully aware that avian safety was going to take a poor second to road safety if the cops caught up with me this time. They'd throw the book at me anyway for obstructing the public highway; and extra hard given that they'd told me I was in the last chance saloon after my previous transgression.

The combination of the car dying on me and possible arrest made me realise how deeply I was foundering on that uneasy middle ground between totally abandoning or shunning mod-cons like cars and mobile phones but still being prepared to use them when it mattered. If I couldn't get back home soon because I was either under arrest, stranded or both, the free-range geese would be easy meat for the fox, the chickens would watch the geese's murder while dying in their enclosed pen from thirst or starvation, and Harry's bursting bowel-and-bladder combo would prompt him to bark long and loud enough for my non-dog-friendly neighbour to consider his own suicide or canine murder but not necessarily in that order (I left my house unlocked and the neighbour knew it).

I clicked the Estafette's long, thin gear stick into first,

waited for the lights to change from red to green – no amber in France – and as I lifted first the handbrake and then the clutch her overheated valves, pipes and pistons whistled in noisy protest. I was sure that if I could just get off this box junction to the cool ground-level calm of the multi-storey car park on Perpignan's Place Arago just 50 metres away, at least I or Patrick da Silva would be able to take stock of the engine, or what was left of it anyway, in both safety and shade – and away from the police who were now just two car length's away from being bang alongside me and my steaming van.

And they were closing fast.

Chapter 1

MY FIRST ATTEMPT AT MAKING WINE WAS AS A TEENAGER WHEN my father's cousin, a GP called Andrew, showed me his home-winemaking kit and explained how he made wine from things like elderflowers, blackcurrants and plums. There was something of a self-sufficiency boom in the UK in the late 1970s and early 1980s and kits like this bought from high-street pharmacies like Boots the chemist were increasingly popular. Andrew, in common with many others, had been inspired by a BBC TV sitcom first screened in 1976 called *The Good Life*, in which a down-to-earth couple called Tom and Barbara Good decide to leave the rat-race when Tom hits forty. They convert their house and garden in deepest suburbia to self-sufficiency, much to the bemusement and chagrin of Jerry and Margo, their upper-crust neighbours, who watch as Tom and Barbara try producing methane from their pigs, Pinky and Perky, and use their vegetable patch to make a wine called 'Peapod Burgundy'. No sooner had we watched Tom and Barbara dig up their TV lawn, than my newly retired dad had dug up the long, Edwardian-style back garden of our home and converted it to vegetables. We didn't get any pigs but there was room for a large chicken coop filled by Rhode Island Red chickens and bantam hens.

My contribution to our self-sufficient urge was to make some wine using the ingredients recommended by my home-winemaking kit: sugar, yeast, water and fruit. The only fruit to hand was cooking apples from several trees in the back garden and these were usually reserved for an acidic tasting apple and rhubarb pudding. Rather than making my first-ever wine from home-grown fruit I opted for a stretchy net bag of supermarket oranges. I asked my dad for some old bottles which I cleaned with boiling water and then sterilised with Camden tablets as cousin Andrew had directed. One afternoon in my putative winery – the conservatory attached to the back of the house – Andrew explained to me that what I had learnt in Bible-speak as 'new wine' really meant one that was newly fermented and still bubbling because it was fermenting and producing gas. This made the bottle explode if it was sealed tight before the fermentation had ended. 'That's why you close the bottle neck with a cork punctured by a U-shaped tube filled with water but open at both the top and bottom ends,' said Andrew, producing an example from one of his trouser pockets. 'This allows the fermentation gas to escape safely upwards while preventing tiny vinegar flies from attacking the wine and turning it to vinegar.'

'I feel like writing to the editors of the Bible to tell them they should change the bit about "never putting new wine into old bottles" to "never putting new wine into fully sealed bottles",' I said, but Andrew pointed out that 'the people who edited the Bible would most probably all be dead'.

Instead of writing to the Bible's editors I directed my energies into winemaking and not entirely diligently. Despite Andrew's firm advice about getting precisely the right ratio of sugar to yeast in the mix, I was far too blasé. I had imagined making wine with a powerfully, sweet raisiny taste and tongue-caressing texture like I remembered from the odd sip of imitation Cyprus 'sherry' (the real stuff now legally comes only from southwest Spain) my parents had allowed me to take from one of a series of decanters on the mantelpiece. They used to drink it from tumblers that were so thin I couldn't get my big nose in fully enough to smell what I was drinking. As for my first wine, because I had put too much sugar in my orange concentrate and too little yeast, whose job it is to eat the sugar, digest it and produce alcohol at the other end, my wine was a disgustingly sweet, vomit-coloured concoction with an odd, slimy texture. Not particularly alcoholic, it was barely even wine. Even I had to admit that the 'orange cream' fillings in chocolates given by the Church congregation to my dad every Christmas for his organ playing, that were so artificially bright as to almost glow-in-the-dark, tasted better than my first wine.

I knew after my teenage orange-wine disaster that I'd never be satisfied unless one day I could make proper wine. And by proper wine I don't mean wine made from supermarket citrus fruit, or from wild berries, hedgerow flowers like cousin Andrew, or from home-grown peapods like Tom and Barbara Good, or even wine made from table grapes. I meant wine made from the sweetest grapes of all, those that only grow on one type of vine, the wine-grape vine or *Vitis vinifera*. But, it's not every day you can just add 'my own wine-grape vineyard' to the more usual items on the day's shopping list like loo-roll, toothpaste and bread and still retain enough sense of realism that for once you'll arrive home with exactly what you wanted. Yet, I had to find a way. Just as my soccer-mad mates still expect to be called onto the pitch from the stands when their local team suffer a run of bad injuries to key players, and friends in the film industry still hanker for the starring role in their own movie, the desire to make my own wine had become not just a craving but a visceral need, one I was finding harder to control the older I got. The need was all the more acute since I had ended up becoming a professional wine taster and wine writer. This meant I was surrounded by wine, albeit other people's wine. As I entered my second decade of tasting and writing articles and books about the stuff, wine had become to me like farts and small children: tolerable only as long as they are your own.

My fortieth birthday and its trusty travelling companion, the mid-life crisis, were heading inexorably my way. What had I done with my time? Could I have used it better? Was I happy with what I was doing? Where had all the time gone? Why did time go so much quicker now than when I was in my twenties? Why didn't time just stop long enough for me to take stock? What did my balance sheet say about me? I was a freelancer who didn't have a regular job or a regular income. I'd written five wine books but, despite winning a few awards for them, had never seen the return I had hoped for. Of all my peers I seemed to be the only one that was neither married nor a father, which suggested I was either unable or unwilling to handle responsibility. Either I had failed to settle down because I was worried that travelling the world in search of the next big wine story would mean I'd never be at the school gates to collect the kids and supervise their homework, and thus would spawn a family of illiterates, or I was using the travelling as the perfect excuse to avoid settling down. The umpire's decision, I felt, could go either way.

I brought up the subject with Andrew, one of my best mates, when I went to stay with him and his wife Emma. The last time I'd really had a heart-to-heart with them was years ago, before they were married or had kids. They'd been living in a tiny box house in a grim city suburb. Now they were living in a medieval country farmhouse in the West Country with open wooden beams, a log fire, a vegetable patch and two adorable daughters. I, meanwhile, hadn't seemed to have moved on at all.

'Mont, your lifestyle of constant travel and never knowing where you're going to be from one day to the next is the perfect recipe for staying single,' Andrew said, over a wine-filled dinner. 'Once you get to our age the nesting instinct kicks in. You may well find a girl who loves the idea of not seeing you for days, weeks, or months on end and not even knowing where you are, but I seriously doubt it.' Emma was nodding her agreement. 'We tried to call you earlier this year to invite you down for the weekend and took ages to find out you were actually in Bolivia. You don't even have a mobile phone,' she said. 'Women are attracted to free spirits, but only up to a point. And, because you don't earn much money as a writer you have the added handicap of still having to live with your family. You're just not seen as a safe bet, that's all.'

'Mont, sometimes mate you've just got to go for it,' Andrew continued. 'You can't say you'll have a family when you get the vineyard or get the vineyard when you have a family. It doesn't work like that. Are you going to come back to see me and Emma in another ten years' time when you're 50 with your dreams still unfulfilled? You think too much. Relax. Just go with the flow. And anyway, what exactly are you waiting for?'

I decided to call my book publisher, Hilary Lumsden, for a summit meeting. We arranged to meet over a coffee on a sunny afternoon in an Italian-owned *caffè* in Covent Garden in London, surrounded by tourists, almost all of whom appeared to be wearing the latest fashion, Birkenstock sandals. Outwardly, the tourists seemed utterly carefree. Anyone looking at me would have said the same. Inwardly, however, I still felt the same as I did ten, even 20, years before, that if what I was doing was not leading me to where I wanted to be, I had to do something else. With Andrew and Emma's words ringing in my ears I felt I had come to a dead-end. 'I've said all I had to say as a wine writer, Hils.' I'd just spent the best part of two years writing a 500-pager, and mentally I was shot. Hils knew my latest, and very much adored, French girlfriend had just left me because I was too committed to my work rather than to her. 'My work – life balance isn't healthy, and writing's not what I want to do anymore. I've studied wine, sold wine and worked with people who've grown and made wine. If I really want to express my thoughts about wine, then I'll just have to make my own. It's the only choice I feel I have left.'

Hils, who was well used to dealing with crotchety authors, took my self-pitying whinge in her stride. 'For heaven's sake Mont, don't give the writing up,' she soothed, in her soft Scottish accent. 'You spent ages getting this far as a writer. Your commitment to wine really comes through in your books and people in the trade are starting to take you seriously. And, anyway, while you're single there's nothing to stop you going off to say Bordeaux and Tuscany to write a couple of wine-travel guides I've got planned for you. Maybe this time you'll find a place you can live your dream and make wine too. After all, you'll meet loads of winegrowers' daughters on your travels.' I gave Hils a big hug and walked to Covent Garden tube. I had a return tube ticket. I threw it in the bin. I walked to Piccadilly Circus and took the bus home instead. I wanted to see the view, to see where I was going for a change. I needed to use my eyes, feel my surroundings more. I had decided to stop watching life from the sidelines, burying myself away like a mole. I was going to use the advance money and travel opportunities I'd get from writing Hilary's travel guides over the next year or so to find, finally, a place where I could make my own wine. If I didn't make a change now, I felt I never would.

Before heading off to Tuscany I accepted an invitation to judge the Organic Wine of the Year Award, organized by the national *Mail on Sunday* newspaper and hosted by the Soil Association, the UK's oldest and biggest organic farming organization, near their headquarters in Bristol. One of my fellow judges was Bill Baker, the Falstaffian owner/proprietor of a highly regarded wholesale wine company called Reid Wines, based near Bristol. Bill was particularly irked by the poor quality of many of the 150 or so organic wines we tasted blind that day. His assessment that it was a wasted day was one I agreed with. When Bill heard of my plans not just to make a wine, but to do it partly by tapping into cosmic energies for healthier vines in an off-shoot of organics known as biodynamics, he roared with laughter, saying he thought the whole thing sounded 'completely barking mad. Load of nonsense. Organic wine – pah! Frankly, you know, you might just as well throw your money away.' Organic wine had a deservedly bad reputation in the wine-trade circles that Bill moved in. The general feeling seemed to be that although there appeared to be some great organic grapes being grown too many were spoilt by earnest hippy types whose apparent lack of personal hygiene mirrored their lack of winery hygiene. For many traditionalists, organic wine came to signify wine with a body odour problem. This made the wines unsaleable in today's cutthroat wine business where clean, zingy, fruity wines were all the fashion.

In Bristol, I had also noticed that all of the wine judges were extra critical of wines *because* they were organic. The attitude seemed to be that as organic winegrowers were so holier-than-thou about avoiding weed-killers and pesticides they should have no excuse not to make stand-out wines, year in, year out. Anyone who knows anything about agriculture in general or winegrowing in particular can tell you that where nature is concerned it is impossible to produce miracles every year. Nonetheless, this was what was expected of organics. Making my own wine was going to be hard enough – did I really want to make it even harder by taking the organic route? It was clear that the only way I was ever going to convince trade buyers like Bill Baker to list my wine was if it was seen as offering good value for money. Bill didn't care about the wine being organic, biodynamic, cosmic, or even hallucinogenic. He just wanted good wine, full stop. Why didn't I just use my long list of trade contacts as a wine writer to sell my wine? At least they'd automatically give me face time if I dropped in with my sales pitch, whereas if I turned up as Mr Organic it seemed I risked putting people off without even being able to get my foot in the door. It made sense at least to sound out those in the UK wine trade who specialised in wines produced from organic grapes.

The UK's two main shippers of organic wine are Vinceremos based in Leeds and Vintage Roots based near Reading in Berkshire. I bumped into the buyer for Vinceremos, Jem Gardener, at an organic open day (again hosted by the Soil Association) after giving a lecture on organic wine. Jem became involved in organics by retailing wholefoods; he then ran the Wharf Street Café in Leeds, which sold vegetarian, wholefood and organic dishes; and eventually bought an organic-wine-import business. Jem is one of the most self-effacing people you're likely to meet, but his business knowledge is daunting. I knew Jem was a vegetarian, and I knew that making wines suitable for vegetarians could be difficult, and making wines suitable for vegans was potentially even trickier. I knew that most wine drinkers thought – wrongly – that if a wine was labelled as organic it was automatically suitable for vegetarians and vegans. Appropriately, Jem and I were standing next to the veg stall and not the organic meat stall when I asked him whether it would make a difference if my wine was suitable for vegan and vegetarian wine drinkers.

'Sales of two organic wines of comparable styles and price points are 20 to 50 per cent less respectively if the wine is not vegan or vegetarian suitable, because wholefood stores, for instance, want their entire range to be vegan or vegetarian suitable. It makes life easier for them in terms of promotion,' Jem informed me. In other words, if my organic wine was not suitable for vegan and vegetarian wine drinkers Jem would be less likely to list it at Vinceremos simply because he'd be less likely to sell it to his clients. And, making the wine vegan and vegetarian suitable could end up costing me more as the wine producer if, say, it was a bad year and I'd picked the grapes earlier than planned to escape bad weather. The wine would taste a little bitter as a result. And the easiest way of removing bitterness in red wine is by chucking in things like egg white, milk, or animal gelatin that render the wine unsuitable for vegetarians and vegans. 'Let me know how it goes anyway,' said Jem as he wandered off across the hall towards the stand where he was promoting the Vinceremos organic wine range for the day. I wasn't confident my wine would ever end up there.

In fact, I wasn't confident my wine would end up anywhere. The main topic of conversation among the producers I was interviewing for the Tuscan and Bordeaux travel guides was the global wine crisis and news of wine's biggest-ever corporate mergers. These showed the big boys felt the best way of surviving a global downturn was by getting even bigger. This meant margins were being squeezed ever tighter for the small fry – potentially me – who remained. There wasn't a wine shop in the UK that wasn't running a promotion, the most common of which was the 'buy-one-get-one-free' or 'BOGOF'. The BOGOF had become something of a sacred cow for Tim Atkin, one of only 250-odd Masters of Wine (or MW) in the world. Tim's readably opinionated and informed column in the respected *Observer* Sunday newspaper had helped him win all the big wine-writing awards several times over. A few years before Tim had given me a huge break by hiring me to write a monthly organic wine column in a trade journal he'd taken over editing called *Harpers*. Tim saw the near-ubiquitous BOGOF as evidence that the wine world had gone mad in a fit of over-production. As European taxpayers handed out cash to the French, Spanish and Italians to rip up vineyards or distil wine in an effort to reduce the global wine lake, governments in places like Australia, Chile and New Zealand were falling over backwards to encourage more vineyard planting because wine earned lots of valuable foreign currency. Tim was as blunt with me on my new-found vocation as a winegrower as he had been as my editor at *Harpers*.

'I think it is a risky project, of course it is. Any project involving nature and farming, is risky... it could go disastrously wrong, it really could. There's a huge global surplus of wine at the moment. In fact, there has never in the history of wine been such a surplus of quality wine.' In other words: we don't need another wine brand to add to the millions that already exist, many of which are sold at huge discount, and even at a loss. The irony was that globally more wine was being drunk that at any time in history. The problem was that European winegrowers were still producing more wine than Europe – the world's main wine market – could drink; and non-European countries had planted so many new and heavily irrigated and thus over-productive vineyards that the world's wine surplus was at breaking point. It wasn't hard to see why, in Tim's words, I was 'facing an uphill task' to get my wine onto a wine supermarket shelf. Planet Wine was a buyer's, not seller's market. Even if he wasn't at all confident that my vineyard would be a financial success, Tim was gallant enough to add that in he'd 'really look forward' to tasting the wine. However, Tim receives thousands of bottles of wine every year, sent by wine producers hopeful of getting a good write-up. He had bottles of wine – some opened, some not – all over the floor of his kitchen, his bedroom, his living room, his dining room and even his bathroom. I could easily see my little offering getting missed.

Even though my dream of making a wine that would dazzle high-street wine buyers the length and breadth of the UK seemed rapidly to be diminishing into selling a few bottles here and there to mates as Christmas and birthday presents, I was determined to follow it through. After all, some of Britain's most successful traders – Tesco, WH Smith, Phillip Green – had started off by selling their wares from the back of a market stall or van, so why should I be any different? And I remembered the first time I proposed an organic-wine-book idea to an editor I was laughed off the phone and then a few years later the same editor had called begging I write an organic-wine book when the organic boom happened. Despite everything I had heard to the contrary, I was convinced there was a market for my organic wine. I just needed to find it.

Tim Atkin commissioned me to write an article for *Harpers* on an English winemaker called Robert 'Bertie' Eden who had a biggish winemaking operation in the Languedoc. While walking around one of Bertie's vineyards in the bright spring sunshine I asked him why, having travelled the world's wine regions, would he buy a vineyard in such a 'backward' region as the Languedoc – backward, in wine-speak, means a region producing mainly characterless bulk wines whose appeal lies in their ability to annihilate alcoholically rather than subtly stimulate you. Surely neighbouring Provence, whose sexy vineyards were often treated as second homes by their celebrity owners, was a more attractive bet?

Bertie said that Provence didn't offer value for money, 'because land is generally worth more as real estate than as planted vineyard. And, I am not looking to make large amounts of cheap, bulk wines from any old vineyard. I want to produce limited-release or small-production wines from select vine-yards, pruned to produce low yields for more complex flavours. To me the Languedoc was the most interesting and per square metre the cheapest place in the world to buy vines. The wine can legitimately call itself "made in France", which still has immense cachet, whatever the critics say. If you are looking to invest in vineyards you must be looking pretty long-term; and if you're looking long-term France is a pretty safe bet. I mean, the tracks and fields I walk across were first planted as vineyards by the Romans.' Bertie's thinking had the perfect logic. Where else would anyone want to make wine apart from France? Australia and New Zealand I considered just too far away from my homeland. South Africa was turning out some decent wines, but what had scared me off buying a vineyard there was the high crime rate. California was a great place to make organic wines, but I ruled it out for now because land, and land taxes, were so expensive. Chile was seriously tempting, offering as much potential as California for less than half the price, especially in southern regions like the Maule Valley which had some of Chile's oldest vineyards and best vineyard terrain. And, although Argentina was getting more expensive by the minute it was still relatively cheap and the dry climate made organics pretty easy. But I had seen with my own eyes how paying backhanders remained part of the business culture there which I don't like, and, besides, Argentina's wines tend to be too high in alcohol (at around 14–15% or more) for me to enjoy them every day for the rest of my life. I had the same feeling about much of Spain, too – great for soft, supple quaffers, not always great for the kind of wines I prefer that have a bit of backbone and zip about them.

This made me think that if crisp, lower alcohol wines were my thing then I should head to Germany. Some of my favourite wines, such as Rieslings from the Mosel region, are among the lowest alcohol wines in the world (at 6.5–8%). But, Germany's strength is her white wines and I was more attracted to making reds, initially at least. I was also unsure I'd be physically able to work in the vineyards along the Mosel or Rhine rivers, which are some of the steepest in the world. I also love drinking and visiting the port, sherry and Champagne regions. Beautiful areas, beautiful wines. However, to buy in to these regions requires very deep pockets. Vineyards are expensive – running into hundreds of thousands of pounds per hectare of prime Champagne vineyard – as are overheads. The wines are often made by pooling the wines from three or more different harvests, which means waiting several years before your first wines can be sold to start the long journey of repaying your initial investment. This is why most vineyards in these areas are owned either by huge corporations or are handed down by their family owners from one generation to the next.

My experience of writing the Tuscany wine-travel guide taught me that Italian bureaucracy was even worse than in France, and that many vineyards had over-inflated reputations and price-tags. Lots of Bordeaux grape varieties planted in places that were far too hot; lots of poor-quality vineyards containing the main Tuscan red grape Sangiovese. Italy was a good place for a holiday home with a pool shaded by olive and orange trees, but not the first place I'd buy a vineyard.

Reportedly, the Italian government was so concerned Tuscan wines were being boosted (illegally) by cheap wines from places like Sicily that it bought several nuclear resonance machines that could analyse wines to pinpoint exactly what part of Italy the wine came from. This kind of thing also happened in France. Lots of rich wine companies in Bordeaux had bought vineyards down by the Mediterranean, and the suspicion was that it wasn't just because the corporate owners fancied a spot of sunbathing. My journalisitic nose was fascinated and irked by that fact that illegal blending went on, as was proved by a steady stream of court cases in which the cellarmaster was usually hung out to dry by the winery's owners who could plead innocence while the cellarmaster received a fine, a sacking and a criminal conviction.

Now, however, my winegrowing urge has made me look at this issue another way: there has to be something intrinsically special about the wines from the south of France if wine producers from more famous wine regions have been prepared to run risks in using them for blending. And, I couldn't be the only dreamer who'd always wanted a vineyard with a view of the sea.

I'd heard a wine-merchant friend called Roy Richards had recently invested in Roussillon – an area whose wines had a reputation for being stuck in a stylistic time warp. It was a region I had visited a couple of times on press trips and was one of those regions worldwide I believed was seriously under-valued but could never imagine realising its potential. I'd first met Roy in the mid-1990s while working at a posh London wine merchants called Roberson. He'd dropped in, wearing a heavy tweed jacket, corduroy trousers and thick wool socks on a boiling summer's day, opened a number of bottles of wines he was trying to get us to stock and talked about them. He had a strong public-school accent, even quoting the odd Latin phrase, but was very down-to-earth. I was the only one of the shop's then three-person wine-buying team to stick my neck out unequivocally and say that the wines Roy had brought – all from the south of France – were better than the equivalents we had in stock. And that even though Roy's wines were marginally more expensive than what we had already in stock we should nevertheless be able to convince our shop customers these new wines were comparatively better value. During my visits to various winegrowers around the world I'd only ever bother asking who their shipper was in the UK if the wines were stand-out in quality. Quite a few had mentioned Richards' name.

I went to see Roy in his Lincolnshire office one day. The only males in the building were Roy, his small dog Boris and me. All of the half a dozen other staff were female. 'Better work ethic than men,' said Roy, 'and better to look at, too.' I asked him about his Roussillon project called 'Le Soula'. In between fielding phone calls from a land line and a mobile that he struggled at times to find on a Victorian writing desk covered by a paper trail of organised chaos, Roy said of Roussillon pretty much what Bertie Eden had said of Languedoc. 'In this part of France vineyards were cheap to buy, had been unfairly ignored historically but were potentially of absolute top quality. Plus, if you could get up into the hills, where it is cooler, you could make wines with real minerality, elegance and freshness.' Roy gave me the name of Jean Pla, a local middleman who helped those looking to buy vines in Roussillon. The first vineyard Jean took me to see was near Maury, the town where Jean ran a wine shop and export business and, with his wife Genévieve, a restaurant called Le Pichenouille. We left the main Maury – Perpignan road and bounced along a rough track surrounded by a landscape that could have been Martian had the large, hot stones the car was scuffing over been red/orange rather than black.

'The vines are wide-spaced to make tractor work easy,' said Jean, immediately into his sales pitch. 'These vines have been weed-killed but to be honest it is so hot here you don't get too many weed problems if you are thinking of going organic. The soil is typical for Maury, black schist, so you get plenty of reflected heat back onto the grapes at night. And, as the site is frost-free and the vines are mature you'll get a consistent and high yield of top quality grapes, year in year out.' This was the kind of detail bank managers thinking of handing out loans to first-time winegrowers (like me) love to hear. And the price was dirt cheap: just a few thousand euros per hectare, a tenth of what I'd pay for even an everyday Bordeaux vineyard, a fiftieth of what I'd pay in Champagne.

'Hang on,' I said, feeling the sweat starting to trickle down my back on what was only a mild spring Maury morning, 'that means that if the numbers you are giving me are correct, it's much cheaper to buy an existing Roussillon vineyard and in its prime producing years, than to buy bare land and plant one yourself.'

'Er, yes,' said Jean with a hint that I should 'stop stating the bleedin' obvious' in his voice. 'That's why so many outside investors are coming here to buy vineyards, avoiding the hassle of buying the baby vines, supporting posts and wires, the costs of keeping the weeds down when the vines are small and the three years you must wait before legally being allowed to make your first wine. Prices are still cheap, but they have doubled in the last three years.'

In other words, if I wanted to buy a vineyard here I should get a bloody move on. Jean lit another cigarette and wandered off to make a call on his mobile and as my eyes followed him I saw the vineyard, that was otherwise a clear bargain, had one major downside: a bloody great high-tension electricity pylon slap-bang across one edge of the vineyard. I explained to Jean that I was hoping to work my vines biodynamically which meant paying attention to lunar and planetary cycles. A power line running over the top of the vineyard would be the surest way to nullify any beneficial cosmic energies. Jean seemed to think I was looking a gift-horse in the mouth, but patiently took me to see another small Maury vineyard owned by an old grower who was taking his grapes to the local cooperative. 'This guy has a choice,' said Jean. 'He can either agree to pull up his vines and accept a fat cheque from the European Union as an incentive to reduce the European wine lake. Or he can take a much smaller cheque from you.'

'Well, isn't that a no-brainer?'

'Not really,' said Jean, a cigarette glued to his bottom lip, and a long trail of ash miraculously glued to the end of the cigarette, despite the wind from his car window being open to provide some airflow in what were now sweltering temperatures. 'It's his life's work. He'd be thrilled if a young guy like you took on his vines. He doesn't have any kids, you see. His vines are like, well... you know.' The old-boy's vines were near a river, which kind of ticked the mental box I had marked 'vineyard overlooking water', but it was so low down I was worried about flooding. And, lots of vines were missing because when they had died they had never been replaced, probably because the old man saw no point in spending money on vines he was either going to soon rip out or sell. Access to the vineyard was poor, too, along a precipitous, overgrown track that Jean could barely get his van along. And, anyway, I didn't want to make wine in Maury which was hot and was best for producing heavy, port-style reds that I couldn't see myself drinking every night and that were a tough sell anyway. More women than ever before were drinking red wine, but not red wines like Maury made.

After stopping in a local café for a chicken-liver salad accompanied by an unfinished glass of local red plonk, I then followed Jean in my hire car up into the hills, away from the valley floor, to the town of St Arnac to see yet another vineyard. At around 400 metres this had a great view, although the sea was hidden behind hills. But, the vineyard – separate plots of red and white grapes either side of the road – was near the loading area of the local quarry. This mined a kind of quartz rock and was the biggest employer in the area. I'd noticed a lot of dust on the road on the way up, and on the vines. Now I knew where it came from. Jean tugged on another cigarette and asked what I thought.

'It has potential. The price seems high though, especially since many of the posts need replacing. Ideally I'm looking for a vineyard where the vines are free-standing, like the first one we saw in Maury but without the electricity pylon. Or a dusty quarry near-by.' At least this quarry was part-powered by a huge wind turbine. Jean agreed the price of the vineyard was high and that the vendor was looking for a 'pigeon', someone with plenty of money and not much sense. He suggested that replacing the missing posts was not that big a deal, but conceded that replacing posts also meant the cross-wires would have to be restrung. 'You could try negotiating,' he suggested, but I'd made my mind up. No deal. From St Arnac it was a short drive along a forest track to St-Martin-de-Fenouillet to meet a winegrower called Eric Laguerre who Jean knew was renting some of his vineyards to Roy Richards' Le Soula, and who was possibly looking to rent out some more. Jean, who was more interested in selling vines than supervising rental deals did this as a favour to Eric and, having introduced us, disappeared, probably realising by now there were bigger fish to fry than me, although as he forced his huge frame into his small van he said, 'If you do ever make a wine, let me know. Maybe I can help you sell it…'

Laguerre was in his late thirties, was tall and fit, and had a Roman look and a long mane of Viking-style hair matted with tractor dust. I'd already been impressed by his red wines which had shown well in a blind tasting I'd been to a year before and which I'd written highly of in the 500-page book I had moaned about writing to my publisher Hilary. Eric invited me into his small winery in the village and let me taste his whole range of wines – oak and non-oak aged red, dry white and pink – and showed me around his vineyards in a old Toyota Land Cruiser built like a Second World War tank. Eric was used to being jolted around driving through his vines, and found it amusing that I should even try to take written notes as I was being hurled about the cab. 'Are you drawing a spider's web with your pen or trying to write some words down?' he laughed. 'My son can write more clearly than that with his crayons....' He told me that he'd taken on the family vineyards after his father died a few years before and had switched from conventional growing using weed-killers and fertilizers to organics. 'We don't really need chemical fungicides here as it's so windy or pesticides as it's too high up for most pests. The only downside is that grape yields per vine are low. Growers in Maury can produce three or four times as much wine per hectare of vines as you will here.' This didn't put me off. Low yields normally (not always) mean good wines, or at least wines with a bit of oomph about them, with deep, concentrated flavours. I asked about alcohol levels in the wines. 'It depends on what kind of grape you want to work with,' replied Eric, stroking wisps of dusty hair out of his eyes.

'Red, initially,' I replied. 'Red wines are easier to make. White can oxidise quickly if you make a mistake and it gets too hot in the cellar at harvest and, besides, people nowadays drink more red than white.'

'In red grapes I've got Syrah which I need and Grenache Noir which I need, plus a bit of Cabernet which I need for my top wine. Are you sure you're not interested in some Maccabeu?' This is one of the white grapes that goes into cava

(Spanish fizz) most of which is grown just the other side of the Pyrénées. It isn't a grape to get excited about. It was a game, neither of us really wanting to get down to the nitty gritty, both of us sensing a deal could be in the offing, but unwilling to make the first move.

'Er, maybe,' I hesitated, not wanting to rule anything out, but determined to stick to Plan A, which was a red wine vineyard. We had been driving for only around ten minutes, on yet another forested but tarmacadam track, which had led us up onto the plateau separating St-Martin from the neighbouring village of Le Vivier. To my left I could see almost the length of the Agly valley from the high Corbières mountains down to the Mediterranean, and to my right were the Pyrénées. Eric clicked the Toyota's hand brake, and led me on foot along an unsurfaced road with vines to the right.

'That's my Grenache Blanc,' he said pointing immediately right, 'and that,' pointing directly in front of us and lengthening his stride, 'is a Carignan Noir vineyard planted by my grandfather in the 1950s. You could take that one if you like. When the *pieds-noirs* (Algerian-born French citizens) came back from Algeria after the civil war against France in the 1950s, they brought a lot of Carignan.' Eric's family had lived in France for generations, but at that time had clearly caught the Carignan bug.

'Why did they plant so much Carignan?' I asked.

'High yields and wines with pretty high levels of alcohol. In those days, after the Second World War which France was still recovering from, and then the Algerian war, it was all about quantity, not necessarily quality.'

'So that's why Carignan got a bad reputation?' I offered, as

Eric led me round a stone cabin with a tiled, gabled roof on the bottom edge of the vineyard, and on into the vine rows.

'Carignan's a good grape, but not if you ask it to yield too heavily and pick it too early. It needs to be ripe. Lots of sun and lots of light. Otherwise the wine tastes of burnt rubber or unripe bananas.'

If Carignan was a grape that needed lots of light, then Eric's grandfather had picked the perfect spot to plant it. This was a high, exposed plateau called 'Planels', or 'mountain plateau' in local dialect. I followed the arc of the setting sun back to where the sun would have risen and saw that the vineyard enjoyed sun from daybreak to nightfall. I had recently tried some pretty decent, if expensive, Carignan-based red wines from Roussillon made either by newly established winemakers who, like me, had come from abroad, or by locals who had decided going it alone was better than being paid nothing for their grapes by local cooperatives on the verge of or in bankruptcy. Even though elsewhere in France growers were ripping Carignan out (more than half of France's Carignan was ripped out between 1979 and 2000), Roussillon's best Carignan reds were even becoming trendy. I was sure that the Planels vineyard could provide something just as good, and better value, if I could keep my costs down.

'What about yields?' I asked.

'It's so windy here,' Eric explained, 'and the soil is so poor, you're looking at maximum yields of 2,500–3,000 litres of wine per hectare. The plot is 2.2 hectares with around 3,000 vines per hectare. So, you'll get just over a bottle of wine per vine.' That's about the same as top Bordeaux châteaux and vineyards such as Latour, Lafite and Mouton-Rothschild produce.

'What about organics?' I asked.

'This vineyard was fully certified organic from 2006 by Ecocert,' said Eric, referring to a body recognised by France's Ministry of Agriculture and thus the EU. It wasn't hard to see that no weed-killers were being used under the vines, as plenty of weeds were growing there, and, as I scuffed my boots into the soil, a reassuringly strong, earthy aroma was released. This suggested the soil was full of the microbes that vine roots need if they are to get the food from the soil that they need for healthy growth.

The vines spread away from the stone cabin southeast-wards across the plateau, which also sloped south, in the direction of the Pyrénées. A couple of lines of fir trees had been planted as wind breaks at intervals, but the trees were still so small they could hardly have any effect. 'Don't you ever water the trees?' I asked Eric. 'Why? They're growing. Let nature take its course. Slowly but surely. That's the best way.' I noticed the vines had been grown initially as if they were meant to stand freely, but that posts and supporting wires had been strung along every row. 'It was done for machine harvesting,' said Eric. 'You can't machine pick bush [free-standing] vines like these if the foliage isn't trained along supporting wires. The vines were planted as bush vines and then the posts and wires were added in and the vines re-trained when machine harvesters came along a generation ago.' This seemed to suggest that the vineyard had been used as a yield donkey by his grandfather or father.

'No, not really,' said Eric. 'It was done to save time when picking, that's all. You'll never be able to use this vineyard as a yield donkey, unless you stick tonnes and tonnes of fertilizer on it. But, because it is so dry and the wind can be so strong, you'd throw the vines out of balance if you did that. The shoots that grow each year would be so flabby that they'd snap in the wind. And anyway, now that the supporting wires are there it means that if you position the shoots correctly between them early enough in spring when the new green shoots are still soft and tender the wind won't break them off and you'll save a lot of potentially lost grapes.' We continued walking, both lost in thought, there being only the wind and birds for company. There wasn't a power-line or main road as far as the eye could see in any direction, and any land not covered by vines was either Holm oak forest or scrub land dominated by brooms, herbs like rosemary, thyme and sage, heather, sun roses and brambles. I could feel my blood pressure dropping in such as tranquil place, and the view to the highest peak across the rippling Pyrénéan foothills, the snow-capped Canigou, was awesome. I decided I didn't need the sea view.

I asked Eric if the stone cabin came with the vineyard. 'Yes and no. The cabin was built by my grandfather. It was where the animals who used to plough the vines stayed before tractors. Grandad would sleep and eat there, too, staying four or five days. That's why there is a chimney, you see? And the animals would drink from the stone-water trough along the side, filled by rainwater from the roof. The cabin was grandad's base, serving all the vineyards on the plateau. Some have been pulled up and are waiting to be replanted by me, or have recently been replanted,' said Eric, as he windmilled his arms around. I now understood that he owned the whole plateau, and all the land surrounding the Planels vineyard was organic. This meant no accidental spray drift from nasty chemicals.

'But you can use the cabin as a place to sleep near harvest

to keep your eye on the grapes, or have barbecues if you are prepared to fix the broken tiles on the roof. You look like you don't eat much, so if you climb on the roof to fix it you're not going to fall through,' he said laughing. This combination of flattery and encouragement I was to learn was Eric's way of getting me to do a job he had been putting off.

'And the cabin might come in useful as a place you can bring journalists to entertain when you come to sell your first wine, *"Laydeez and genteelman, zis iz ze wine by ze Château Monty!"*,' he trilled to his imaginary audience.

I asked Eric how much it would cost to buy. 'It's not for sale, unless you offered me big zeros, and even then I'd feel I was selling the family furniture. You just won't find a vineyard in a spot like this anywhere else. That's what my grandad said, and it's still true. If you buy vines there's quite a bit of paperwork that costs time and money. Vineyard prices are going up here as word gets out that this is an undiscovered, undervalued region. If you want to buy vines Jean Pla will find you something, but he's probably told you already it makes better sense to buy a substantial chunk of vines, as your legal costs will be pretty much the same if you buy a couple of hectares or 20. If you buy vines and decide the wine they make is not to your liking or are sited in the wrong place, you're stuffed. You'll find it hard to sell them if word gets out you think they are rubbish, unless you know a "pigeon". But, if you buy your own vines and prices keep going up the way they have been, you could sell in maybe five or ten years for a good profit. You can't do that if you rent. However, renting is much cheaper initially and I'll offer you a fair deal, and quickly. Your risk will be much less, too. We do get hailstorms here, which means that if you buy vines and plan to pay the bank back with profits from your wine and then get hailed on in your first year you'll really be in the shit. You'll have no grapes for two years from those vines as the hail destroys this year's grapes and the grape-bearing buds for next year too. If you rent vines and hail strikes you'll be able to get out and forfeit one crop, while renting vines somewhere else which will allow you to make back what you lost fairly easily.'

I am a terrible decision-maker, so I asked Eric what he would do with my small budget and lack of experience.

'Rent. See how you go. You like your freedom too much to commit straight off. I can see that, the way you ask questions. Typical bloody journalist! Ha ha. That's why you're not married yet!' Eric, who of course had a gorgeous wife and son, already had me worked out. 'And, anyway, I can see you like this vineyard, and the only way to farm it is to rent it. If you take it, it will give me a bit more time for my other vineyards. But I won't offer you a second chance.'

Eric had barely finished speaking as I held out my hand. 'Done,' I said. 'Good,' he said. 'Château Monty. Ha ha!'

Chapter 2

As SOON AS ERIC AND I HAD VERBALLY AGREED THE RENTAL DEAL for the vineyard I began planning my move to St-Martin-de-Fenouillet. This would be from my adopted home in Tuscany, where I'd been living on and off since writing the Tuscan wine-travel guide for Hilary. I'd ended up renting a flat in a hilltop village in the shadow of an extinct volcano, Mount Amiata, Tuscany's highest peak south of Florence. The volcano's dense, unsculpted forests of pine and chestnut gave way to a more manicured landscape, the cypress-lined driveways leading to the vineyards of one of Italy's most prestigious winemaking zones, Montalcino. Its red wines were named after an especially concentrated form of the Sangiovese grape, the 'Brunello' or 'little dark one'. They were far too expensive to drink every night at home, and, anyway, the girl I had settled down to live with in the flat, Silvana, was teetotal. Her explanation was, 'I asked for a spoonful of beer from my grandfather when I was 14 months old and apparently vomited for the next three days.' Co-habiting with Silvana fulfilled to some extent Hilary's prediction that writing just one more book for her would be the best way to meet a winegrower's daughter, although, in fact, neither of Silvana's parents were vineyard owners. Silvana's mother, Francesca, did work for a wine-making and olive-oil business, located about half-an-hour's drive south of Siena. Run from an old abbey and as a charitable trust it was only known locally. The vineyards and olive groves Francesca worked in had mostly been bequeathed by church-goers in their wills. Many were childless, having either lost partners in the Second World War or had failed to find one afterwards. Savino, Silvana's father, was a craftsman and worked mainly nightshifts in one of Tuscany's many ceramic factories.

Silvana's parents, like many others living in Tuscany (and anywhere else north of Rome for that matter), were originally from Italy's poorer, southern half and they knew the value of a good education. Fortunately, Silvana did well at primary school, excellently at secondary school and exceptionally at university. Her fellow students sometimes called her 'the Martian' because of the way her near-photographic memory allowed her to absorb effortlessly book-loads of information.

To pay for her university studies Silvana held down a full-time job at one of the Montalcino wine zone's most famous wineries. She'd set the alarm for 4 am, spend three hours studying at home, then drive to work for a ten-hour day in the office working on the winery budget. Each evening she'd study for at least couple more hours before a normal night's sleep – normal meaning no more than five hours. She was the youngest ever Italian to combine an accountancy doctorate (aged 26) with seven years' work experience.

Silvana's boss, the winery's owner, was a radiant and kindly Italian countess whom I had met while researching the Tuscan wine-travel guide. She suggested that her Christmas party, to be held in her wine cellar, was the perfect opportunity to introduce me to Silvana. I'd spent the previous night celebrating the end of another chapter of the Tuscan book with the countess. She'd wisely retired to bed early, leaving me with her winemaker. His suggestion that I taste (but had drunk, of course) a bewildering number of wines into the early hours had left me with the hangover from hell. I had to concentrate hard to avoid breathing the fumes of last-night's carefully selected wines and the late-afternoon's carelessly made coffee over the countess as I kissed her cheek in greeting. I then had to refocus my swaying body by aligning my feet with the parallel lines made by the red tiles on the winery floor. A line of metal fermenting tanks, the evening's five-piece live band and an enthusiastic winery staff (all eager to meet me it seemed) soon came into soft focus view.

'Monty, this is Silvana,' said the countess, as the wall of noise bouncing off the stainless-steel sides of the tanks from the live band nearly pushed me over the edge before I'd even shaken her hand. 'Silvana, I want you to look after Monty and improve his Italian,' she continued, lingering long enough for both of us to register what appeared to be the knowing smile of a matchmaker on a potentially successful mission.

I had no idea that Silvana's computer-like brain had stored on its hard drive the fact that we had already spoken on the phone, something of which I was ignorant. A few weeks' previously when I'd had to call the winery to get travel directions, I'd introduced myself as a journalist and spoke French. The countess had merely given me a phone number without letting me know it was Silvana's direct line. I'd assumed that whoever answered would follow the 'Italians generally speak French and not English as a second language' rule. This assumption had not gone down well with Silvana, even though she spoke very good French, because she had just sailed through an English-language course in London that the countess had helped her organise. Silvana had given me the necessary travel directions and then asked for the phone number of my non-existent mobile, 'just in case'. Soon after this the phone conversation came to a polite but abrupt end, Silvana apparently telling her office colleagues as she hurled the phone down that 'some English cretin who thinks he's too famous to give out his mobile phone number' would be arriving for the Christmas party. A journalist without a mobile phone was simply unthinkable, especially in Italy, where most men of my age communicate using two mobiles, one for their wife and one for their lover.

All day, and in between bouts of nausea, I'd been practising the kind of verbal greeting I supposed would be needed at an Christmas party in Italy. After a month-long intensive Italian language course in Siena I could just about trot out this hopelessly unambitious stock phrase in the vernacular: 'Good evening. My name is Monty Waldin. I am English. I am sorry, but please can you speak slowly as I don't speak very much Italian.' At this point a luminous smile seemed to flicker across Silvana's face, one she did her best to hide by taking a sudden interest in the winery ceiling, thinking, I suspected, that my claim of not speaking much Italian was a gross understatement.

'How did you find studying in London?' I asked, hoping to detain Silvana, telling myself that here was a great opportunity to speak a bit of Italian and that her unusual and totally arresting combination of girlish beauty and womanly poise was secondary, indeed irrelevant.

'The language school had good teachers, but I was often kept awake by the noise of drunk English men in the street outside. People drink a lot in your country, no?

'Well, there might always be one or two who occasionally... exaggerate,' I said. I was caught in the dilemma of wanting my eyes to adsorb the positive effect of Silvana's porcelain skin, delicate hair and luminous eyes on my hangover while at the same time hoping that because Silvana was a good deal shorter than me she'd be unable to register just how bloodshot my eyes remained from the previous night's alcoholic exertions.

'You know, if you ever want to improve – practise – your English, we could always meet over a coffee sometime.'

'Maybe you could explain the difference in English between "could", "should" and "would"?' Silvana's attention, that had clearly been wavering, was now fully focussed on me.

Help, I thought, I only speak English, I don't know how the bloody language works – why is she asking me this? I waffled hopelessly and painfully providing irrelevant examples of how the verbs can, will and to be become could, would and should in the conditional until Silvana did the honourable thing and left me with only the band, and a shirt still bearing the vinous battle scars of the previous night for company. I was in social Siberia as far as the Christmas party was concerned. I'd completely blown it with Silvana.

Harry's stubby little tail-come-bottom was parked between Silvana's and my head as we awoke in St-Martin-de-Fenouillet's recently opened guesthouse-restaurant, the Auberge Taïchac, after a 12-hour drive around the Mediterranean the day before. Silvana's work commitments meant we had less than two days to check and sign the vineyard rental papers (which ultimately went without a hitch) and sort out the budget for my first wine. Silvana was there to provide some legal counsel on the rental agreement, her professional expertise on the budget and general moral support. When I had first told Silvana about my French vineyard she had naturally donned her accountant's hat and offered to do me a rough budget. Never having done a budget before, and due to the fact that Silvana had a full-time job and I suddenly had a lot of travelling to do, I'd set aside our short time together in St-Martin-de-Fenouillet for the task, assuming (wrongly) she'd need to see the vineyard before doing the budget for it. On the way to collecting her from her office in Siena for the night-drive ahead I'd visited Silvana's favourite organic-food market in Siena in search of treats. These would sustain her throughout what promised to be a heavy weekend of driving and number crunching. Day One was to be devoted to what I had grandly called 'Plans and Possibilities' for the French vineyard, with Day Two given to a 'Cost – Benefit Analysis' – a term Silvana used often and that I knew was accountancy-speak for what was sensibly affordable, and what wasn't.

Through her job Silvana had done hundreds of budgets for wine producers, and she made it clear from the start that budgets are about numbers rather than emotions. We hadn't bothered to close the hotel curtains as we'd arrived so late and in darkness the night before. Thus we had been awoken early by the bright mid-autumn sun beaming across mountainous evergreen oak forests so apparently soft we felt we could almost dive into them unharmed from our room's balcony. The thought must have been particularly tempting for Silvana who'd been stuck all week in an office, and then all the previous night in the car. Harry's jaws meanwhile were dangerously near Silvana's favourite, highly chewable pencil as she marked out a spreadsheet on the back of a recently emptied packet of organic chocolate biscuits, perched via the duvet on her knees.

'Monty, it's sweet you thought your budget would take a whole weekend, but it won't, just a couple of hours. To do your budget I don't need organic biscuits and all the other treats you tried to hide from me, nice surprise though they were, or would have been had you not left the receipt on the passenger seat! You've made the classic mistake of creating an unnecessary cost, expensive treats, for no benefit. Unless you can get that cost – benefit concept into your generous but hopelessly impractical brain I can see your vineyard turning into an expensive night-mare before you've picked a single grape.' Silvana scribbled something down before she suggested that, 'we'll start by going through the kind of costs you'll need to cover the growing of the grapes in the vineyard and of course picking them, then the costs of turning the grapes into wine, and finally the costs of bottling, labelling, marketing and selling the wine. At some stage, not now, we'll look at tax liabilities and legal costs, too.' This sounded expensive, complicated, risky. Why didn't I just go back to selling other people's wines by working in a cosy wine shop on fixed hours and for a guaranteed salary?

'Look, about the biscuits... I can just tell Eric I've changed my mind, take him and Corinne and Paul out for a nice lunch, with you as well, and admit that maybe this whole thing isn't for me, no harm done.'

'Pruning,' said Silvana, ignoring and snapping me out of my wistful fear, 'requires tools in the form of pruning scissors and shears, plus labour.' Pruning was unavoidable. Pruning is the way winegrowers can control vines to produce the number of grape bunches they want and in such a way that the vineyard remains easy to spray and pick. An unpruned vineyard would still produce grapes, but the vines would soon become so unkempt and sprawling that it would be impossible to spray them – or even pick them – efficiently. Pruning vines in the right way helps ensures a regular, healthy crop.

'Okay, I'll borrow a pair of pruning scissors to prune the smaller shoots, and a pair of larger shears to cut off older, larger pieces of dead vine wood,' I said. If left in place these old bits of wood can provide a home for fungal diseases and even pests like mites. They hide in the bark in winter ready to attack the vine in spring. 'I'll pick up some second-hand ones on the cheap – no point wasting money,' I said.

'No,' said Silvana calmly, 'you need to go out and buy new scissors and new shears that you know will be sharp otherwise you'll damage the vines and tire yourself out. Shall I budget for some labour costs, too?'

'I'll do the pruning myself rather than pay someone else,' I said. 'Pruning isn't difficult. It's just dull, time-consuming work that takes place in the bitter cold. I just need to check with Eric how he usually prunes the vines for some tips, so as not to injure the vines by cutting the wrong bits off them.'

Silvana's next question was, 'What about disease control?' All wine-grape vines need to be sprayed at some stage each season to prevent disease. 'Your vineyard is mainly Carignan, which is very prone to powdery mildew.' Silvana, despite not drinking wine, had clearly been doing some wine research on fungal diseases. Powdery mildew (or *oidium* as it is sometimes called) covers the vines with a cobweb-like, ash-grey powder and prevents grapes from growing and ripening to their full potential. Cabernet Sauvignon and Chardonnay are other grape types that suffer from powdery mildew, but Carignan is particularly weak against it. Luckily, powdery mildew is easily prevented by spraying vines in spring with sulphur dust dissolved in water, or by dusting the vines with sulphur powder in summer. This kind of sulphur dusting/spraying is allowed for in organic vineyards, firstly because sulphur is naturally occurring and secondly because the spray works like a condom, forming a physical barrier between the vine and the mildew, thus leaving no residue in the wine. Non-organic sprays like systemics act like the contraceptive pill by penetrating the vines and these are not allowed in organics because of potential residues.

'Depending on the weather conditions I'll need to spray the vines with sulphur anywhere between four and eight times, beginning in early spring and up until the grapes are full-sized, say every 10–14 days or so. I'll need less sulphur in spring than in summer,' I said, explaining that this is because in spring the vine's new green shoots are smaller than in summer when they are fully erect and provide a bigger surface area to protect. Silvana factored in the cost of buying the sulphur then asked whether I was 'going to spray by hand or with a tractor?' knowing full well I didn't have a tractor and wasn't likely to get one either. 'I'll try and do as much by hand as possible,' I said, knowing I was going to have to ask to borrow her father's copper, pump-by-hand back-sprayer rather than buy an expensive new one. 'I'll also spray the vines with herb teas, made from plants like stinging nettle, chamomile and common horsetail. I can cut these locally and for free.' Silvana scribbled some notes on what looked like a small shopping list. 'When you cut the plants have you thought about how you are going to dry them. Do you have a rack, bags in which to hang them, a place in which to hang them, a large enough pot to boil them in and containers to store the tea concentrate in? You'll need containers with handles to make them easier to carry, you know.'

'Hey, stop unnecessarily breaking my balls, Sil! It'll be fine. I'll scrounge what I need when I need it. If I need to borrow some big buckets I can always give whoever lends me some tea as payment.'

'And presumably you'll spray it on their crops for free as well, will you? Look,' said Silvana, in a tone of conciliation, 'all I am trying to get you to understand is here you are in the south and you are in a foreign country. You can't expect people to do you favours for nothing, you know, even if it is for something small like lending buckets. Just be careful, okay?'

'Okay.' I didn't mention to Silvana that she had forgotten to factor in the costs of replacing vines and of the vineyard's support posts and wires. I knew that Eric had piles of old posts and wires that I was sure I could recycle for free if during pruning I came across anything that needed replacing. Silvana's next question concerned how I planned to protect the grapes from the wild boar. The boar could decimate my whole crop in a single night. I didn't have a hunter's licence so couldn't shoot them. 'What I can do is help erect the portable electric fences when the time comes with Eric. He already has the equipment and will fence his vines that are either side of mine and rig it all up to one battery. It makes no sense both he and I fencing our own plots.' This kind of practice between neighbours was quite common in Tuscany where boar attacks were also a big issue. 'And will Eric give you electric wire and insulated posts for free?' Silence. 'So, let's factor that in as a cost you'll have to assume, Monty.' More silence.

Silvana pressed on. 'The only other vineyard costs, apart from the cost of the actual rental, is picking the grapes and controlling weeds.' I said I thought it would take five people less than a couple of days to pick the grapes, easily. 'And your estimate is based on what, exactly, Mr Monty Waldin?' When Silvana used my full name there was never a trace of comic irony. She knew I was guessing. She reeled off statistics for how long vineyards planted with the same vine spacing as mine, yielding the same amount of bunches as mine and on terrain such as mine would take to get picked. 'Twelve people for one day, plus one person collecting the filled grape bins and loading them onto the tractor, plus one person driving the tractor to the winery.' This didn't seem much of a difference in man-hours, but labour costs are especially complicated in France due to the cripplingly high social-security costs that employers are responsible for paying. Silvana calculated I'd be paying more than double what I had anticipated. 'And that doesn't include costs to cover picnic lunches for them.'

This still left weed control – a big headache for organic growers who are not allowed to use the cheap option of weed-killers. While stretching out after the previous night's long drive I'd seen a hand-written advert on the Auberge Taïchac's front door for a local couple who ploughed weeds off by horse. I felt this was worth investigating. 'It won't be cheap,' was all Silvana could say, in what was becoming a near constant refrain. 'Horses are more than three times as expensive as humans...' The thought that maybe I should have been born a horse crossed my mind, but Silvana was pressing me about where I was going to make my wine.

I'd rented a vineyard but hadn't yet rented space in a winery, but was confident I could use the local cooperative (which had space) for minimal cost. 'I just need to rent a couple of vats, one to ferment the grapes in and one to move the wine to when fermented, plus I'll need to rent a couple of hoses and a pump to move the wine around. Do you know how much that'll cost, Mr Waldin?' I said in my imitation of Silvana's voice, one that was good enough to raise, miraculously, the first Silvana smile of the day. 'No, Silvana,' I said, answering my own question, 'but I'll find out and anyway it won't be expensive. The cooperative has loads of spare capacity.' Silvana's smile had not completely gone, I was relieved to see. 'Hmmm. Okay. But factor in some money for the materials needed for cleaning and disinfecting the pump, hoses and vats,' Silvana advised. 'No point in allowing the wine to taste dirty, when you can avoid it for minimal costs. Cooperative wineries are never the cleanest.' However, and as I wasn't planning to age my red in expensive oak barrels, wine-making costs appeared fairly minimal and straightforward.

I was at a disadvantage though when it came to bottling. 'Manufacturers give bigger discounts for bigger volumes,' said

Silvana, speaking with the natural authority her day-job conferred, 'so unit costs for dry goods, things like bottles, corks, bottle labels and the cardboard boxes the wine gets shipped in, come down the more you buy. You're so small scale you'll be unlikely to get any discount.'

'Couldn't we revise your estimates, Sil, as they seem a bit pessimistic? I'll be able to wangle a discount from someone, especially as I am trying to make as environmentally friendly a wine as possible. And, an artist friend will probably design my wine label and even a website on the cheap. Plus, I do have pretty extensive contacts with wine-writing colleagues, so I won't need to wine and dine just to get some press coverage. Plus, I know enough trade buyers to sell the wine over the phone, or by sending the odd wine sample for them to taste by post.' Silvana gallantly kept her obvious exasperation in check, merely warning that, 'Things like that can unexpectedly chew up lots of budget without you really noticing, Mont.'

Silvana then turned to the money coming in from the sale of the wine. 'Once you know roughly how many bottles you can make and how much you want to sell each bottle for you can calculate your potential income. For the moment I can do rough calculations based on what Eric says the vineyard normally yields, which is around 8,000 bottles. Obviously between the moment you generate your first cost, the purchase of some pruning scissors, to the moment the first cheque clears from the sale of the wine – and remember most trade buyers will want 90 days credit – will be about 18 months. What you don't want to do is run out of money half way through, when the wine is made but you have no money to pay for the bottles, for example. It's called cash flow.'

Cash flow was not my strong point. Silvana knew I never checked my bank statements to see what I had spent, but (nearly) always managed to stay in credit by only roughly spending as much as I thought I was earning. There was also one potentially not inconsiderable cost I kept from Silvana: that the wine was going to be biodynamic. I had written the first-ever book on biodynamic wines and virtually all my favourite wines – some from famous wineries, others from unknown ones – were made biodynamically.

Biodynamics is the oldest (some say the most extreme) form of organics. It originated in 1924 when some European farmers asked Austrian scientist Rudolf Steiner – of Steiner Waldorf Schools fame – for advice as to why their soils, crops and livestock were getting weaker. Steiner pointed to the recent industrialisation of farming: we had lost our connectedness to the crops we were growing because our mind-set made us think only about material things. Putting one tonne of fertiliser on the land may give us one tonne of food, said Steiner, but as that tonne of food would have come essentially from inert or lifeless fertiliser the food would lack vitality or soul. The more we allowed ourselves to eat lifeless food, the more likely it was that we would continue, unthinkingly, not just to produce it but ever to ask ourselves the question, 'Why are we so happy producing this lifeless food?' My favourite biodynamic fact is there's never been a case of BSE or mad-cow disease in a biodynamic cow. Biodynamic cows never undergo the unnatural process of having their horns removed (which weakens them). Nor are they allowed to eat meat, least of all their own, ground-up and disguised as feed – Steiner even predicted feeding a cow its own meat would affect its brain.

With that in mind I felt that Steiner's idea that by dumbing down our food we had dulled our spirits and lost our respect for nature, the soil, crops and livestock made sense.

Steiner's answer to arrest this vicious cycle of bad food/bad farming was biodynamics. The 'bio' bit comes from swapping the inert chemicals of conventional farming in favour of nine biodynamic farm treatments or preparations. There are three sprays made from cow manure, the mineral silica that is obtained by crushing quartz rocks, and a herb called common horsetail. These go on the crops, or the soil, or both. Then there are six medicinal plants, all of which are fairly easy to come by, and all of which biodynamic growers use in their compost piles. These are the flower heads of yarrow, chamomile and dandelion; crushed oak bark, stinging nettles (stalks and leaves) and tea made from valerian flowers. The combined presence of these six medicinal plants or 'compost preparations' in biodynamic-speak is what transforms normal compost into biodynamic compost.

You must use all nine preparations regularly to get the full biodynamic effect, which as far as wine is concerned means wines having a vitality and a real sense of place. In other words, wines that are really individual; like the difference between a bland egg with a barely yellow yolk from a battery hen or an egg laid by a free range hen on wild, unpolluted land with a yolk as bright and vibrant as the noon-day sun. I was convinced that biodynamic farming was not necessarily more expensive than its organic or even conventional equivalents. You just had to learn to spend what money you had in a different way – like making biodynamic compost from the manure of your own cows rather than buying in fertiliser.

'Come on,' I said to Silvana, 'I'm bored of budgets, spreadsheets and numbers! Let's walk up to the vineyard.' Harry jumped off the bed and we stumbled into our jeans. We climbed towards the crossroads on the plateau on St-Martin's southwestern side, where the pastures were full of large, round parcels of winter silage wrapped in blue plastic for the livestock. Here we turned off the main road, between St-Martin and Le Vivier, east along a rough cinder track with the mountain wind as persistent as ever, but now at our backs.

'Those vines are a bit messy,' said Silvana, at the first block we came across, 'as if they have been abandoned. They're enormous. Yours won't look like that, will they?' In fact the vines, that were strung along support posts and wires, were not unusually tall but they were big in the sense of appearing almost overgrown – their lush foliage trailing so thickly in every direction that the supporting posts and wires on which they hung were completely obscured. The soil, however, was completely bare with not a blade of grass in sight.

'That looks like a classic example of back-to-front wine-growing,' I said, perhaps the first really confident statement I had made all morning. 'Vines made ridiculously green from chemical fertilisers growing on soil made unnaturally bare by weed-killers. It doesn't add up. How can you possibly make a credible wine by growing grapes like this?' I asked, swinging my arms around to no audience at all, Silvana and Harry having carried on walking. Photographs of artificially clean and tidy-looking vineyards full of blue skies, green vines and clean soils represented the picture-postcard image of winegrowing – the kind of images I'd seen in the first wine magazines I'd ever read. The implication was that wines should be judged on what the vineyard looked like.

'Look how obviously that soil is eroding,' I urged Silvana, who hadn't taken its dull, pasty and structureless texture as quite the affront I had. 'If the guy farming it had left some weeds to grow there he'd still have some topsoil left. With no weeds or grass left what does the soil have left to hold on to? Removing weeds in the vineyard is like removing trees from the jungle. Rain washes all the soil away, causing flash floods, destroying eco-systems…'

'But we're not in the jungle, Mont. We're in St-Martin in France having a nice walk with Harry.' Silvana was worried about how much it would cost me to plough weeds out from certain areas of my vineyard by horse, and knowing, too, that I knew she knew I was trying to make my pro-horse case. I hoped the fact that several of the local vineyards had, like mine, stone cabins where the animals that used to work the vines would be tethered would bolster my case, if not financially then emotionally. Who could resist a horse? Working horses were replaced in the 1950s by tractors, a process encouraged by cheap loans offered by president Général de Gaulle's post-war government. Tractors and tractor-mounted spray-rigs allowed weeds to be killed cheaply using chemicals. 'Using weed-killers is the first step on the chemical treadmill. Everything's fine for the first few years, as weed-killers are quicker and cheaper than ploughing weeds away than with a horse.'

'What do you mean, everything's fine when you first use weed-killers? Why don't you just use weed-killers at Château Monty then if it is so much easier?'

'Well, in the first few years the weed-killer is decomposing so many different types of weeds in the soil that enough food is being provided for both the soil and the vines. However, the weed-killer burns the soft, earthy bit or "humus" out of the soil leaving hard, stony bits. And, as there is no longer any grass left on top, the soil is more easily compacted when tractors pass. As the soil texture becomes physically harder, and the soil becomes more acid, fewer weed types are able to grow. You usually end up with just one or two weed types – such as bindweed (*Convolvulus*) – that grow on compacted soils. With only a single main type of weed growing and then decomposing the vines start to get hungry. The winegrower then thinks about buying some chemical fertilisers.'

'You sound like you won't be using any of them,' said Silvana. The flat cinder track we were on had given way to the unsurfaced one that led directly up to the gentle, but partially exposed, rise to my vineyard. 'Fertilisers make sense if you've started using weed-killers. They give vines a quick boost. The vines produce longer shoots, bigger, greener leaves and lots of grapes leaving any vineyard neighbours still ploughing with horses envious.'

'Of course they are,' said Silvana. 'Technology is moving on and they are being left behind because, just like you, they are being stubborn, stubborn, stubborn! Why not leave farming to the scientists rather than people like you who behave as if the earth was still flat?'

'Okay, hear me out. The flat-earther, back-to–the-land, horse-ploughing farmer is only jealous until of course he sees how the neighbouring vineyard with no weeds and just big vines is an illusion because the vines start attracting pests and diseases.'

'Says who?'

'Says I,' I said, not sure and not for the first time with Silvana – whose English was getting better than mine – that I was speaking my mother tongue correctly anymore. As we approached the vineyard the crimson and gold of the vine leaves in autumn was more arresting than the fractured and bleached pink of the tiles on the cabin roof. 'Look, I've read the science and more importantly I go on my own experiences, for example when I worked in Bordeaux as a teenager. This taught me that the more chemicals you throw at a vineyard the more chemicals you'll need to throw at the grapes once you get them into the winery to make the wine. Chemical fertilisers feed vines directly because when it rains the fertiliser pellets dissolve to be taken up by vine roots. This means that the vine can get a whole year's supply of food in one or two large, immediate hits. That's a bit like asking you to eat 365 lunches in one sitting.'

'Well, *you've* certainly never complained when my mother offers you your fourth helping of pasta followed by unlimited bread, cheese and salami and a double helping of fruit tart...'

'Exactly,' I said. 'Exactly what?' Silvana replied. 'I eat, or drink, when I need to. If I can't eat what Francesca offers me, I don't. That way I stay healthy. But, if she forced a year's worth of food into me in one go I'd grow too much too quickly and then suffer from heart disease, weak bones, lethargy and so on. It's the same for vines. Fertilizers make them grow so unnaturally quickly that they become weak and attract diseases. The grapes may produce lots of sugar but they lack colour and the right amount of acidity – that then has to be corrected in the winery. Fertilisers make the vine's trunk, leaves and even grape-skins balloon because the plant's cells get stretched. Stretched cells are too weak to stop diseases such as mildew, or pests such as spider mites from puncturing the leaves. Pests and diseases are simply nature's way of killing off something that is already in the process of dying. That's what biodynamic winegrowers say anyway – it's better to prevent diseases in the first place rather than to eliminate them with chemicals.'

The weed-killer salesman, I noted, would have been horrified to see how many weeds were growing in my vineyard, but I was reassured by their presence. They showed my vineyard justified its official status as certified organic. This took three years to obtain and had to be maintained each year.

'Monty, I'm sorry, but why don't you just plough the weeds away with a tractor instead of a horse? It would still be organic.'

'I could do, but lots of French winegrowers are going back to ploughing with a horse.'

'And you have to copy them, do you?', said Silvana. 'You're supposed to be a leader, not a follower!'

'Okay, but the horse thing is a good idea because it's less aggressive on the vine's fragile topsoil roots, less likely to compact soil and less damaging to the soil's ecosystem...'

'And much more expensive than a tractor,' came Silvana's voice of reason.

To the south, the distant peak of the Canigou was hidden by puffy cloud. Clearly visible, however, was a 50-metre-high radio mast – its needle-like form pinned to the ground by wires – on the range of hills nearest to us, to the southeast. Behind the hill lay the village of Felluns, where a local farmer with a herd of organic cows lived. His cows were grazing the lower slopes around the transmitter. Even though the cows were a ten-minute-walk away and downwind we could easily hear the jangling of the bells around their necks.

'What would you say budget-wise about getting a couple of cows, to produce manure for compost so that the vineyard becomes as self-sufficient as possible? The farm becomes self-reliant, so whatever is grown tastes of a real sense of place. It's like organics, but a bit more profound. It's called biodynamics. With your own cows you're halfway to becoming truly biodynamic. You can dilute their manure in water to make a soil spray that softens the soil enough for vine roots to dig deep down for the kind of food they need to make the best wine. You can recycle cow manure into compost to give the soil enough structure so it doesn't erode and is full of microbes and life and...'

'Very sexy,' said Silvana, trying to snuggle her tiny frame into my coat to get away from the wind.

'What, manure?'

'No, you. I didn't know my ice-cold Englishman could be so passionate. About cow shit!'

'Well, of course I am passionate about cows. Biodynamic farmers say that just having animals on your farm conveys some kind of intelligence to it. I suppose their presence just makes us humans more connected, more sensitive, more spiritual.'

'I always thought it was that tiny little brain of yours that controlled what you did. Now I can see that you really are a typical man, hard on the outside but much softer on the inside. I didn't know biodynamics was like a religion.'

'It's not, and anyway you know I am not religious.'

'I'm sure you only say that as an excuse not to get married!'

'I don't want to get married in a church, that's all. I'm

spiritual about things and that's not the same as being religious. A cow is an object, a thing, a physical being but in biodynamics we say that there is no matter without spirit and no spirit without matter, and I agree. When I see those cows over there I feel I want one, almost need one. They're just nice. And having some around will make me a nicer person.'

'Monty, even if you were surrounded by every cow on the planet you would still be grumpy, always screaming about what a terrible state the planet is in, always complaining about how much boring wine is made every day and so on – always complaining about something. That's just you! It's one reason I wanted to be with you. You care passionately about things. Even if you don't care enough about me to get married! Save the money from the cow to pay for a wedding!'

'Now you're just be silly, Silvana!'

Silvana threw some numbers at me. A cow, it turned out, was as expensive to buy as a reliable second-hand car; much harder to transport and provide documents for and was effectively as expensive to run. Prices of winter hay that cows eat at the rate of ten or more kilos a day were rising steeply, due partly to a series of bad harvests caused, it was said, by climate change. 'And besides,' continued Silvana, 'where would you put your cows? In the village's main square, or in the mayor's office?' I maintained radio silence, not having thought this part through quite fully enough.

'The only possible place would be on that spare land of Eric's over there,' said Silvana, pointing to a strip next to the horseshoe-shaped track running towards the radio mast and Felluns. 'One cow could eat all that in less than a day. And a single cow on her own will get lonely. Cows are very sociable creatures. So you'd need more than one. You'd have to fence them into a semi-permanent paddock. That's really expensive and, anyway, I doubt Eric will want his land fenced or covered by cow and feed sheds because he's bound to replant it with vines in a few years' time. What are you going to do if the cows escape, which they are bound to do at some point? Will you insure them or trust to luck? And who'd milk them every morning and every evening, especially if you are away for a week in England selling your wine?' I was sure Eric would have been delighted to have had cows grazing and feeding the land with organic cow manure for a few years before replanting it with vines, but I could see Silvana's logic that it was uneconomic and impractical. Even in the short space of time we had been talking, the cows opposite had been constantly on the move, grazing off this hill pasture until they'd disappeared from view in search of more food.

'Monty, listen. You want to start small which means even a single cow is too much. And as an economist I see your main goal is to make wine that you can sell at a profit. Saving the planet should be part of that, but not, or not yet anyway, the be-all and end-all. It takes years to get organic, let alone biodynamic, farming right. You're trying to get there immediately. And besides, if you set the bar too high by making out you're the complete biodynamic-wine package straight away people are going to have unrealistic expectations of your wine. I am sure you can buy some organic compost from somewhere. They even sell it in supermarkets in big sacks, so it's likely if you spoke direct to the supplier you could get it delivered in bulk.'

We took a different route back to the village and on arriving we saw a mule calmly standing outside the Auberge

Taïchac's front door. The mule, whose name we later learnt was Bob, made a habit of escaping from his paddock on the edge of the village. Seeing his owner, a guy called Jean-Luc, trying to pull Bob with all his might, just to try and budge him from the main square back towards his paddock, made me realise what a commitment cows would have been. At least when Harry escaped I could pick him up. There was no way I'd be able to do that with a couple of cows.

Even if two cows landed in my lap for free I'd still have to wait one year before I'd be able to spread their manure, in the form of compost, onto the vineyard. This is because compost takes a minimum of around three months and more usually six to decompose into something usable by a vineyard soil. Now I needed to find a local source of compost that had the official organic certification. One of Eric's conditions when he rented me my vineyard was that I maintained its official organic status, and this implicitly ruled out non-organic compost. I called a local agricultural supply depot, run as a kind of cooperative, which put me in touch with a municipal compost maker located at St-Hipployte, a ten-minute drive northeast of Perpignan city centre and not far from the Barcelona – Perpignan motorway. Its compost was made by recycling green municipal waste, mainly lawn clippings from public parks, tree prunings from roadsides and even dead flowers from cemeteries. As bio-dynamics was all about recycling dead stuff so as to bring life back to the soil this didn't put me off. The compost-making area covered the equivalent of several football pitches and the compost piles themselves were each as high as a normal family home. From afar they looked like huge piles of driftwood mixed with seaweed, while the bulldozers shaping them moved sideways like rusty coloured crabs caught on an artificial beach of reinforced concrete.

The site foreman explained how, 'Water sprinklers keep the piles moist while warm air is vented via tubing into the centre of the piles from underneath. Warmth and moisture are essential to encourage the microbes responsible for breaking down compost. Orienting the piles on a north – south rather than east – west axis means both sides of the heap get the same amount of warmth, ensuring the piles rot down more steadily and evenly. After a few weeks we turn the piles and sieve their contents in a rotating drum to remove anything over-size, usually bits of tree trunk or large branches. What's left is the compost.' This was nearly black in colour, and in my hand had the fine, crumbly texture of dryish peat moss. I accompanied him and he gave me copies of the municipal compost's organic certification.

Before leaving for Italy I had signed a purchase order, delivery date to be confirmed, for 15 tonnes or a lorry load of compost, this quantity being the minimum allowed. The compost analysis revealed the correct 'C:N' (or carbon to nitrogen ratio), carbon being the food of choice for the kind of soil micro-organisms I wanted to encourage. Fifteen tonnes would give me enough for the vineyard if spread at the recommended rate of around five to six tonnes per hectare, with a tonne or so extra for the vegetable garden I was planning.

'But Monty,' said Francesca as she drove me to the seaside town of Grosseto on Tuscany's Mediterranean coast, three days before I was due to return to France for good, on a shopping trip for vineyard attire such as some strong gloves for pruning and some waterproof trousers for compost spreading, 'what I don't understand is you want to be biodynamic and to be biodynamic you need the compost to have these six medicinal plant preparations in, so why are you using only organic compost?' Francesca had a huge vegetable garden at the back of the family home and was asking almost daily for tips on how she could manage it in a greener, more organic way.

'If you can't get the six biodynamic compost preparations into your newly made compost piles in time for the composting process to begin, there is a short-cut. You make what is called biodynamic barrel compost. Whereas it takes anything up to a year for a normal compost pile to become ready, only a month or two is needed for barrel compost. You make it by stirring the six biodynamic compost preparations into some fresh cow manure for an hour or so. Then you put the mixture into a barrel you've half-buried in the ground. If you want you can even stir in some ground-up eggshells.'

'Eggshells?'

'They help diffuse the radiation that interferes with plant growth, like the fall-out from Chernobyl. You leave the mix in the half-buried barrel and after one month your so-called barrel compost is ready. You crumble it into warm water, mix it for twenty minutes then spray it onto the soil in the vineyard. The soil should be warm, like in early autumn or mid-spring. The microbes in the barrel compost would need some warmth to multiply. And you should time the making and spreading of the barrel compost according to lunar cycles, as biodynamic growers believe that what's going on above their heads in the cosmos is just as important as what's going on in the soil beneath their feet.'

'Like sowing on the new moon and harvesting on the full moon, I suppose?'

'Well,' I said, 'that's the easiest moon cycle to follow as you can see the size of the moon clearly from earth. But, the full- to new-moon cycle is only one of several moon cycles biodynamic growers pay attention to.'

'Such as?' asked Francesca, as the Mediterranean came into view between a break Tuscany's irregularly shaped coastal hills.

'For example, the barrel compost is an earth remedy. It helps the soil. So, you're supposed to make it when the moon is standing in front of the constellation of Virgo the virgin, which is an earth sign.'

'Like astrology, then?'

'Er, no, not exactly,' I said, unable to explain in Italian an astronomical term called the precession of the equinoxes. The dates given for the star signs from the tropical zodiac that people still read today in their daily newspapers were drawn up by the ancient Greeks. At that time the sun stood in front of Aries at the moment of the spring equinox, March 21, in the northern hemisphere. However, as the sun's point at spring equinox is constantly moving backwards, the sun is actually now in front of Pisces on March 21, and by 2375 the sun will be in front of the constellation of Aquarius at the spring equinox. 'Biodynamic farmers use astronomy – the actual positions of the sun, moon, other planets and stars – not the imaginary positions of astrology. In fact, the person who developed the biodynamic barrel compost, a German farmer called Maria Thun, produces her own biodynamic 'planting a seedling' calendar. I can get you a copy in Italian if you like. It's printed in all the European languages and only costs as much as a trashy paperback book. I've planned my compost spreading in France next week to coincide with lunar movements, too. I have one chance each month for an optimum day.'

'Do you really think it works?' ask Francesca.

'Yes, of course I do, otherwise I wouldn't do it,' I replied. Grosseto could scarcely claim to be anywhere near being considered Tuscany's most beautiful coastal city, but it seemed lively enough today, standing under crisp, late morning, wintry sunshine and before a flat, effortlessly blue Mediterranean.

In order to park, Francesca turned the people-carrier onto a normally busy, but seemingly empty, one-way street. As she made the turn I could see in slow-motion a small white car hurtling towards the side on which I was sitting. The face of the driver, a man in his early twenties, was not visible as he appeared to be looking across the passenger seat and out of his side window, rather than straight ahead. He was holding a mobile phone to his ear and driving with one hand. Time, as the saying goes, stood still. Silvana and I had already had one car smash in Italy a year before (not our fault) and the police had told us we'd been lucky to leave the crash scene relatively unscathed. I wasn't sure this was going to have quite such a happy ending as I braced myself for the impact, after which our car left the ground. The car was pushed so far off the main road that it had flattened a lamp post and part of the wall beyond the pavement. Somehow we hadn't hit a single pedestrian, although we were surrounded by them as soon as the car had come to a stop. The car's front and left side were crumpled like a piece of aluminium foil someone had used, scrunched up, and then decided to try and re-use. I could walk only a few steps before

I felt my back seize up. I knew I had to get horizontal, but to do this required an excruciating manoeuvre into the back of the car via my elbows and knees, my backside in the air, whilst my nose ended up in the magazine rack behind the driver's seat because my back was now banana-shaped and in spasm. I remained there until a female ambulance woman grabbed my head to stop me moving my neck, strapped me to a board-like stretcher and placed me in an ambulance. It seemed to take an eternity to pull away, leaving Silvana's mother to argue with the local police about who was responsible for the accident.

'It's okay, treasure, it's okay,' the first ambulance woman on the scene kept repeating. 'No, not really,' I whispered, my mouth feeling suddenly and inexplicably dehydrated, my bladder (also inexplicably) apparently fit to burst. 'I have to go to France,' I insisted. 'Yes, I am sure you do my love, we all want to go home, but not today,' she said, as she ran her fingers and their pungent smell of nicotine through my hair. 'Look, I'm English, I'm not French,' I whispered through my teeth, as the first feelings of claustrophobia induced by immovably tight straps pressing down on my bladder. 'I can stay in hospital for a few days if you want as long as I can leave for France on Saturday. I can't miss next week's moon. I'm a wine expert, I'm making a wine in France and...'

'Yes, of course you are, my treasure. Did you have any French wine today yet, any alcohol at all?'

'No, no, just an espresso for breakfast. I can't stay here. If I don't get the compost on at the right time my entire soil programme will...'

'The doctor will have a look and decide when you can get home to France,' she said, swabbing the soft centre of my right arm, and then inserting a needle and drip-feed attachment, 'but I want you to relax. Don't worry, the moon will still be there when you wake up, and long after that, too, I don't doubt.'

Chapter 3

'RIGHT. PUT YOUR CLOTHES ON THAT CHAIR AFTER YOU'VE TAKEN them off, then lie on the table. Head-end furthest from the door, face-up and with your underwear on. Good, you're wearing proper shorts. I once had an elderly patient with a cancerous testicle winking up at me from the side of his boxer shorts throughout a session. Very distracting. Take off your wristwatch, too, as I may pivot you around later by moving your forearms. That's if we can get your lower back loosened of course which, looking at these X-rays...' This was how the first of what would be regular visits to chiropractor-osteopath Frédéric Py began. Fred, as he preferred to be called, had an office just off St-Paul-de-Fenouillet's only car and bus park. This area was transformed once a week by the bright stalls of the Saturday market. Tonight, however, no one else was to be seen as I crossed the square, struggling in the faint fluorescent light of those streetlamps that were working to read Fred's name on the brass plate on the front wall. It was more than a month since the car accident. Fred's treatment rooms were an agreeably bright and warm contrast to the dark, mid-January cold outside. From my now horizontal position I could hear the half-dozen X-rays of my head, neck and back being slid carefully out of their large, square brown envelop – vital pieces of evidence being presented to the presiding judge.

'Hmmm, bit of a mess.' Fred lifted my left knee and put his right arm under my left buttock so that the palm of his hand supported an area around the base of my spine, while his fingertips massaged the space between two spinal joints. It didn't feel invasive at all, as if he was barely touching me. 'Who was driving, your mother-in-law, wasn't it?'

'My girlfriend's mother, actually. Silvana and I are not married. It wasn't her fault. The accident I mean. Our car was hit from the side. The guy was talking on his mobile phone. I was sitting on the side that got hit.'

'And the hospital doctor advised you to…?'

'Thirty-five days of rest, ideally a couple of months, of not putting any pressure on the back. That's about it. He said there's not much can be done with this type of back injury. Just hope that when the fracture heals my back heals straight and not like a banana. Maybe you can help work on the muscles and joints around the injury.'

Fred's constant chat peppered with wry observations or outright jokes would only ever turn, I would learn, more serious when giving me his professional opinion. The cheek-scrunching smile would retreat as if pulled upwards by the action of Fred's dark eyebrows being raised. He would speak more slowly, too, so that whatever point he was making would be understood.

'I can certainly try, Monty, but whether I can make it any better… So, why didn't you let doctors in Italy follow your progress by staying there rather than coming to France? Your French is very good by the way. Especially for an Englishman.'

'Thanks. I must be relaxed already as my French falls to pieces if I am tired, stressed, distracted. I'm here to make a wine, my first, from an organic vineyard I've rented from one of your patients, Eric Laguerre. He said you might not be able to make my back any better, but that you won't make it any more painful that it already is.'

'That's kind of him,' said Fred, continuing to work his fingertips into my spinal joints, now gently moving my lower back through the movement of his upper chest on my raised right hip. To lie on my side in bed had been nearly impossible for the last several weeks, but now with Fred's support I could almost do it without flinching in pain.

'Very nice couple, Eric and Corinne. Their son Paul and my son are best friends at primary school here in St-Paul. But Monty, you'll never make a winegrower, no my friend, not with a back like you've got. Mind you, I suppose, even without the fracture in your back growing wine is a sure way to damage it permanently. So you can't win either way!' said Fred, not trying to contain a conspiratorial laugh as he looked right down on top of me as he pushed an electric button that made the couch slowly descend.

After our first session together, that Fred said would take at least an hour, he offered to show me his wine cellar. 'It's behind one of my physiotherapy studios. It's at ground level, no stairs to get up or down, so don't worry, you'll just about make it there even in your state! I haven't paid for most of the wine in there. Many of my clients are winegrowers and they always bring me a bottle or two. Worn disks in the lower back are one of the most common problems I see. That's what Eric has. It's all that repetitive bending down in the vineyard, heavy lifting and tractor driving that does it. You won't be doing any of that for a while, at least, as it's winter.'

'Well, actually, I've got 15 tonnes of organic compost to spread. I'm taking the vineyard beyond organics and farming it biodynamically.'

'Ah, biodynamics. Interesting. You a hear a lot about so-called alternative methods when you study complementary medicine like I did. Same guy behind biodynamics who set up Waldorf-Steiner schools, right? If we had a Steiner school in St-Paul for my kids…,' said Fred, as he walked from one side of the couch to the other for perhaps the eighth time already that session.

'Yes, Rudolf Steiner was behind biodynamics. In bio-dynamics, working with the forces exerted by the moon is quite crucial and tomorrow the moon is descending which is ideal for compost spreading. I missed the last time the moon was in the right place due to the accident. If I don't do it this time…'

'And what machinery will Eric lend you for 15 tonnes? Sitting on a tractor bouncing up and down on that mountainous terrain twisting your back round to see the compost spreader behind is the perfect way to inflame your already over-heated back muscles.'

'Er, I was going to use a wheelbarrow and a shovel to spread the compost and, if I have time, a rake to rake it in. I am trying to do as much by hand as possible.'

'You English have some funny ideas, that's for sure, and that's the best one I have heard in a while.' Fred was now standing directly behind me and holding my head in both hands and moving it as one would a door on a rusty hinge that needed oiling. 'Monty, listen, your back has suffered a trauma and the muscles around the injury are tight because this is the body's way of telling you to slow down, to take it easy. Zen, you know? You must be making an expensive wine if you are prepared to risk your back and do all this compost spreading by hand.'

'I know there are quite a few emerging wine producers in Roussillon now making a splash with expensive wines but the market for these wines is already cooling. There's more wine of good quality being drunk than ever before worldwide – wine being seen as healthier than spirits and not as hard on your bladder as beer. Plus, more women are drinking wine now as it is less fattening than spirits mixed with sugary soft drinks like lemonade or cola. But, heavier styles of red wines, such as Maury from down the road, are out of fashion.' I was starting to move my arms freely, like I did when I gave a talk on wine, except I usually did that standing up and without Fred having to grab one of my arms and lie it down next to me to stop me thumping him in the midriff as he went about his work.

'Tell me about it,' said Fred, as he pulled my torso up from the couch and gently rotated me. 'One of my relatives worked as a house-fitter after the war and he told me that in Maury the winegrowers could afford the finest marble for their kitchens and bathrooms. After the war, strongly alcoholic, sugary reds like Maury were seen as a luxury – but an everyday one – and Maury was easily the easily richest local town.'

'Yes, but Maury didn't adapt when tougher drink-driving rules and health issues meant sweet, alcoholic reds went out of fashion. However, Maury is small, a drop in the global wine lake. All these new irrigated vineyards in places like Chile, Australia,

Argentina, South Africa producing massive amounts of wine – they've helped push the price of wine down, which is great for wine drinkers but not so great if you try to produce expensive wines. The latter can be good but many just have fancy bottles and smart labels and are not worth the money because often the people who make them have jumped on the 'wine-is-trendy' bandwagon and are trying for a fast buck to pay for the new vineyards they have planted. The only style difference in the cheap-wine range is the top-tier wine that is aged a bit in oak barrels. Other than that it's mainly down to fancy packaging as both the cheap bottle and the most expensive one come from the same, often very young and over-irrigated, vineyards. The woody flavours are there to disguise this, and the over-elaborate packaging just confirms my belief that expensive wines like these are often mutton dressed as lamb.'

Fred had made me sit on the side of the couch, legs dangling off the floor, while he stood behind me to see just whether the curve in my spine was straightening as we came to the end of our first session. 'What makes your wine so special?'

'Not much right now. I haven't done a minute's work in the vineyard yet. But my aim is to make an easy-drinking, smooth red wine – the kind of wine that slips down easily with your evening meal after a hard day's work but that doesn't cost the earth. So, I won't be ageing it in expensive oak barrels. Is cutting down a tree just to give a wine a bit of flavour justifed? Wine snobs only exist because so many winemakers over-elaborate something that is really simple. Wine can only ever be red, white or pink, sweet or dry, still or sparkling. Wine is just one more nourishing part of a meal: like the bread in the basket, the salad, the vegetables, the meat or fish or whatever. It's something to be drunk, enjoyed and forgotten, but not worshipped. It's not the be-all and end-all. It's only bloody wine after all.'

'And you're going to risk your back tomorrow to follow the biodynamic moon, just to make an everyday wine?' I'd felt I'd made major progress, even in the half hour or so under Fred's control, but, in fact, my back was still very badly twisted as the uneasy 'oooooh' that emerged from Fred's lips as he ran his forefinger up and down the straight line where my spine should have been made clear. Fred told me to lie down again on my back.

'Well, I can't just lie in bed all day, partly because the Italian doctors told me to keep active, and I go nuts if I do nothing. The pleasure I get from knowing that putting this compost on the soil means a little bit more of the planet is being fairly treated because I am giving something to the soil before taking the wine from it makes me feel good. If my mind is feeling good, the body will follow.'

'If you carry on talking like that you'll be doing my job next!' said Fred, who had spent several minutes lightly putting his fingertips on my temples, as if he were trying to feel what was going on inside my head. 'If your mind is not right your digestion is also affected, and as your internal organs are all scrunched up due to the impact we need to make some space for them,' said Fred, as he dug his fingers up under my ribcage, which was momentarily uncomfortable as it felt like the whole centre of my body started to relax for the first time in weeks. 'My advice to you for tonight is go home, relax, have a light dinner of rice so your body doesn't have to digest anything difficult like red meat, pizza and so on.'

'Can I drink wine?'

'Yes, a bottle of wine won't hurt you,' said Fred, grinning, 'but only if it is a very good one! You can choose one from my cellar if you like. And if you are determined to spread the compost tomorrow do some light stretching before you start to get the blood moving, blood being the oil that's going to unblock your seized engine. But, I think you are taking a big risk, Monty, really I do.'

When I finally dipped my shovel into the pile of municipal compost left by the supplier at the side of the vineyard, as per my instructions, I experienced mixed feelings. The emotionless winter sky overhead made the leafless vineyard seem much larger, more nakedly aggressive, than I had remembered it, despite the morning's softly flickering light. I couldn't predict how long the stonewashed blanket of cloud would stay high enough for the peak of the Canigou in front of me to retain its status as my unyielding landmark. Freshly slipped off the back of its lorry the compost pile resembled a beached brown whale that would require hours of slicing apart with a shovel to get it where it needed to be. I was at least two months behind schedule and the soil felt colder in my soft palms than I had wanted it to be for compost spreading. Warm autumn soil is more receptive to fresh compost than a cold winter one. Yet, it was a big relief to feel that I was finally getting down to the business of growing my own wine. This had seemed an impossible moment ever to hope for when a few weeks before I'd spent six hours strapped to a hospital trolley waiting for the results of my X-rays to be given back to me by a very serious-looking Tuscan doctor. His diagnosis, spoken with a lisp and in a strong Tuscan accent that made it hard to follow, was that although the fracture in my back would heal the back itself would be prone to developing bends and kinks. This had left me not knowing whether to laugh or cry.

Although my shovel slipped easily enough into the pile of crumbly but not dry, dark-brown-to-black compost, I was acutely aware that I could barely twist my shoulders in the way I normally would have done when shovelling. Usually I liked to get my nose as close to what I was shovelling as possible, to check if the compost smelt as it should: clean and earthy rather than of rotting food. The corset I was wearing supported my torso (and conveniently held in my expanding middle-aged spread), but restricted my ability to bend and generally made working uncomfortable – both physically and mentally. It was as if the corset was reminding me that one false move would see me suffer an agonising relapse as the muscles seized up for another couple of weeks, leaving me barely able to put one foot in front of the other. It wasn't long before I could feel the cold sweat trapped between my warming back and the corset running up or down my spine with every half-bending or half-straightening motion.

I remembered the first time I had collected leaf-mould with my father, shovelling the fallen leaves from the trees in the pasture between the back of our house and the playing fields of the primary school in Winchester which I attended and where dad taught. My job was to pat the leaves down into the wheelbarrow as firmly as possible, so that each trip back home to our vegetable garden was a full one. At least trips with a filled wheelbarrow today were downhill, as I'd asked the compost-

maker to dump the truckload at the top of the vineyard, on the
north side. Gravity provided an invisible helping hand, pulling
the wheelbarrow in the direction of the Pyrénnées, its
mountaintops more easily resisting the day's strongish icy winds
than the peak on my woollen hat which bent to its left or right,
according to whether I was moving up or down yet another vine
row. The heavy working boots I was wearing had been given to
me by Californian winegrower Bobby Fetzer when I did a six-
month long work experience on his biodynamic family vineyard.
I remembered that he had once said to me, 'The best noise a
vineyard can hear is the sound of the winegrower's feet.' My own
vines were hardly likely to confirm the wisdom (or otherwise) of
Bobby's words, but even after only two hours of wheeling
compost I felt I was getting to know the vineyard in a way that
never would have been possible from a tractor cab. How the sun
fell across it, where the *tramonata* or mountain wind blew from
and in which spots the vines were potentially weak due to rocky
soils or where the vines might be growing too strongly due to
wetter soil. As the vines were un-pruned it was quite easy to see
where weak spots might be. Vines that had either lacked food or
water or both had produced shorter than normal shoots the
previous year. These shoots had only grown as high as the
highest supporting wires strung between the vineyard posts.
The weakest vines were found on a slight bump in the land
running across the slope, where topsoils were thinnest. This
area was given extra handfuls of compost taken directly from
the wheelbarrow. The compost was sprinkled in little piles either
side of each vine and in the same direction of the vine row. Less
compost was needed the further I descended down the slope, as
this was where the soil was richest and more obviously capable

of holding water, but I put compost there all the same. Here its effect would be to allow the soil to absorb the rain to prevent precious soil being washed away.

Spreading the compost right next to the vines was one advantage of doing it by hand. You'd never get this close with a compost-spreading machine, which tend to spray gobbets of compost everywhere. Next to the vine is where the vine's small feeder roots are found. Stimulating the soil in this area made sense if the rest of the vine's root system – the deep tap roots that it puts down vertically into the ground, and the more extensive feeder roots that push horizontally in the topsoil between each vine row – is to benefit. The other advantage of compost spreading by hand is that it saves a lot of money on tractor fuel and that the tyres are more likely to compact the soil than human feet and a wheelbarrow. Saving fuel also means not releasing any carbon dioxide into the atmosphere, a double bonus when it comes to compost spreading as the processes involved in making the chemical fertilisers used in conventional agriculture make them the biggest source of carbon dioxide emissions in agriculture and the biggest source of nitrous oxide worldwide. I can't remember exactly how many of the ultra-strong painkillers Eric had given me I had taken by the end of the day when I crawled into the bath in my rented house in St-Martin.

When looking for a house to rent Silvana had described the one I had ended up with in her inimitably concise way as 'not perfect, but perfect for you at this time'. I couldn't rent a flat in Tuscany while also renting one in France and as Silvana didn't want to live in our Italian flat on her own she moved back in with her parents. She planned to use the money she saved on rent to come and visit me in France as often as her hectic work, teaching and study schedule would allow. My share of the Italian rent would be used to find somewhere in St-Martin.

'There seem to be lots of unoccupied houses in St-Martin, so it shouldn't be too difficult to rent one,' I had said to Silvana over coffee at the Auberge Taïchac during the weekend we came to France to sign the vineyard deal with Eric. 'Yes, Monty, but probably French people do like they do in Italy. They own a house in a small village like St-Martin and come here with their families only for the summer months and spend the rest of the year in the city. I heard someone talking at the bar yesterday about the presidential elections due next year.'

'I'm only looking to rent a bloody house, not stand for president of the fifth republic...'

'No, listen to me for once. It seems that in St-Martin around 80 people are registered to vote here, even if only half that number actually live here all year round. That's the point. So, most of the houses here won't be for rent, even if they're empty. And you have to be French to become president. The only thing French about you is your big nose!'

Silvana had put the word out that we were looking for somewhere to rent and it seemed we had just two choices. To find the first house we had to go through a guy called Jean-Luc Rochette. Jean-Luc, whose good looks could be described as boyish, chiselled and often flecked with paint, owned Bob. This was the escaped mule we had seen in the main square the day before. On the back of his pick-up Jean-Luc had a mule-shaped sticker in the vertical yellow-and-red-striped colours of

Catalonia – many people in this part of the world consider themselves Catalan first and French (or Spanish) second. Bob the mule, we discovered, lived with another mule called Blondie in a paddock Jean-Luc and his brother Eric had built amongst the oak forests on the highest edge of the village, at the back of Jean-Luc's house. Jean-Luc spoke excellent English, but with an American accent having lived in Las Vegas for many years while working as a painter and decorator. 'Vegas has one of the fastest growing populations in America, so that meant plenty of new homeowners in need of painters and decorators like me. I've just finished decorating a newly renovated ruin here in the village that is available to rent and that belongs to my brother, Eric,' Jean-Luc told Silvana and me. We had accidentally-on-purpose made sure we bumped into him the next time we saw him about the village, mule-less but with brush and paint-pot in hand. Eric Number Two as we learnt to call Jean-Luc's brother (vineyard-owner Eric Laguerre being Eric Number One) showed Silvana and me the house with his wife Sylvie. The mayor's daughter, Sylvie worked as a pharmacist in Perpignan, although I guessed that as her natural beauty radiated whether she was smartly dressed on in her jogging gear (both her parents regularly completed marathons) she could quite easily have become a model. Her husband was more of a jeans-and-T-shirt kind of guy. He didn't seem too bothered about how long his hair was and was, like many of the villagers, a rugby fanatic. 'You know, Perpignan is the only place in France where we play both 15-a-side, or rugby union as you call it in England, and 13-a-side, or rugby league.' I wasn't a natural rugby fan, but with the rugby world cup due to be hosted in France in the summer I realised I'd have to brush up on my rugby knowledge. Even knowing a few facts would help as a conversational ice-breaker. As well as running a number of property businesses, Eric had another passion. In a hangar near to where Bob the mule lived there were over half a dozen pick-ups, jeeps and other classic cars. Eric and Sylvie's labrador, Cooper, had (it appeared) been named after the Mini model of that name that Sylvie regularly drove to work.

'This house has the most modern interior of any small country home I have seen in France,' I said as Silvana and I followed Eric Number Two around the house. Harry and Cooper had decided it was more fun chasing each other around the main square, with Sylvie dog-watching despite my pleas that nothing untoward would happen. 'Harry had his balls cut off when he was small,' I explained, 'because he came from the top breeder of Jack Russell Terrier's in California who didn't want Harry's new owners to breed from him. Anyway, he lived for four years with a big Ridgeback called Marlowe who had both his balls, just like Cooper. So, Harry shouldn't feel too threatened or jealous.' Silvana glared at my lack of tact, but Eric Number Two and Sylvie just laughed. 'I went to see Harry in Los Angeles before I adopted him from a schoolmate who was having a baby and couldn't handle two dogs anymore. That's how I know.' Harry was so enthralled by his new canine friend, Silvana and I had a job steering him back to the hotel after our first house visit was complete. 'Well,' said Silvana, in post-mortem mode, 'lovely modern kitchen. Clean bathrooms. Shower and full-size bath. Brand-new washing machine and tumble dryer. Well-designed spiral staircases to make the most of the living space. Lots of space for storage, too. New beds and mattresses. Nice and bright. Easy to heat, and well insulated.

The only problem is the rent is around double what I had budgeted.'

The only other house for rent in the village was two doors up from the one we had seen, and it had been inherited by Eric Number One from his grandfather. Eric Number Two had even suggested we look at this house. 'It's not as modern as the one I have, but is much cheaper.' Bearing in mind that Eric Number Two was recommending a rival bidder if you like, his description of the second house as being 'not as modern' as his was a delicate understatement. There was no central heating, no washing machine, the windows were rickety and the curiously turquoise shutters were in places rotting off their hinges.

'Our last tenant was a writer and had a dog,' explained Corinne, Eric Number One's wife as she showed Silvana and I around. 'He bunked off one night without paying the rent or bills. He, or rather his dog, did leave us with plenty of gifts on the mattresses.' Egregiously stained, these were leant against the wall of the largest of the three bedrooms. All had parquet rather than tiled floors that would make them slightly warmer under foot for someone like me who hadn't owned a pair of slippers since leaving prep school aged 12. The house was, however, light, had three spacious floors and, most importantly, was cheap. After the discount I eventually haggled out of Eric Number One it was less than half the price of Eric Number Two's more modern house. As I fitted the potential profile of a non-rent-paying dog-owning writer, I allayed Corinne's fears by agreeing to pay rent up-front promising that because Harry would be with me 24/7 there was no danger he'd be messing in the house. The back of the house overlooked one of Eric's storage cellars and the hills, behind which were the Agly river and the town of St-Paul. The basement area at the front of the house formed the only way in and opened directly onto the cobbled backstreet that led down to the main square. 'That was where, up until the 1950s, the horses, mules, or oxen that worked the family vineyards were housed in winter,' explained Eric, as Corinne, Silvana, Harry and I passed him on the way up onto the first floor. Eric was lying on the speckled-egg marble floor of the hallway on the middle floor in an orange jumpsuit. He was surrounded by bundles of white tissue-paper stained red by the heating fuel Eric was trying to mop up from a sometimes blocked, sometimes leaky fuel line. This ran along a metal-overspill tray at the base of an enamel-topped stove-come-heater that was the house's only form of heating. The heater was sandwiched in the wall cavity between the staircase leading up to the bedrooms on the top floor and the stairs down to the basement. All the other houses in the street had similar basements, although this was the only one that, seemingly, had yet to be converted into either a garage or an artists' studio.

'You haven't seen it yet but there's a fuel tank in the basement,' said Eric, lighting a taper that he had already wetted with industrial alcohol from a clear bottle before dropping it into the heater's central cavity. The fire didn't take, prompting Eric to exclaim, '*merde de merde de chié de merde!*' to himself. 'You'll need to fill the tank up if you want to stay warm this winter. I'll give you the number of the supplier in St-Paul. He's coming to fill my fuel tanks for the tractors in a couple of days.'

'How much do you think I'll need?' I asked, not having any experience of fuel heaters like this before.

'Say a couple of hundred litres.'

By the time I clambered out of the first bath I had taken in my new home, the fuel had been delivered. The only way of paying the bill was cash there and then. The bill was what I would normally spend in a year on heating at home in England. The room in which the fuel was stored at the bottom of the house had no spare space, Eric having dumped piles of old furniture there. The smell of fuel was not quite over-powering enough to make your clothes smell of it after a brief visit, but you'd need a strong coffee afterwards to remove its presence from the back of your throat and nostrils.

I spent the first couple of days after compost-spreading getting my bearings in the house, shunting my possessions around as best I could, arranging for the phone line to be reconnected and putting up some makeshift curtains that Corinne had found for me. 'It's a small village, Monty,' she explained, 'and you don't want people knowing what colour boxer shorts you're wearing every day.' Although nearly as short as Silvana, Corinne insisted she'd be the one to perch on a chair and stretch up and backwards to hang the curtains on the occasionally rickety curtain rails. 'Your bad back,' she said, simply. She also showed me how to turn the water and electricity off in an emergency. Gas for the cooker in the kitchen as is normal in rural France was supplied by refillable gas bottles. 'We have red and blue bottles in France. For this gas cooker you need red ones. The petrol stations at either the supermarket or the main garage in St-Paul have them. But, they're heavy to lift.'

Fred Py had said he wouldn't see me for at least 14 days after our first back-mending session. 'The back will heal itself naturally. All I can do is to guide it the right way but only every so often, not every day.' My problem was I had to try to get the compost raked in. I didn't just want it sitting on the soil surface, where it would only do a little bit of good. I needed to get it into the first couple of centimetres of topsoil if it was to feed the soil so that the soil could then feed the vines. I could feel that the act of compost spreading had undone some of Fred Py's fine work and I was going to have to undo more of it to ensure the money spent on compost did not go to waste. However, when I arrived at the vineyard, corset pulled tight once again against the cold, rake in hand I could see the vineyard had been lightly ploughed with tractor-mounted disks. The blots of dark compost had now been covered by bright soil. I caught up with Eric outside his house as he was preparing for lunch. 'I'm really sorry, Monty,' he said, holding his hands up as if I was pointing a revolver at him. 'I just went onto autopilot. I was ploughing all my vineyards on the plateau, as I do every year, and I did yours as well by mistake. Come in and have a bite with me and we'll sort out some kind of refund on the vineyard rental. I'm sorry, I know you want to do as much as you can by hand.'

'Listen, Eric, it's fine. And, besides, spending a couple of days raking it in by hand is not the kind of thing my back needs right now. Fred Py is already going to kill me for shovelling so much compost.'

'Well, to be honest, I saw you walking around the other day – there are 80-year-old men in this village who are less stooped and quicker on their feet than you. Corinne said you couldn't even hang a curtain. I did the first couple of rows in your

In an act of love, Monty tries to cure Silvana's homesickness for Tuscany by impersonating the leaning tower of Pisa.

Harry gets in on the winegrowing act by showing Silvana his newly rented dwarf-vine vineyard, designed for small dogs.

The Taïchac castle east of St-Martin. Spring snow helped slow the vines down after far too warm a winter.

St-Martin-de-Fenouillet lies in the 'Fennel' hills above the Agly valley, less than one hours' drive from Perpignan.

Pascal and Dominique prune my vines on the Planels plateau.

Pascal holds up what he has just pruned: last year's vine shoots.

Eric stockpiles Grenache Gris cuttings during winter pruning ready for use as grafting material should any existing vines die.

Arnaud guides Cajolle and plough as close to the vines as he dares while ploughing out inconvenient weeds.

'We haven't seen a vineyard ploughed by horse in thirty years,' several villagers remarked when seeing this.

Marmaduke's desire for complete colour coordination meant only a silver water bucket would do for the goose house.

Petronella considers calling her lawyer on being shown the size of the swimming pool.

Petronella (foreground) and Marmaduke were a formidable double-act, especially when performing the synchronised goose routine.

John Holms prepares to cut a hatch in the chicken shed for the hens to jump through.

Daniel Salinas prepares to clean out the allotments' irrigation canal.

John now realises the hatch is too small for him to be able to raid the chicken house for eggs.

The raised bed system allows you to sow, plant and pick your crops from the safety of the garden path.

The garden, plus chicken run (top left) and goose run (bottom left) in full bloom.

Harry gives me his 'isn't it time for a walk, dad?' look in an effort to drag me away from my writing desk.

Harry rehearses his response for when the French traffic police next try to impound the Estafette for its unroadworthiness.

vineyard by accident. Then I remembered I was renting it to you, but I carried on. It's great what you did with compost, investing so much in the soil. And, at this time of year, some tractor work won't do any harm. Raking by hand will. But, if you think I over-stepped the mark, a refund is no problem. Honestly.'

I thanked Eric, refused his offer of a discount, left him to his lunch and had my own, secretly relieved that a genuine error on his part was going to save me a couple of days of spinal agony. The way Eric had ploughed in the compost had put it exactly where it needed to be in the topsoil – any deeper down into the soil and the worms and other topsoil microbes would never be able to get to it to mix it in properly. I couldn't have done a better job myself to be honest and, as I made my way to the allotment, rake and shovel left at home, I experienced a feeling of elation for the first time since before the car crash.

I hadn't known the house I had rented came with its own vegetable plot at the bottom of the village until Corinne mentioned it when she came round to do the curtains. 'On Sunday, everyone who is going to grow vegetables down there is due to meet and clear out the water canal. The guy organising it is called Daniel. You can't quite see his house from yours, but I'll show you where he lives and you can sort it out with him.' Daniel turned out to be the wiry, tall man I had seen around the village clutching bags of snails. He was a retired postal worker from Paris and now lived in St-Martin with his wife. He had collected the snails by coaxing them out of their favourite hiding places in the stone wall that formed one boundary along the side of the allotment area. Between this wall and the small stream were around a dozen vegetable plots. Eric Number

One's, or rather mine, was at the far end, along a bumpy, unsurfaced track by the wall only wide enough for one person to pass comfortably at a time.

'You clean the snails by putting them in a salt bath,' Daniel explained, as we began clearing the narrow irrigation canal that ran along the path. 'You do this a week after you have caught them, but you don't give them anything to eat in the meantime. The salt cleanses them of any impurities. Then you de-shell them, trim off the bits you can't eat and cook them. Not too hot though. Otherwise they'll be too tough.'

Daniel's staccato-style Paris accent made his French easier for me to understand than the local dialect, which at times seemed a mixture of Catalan, Spanish and medieval Mediterranean French. After we had cleared the canal, Daniel scraping the bits of earth, twigs and fallen leaves out of the canal into a bucket; me emptying the bucket onto where I had decided my allotment compost pile was going to be, we wandered up to the water reservoir that fed the canal. This was (logically enough) upstream from the allotment area. A solid metal plate fixed between two waist-high stone walls stopped the stream's flow, forming a natural dam. 'To get water to flow into the irrigation canal,' Daniel explained, 'you either take out that wooden post-end blocking the hole at the bottom of one side of the wall, or put one of those large pieces of hose in the water until full, block one end with your hand, lift the other over the wall above the canal and let go. The water will be sucked over the wall to run along the canal. There is a slight slope from here to the stone water-collector we passed at the other end of the allotments. This collects any overflow for the gardens at the other end when the system is in use.

Anyway, to get water from the canal onto your garden just un-block one of the holes at the side of the canal where your part is. You should have three, one at each side, and one in the middle.' Sure enough, Daniel showed me where my three holes were. These had been blocked by scrunched-up plastic carrier bags and various-sized stones covered by a couple of large handfuls of compacted earth, now overgrown by grass.

'But what do I do when the water comes in? I don't want to flood the whole garden,' I asked.

'You won't flood the garden. You simply sow your crop seeds, or plant your transplants, in furrows along which the water runs. With a hoe you can direct the flow of the water by blocking or opening a furrow by piling or removing a bit of earth.' This was the same system I had seen used in South American flood-irrigated vineyards, a system perfected by the Incas. The problem with it was that quite a bit of water went to waste, or simply irrigated the weeds that would inevitably colonise the furrows that had been dug. And there was no real control over exactly how much water each vegetable plant had.

'People here have been using this system for about 300 years, Monty. I wouldn't worry too much,' said Daniel. 'The water always runs out down here at some stage during summer, even though only around half a dozen of the allotments here are maintained. Just hope that it runs out in late summer, not soon after Easter, that's all.'

I knew water use was a big issue. The last three winters here had been very dry and some local villages had had to truck in drinking water for the villagers. The area of Roussillon on the flatter land nearer the coast is a big area for fruit – peaches, plums, apples – and the lack of ground water over recent years had hit yields there as well as for the winegrowers both near the coast and up in the hills around places like St-Martin. As I wasn't convinced about the flood irrigation system, I resolved to find a way of watering my vegetables by hand. 'Watering by hand is a good idea,' Daniel said, adjusting what looked like a corporal's cap on his head, 'especially as you're not growing vegetables commercially. But, with a back in your condition, doing it by hand means that you, rather than gravity, will be bearing the load.' Everything Daniel said made perfect sense, of course, but I was sure of two things. First, my back would get better and it would only get better if I refused to spend all day lying in bed complaining about it. Second, I was sure I could save water by digging my own water pit that could double-up as a pond for some chickens, ducks, or geese. The eggs, or meat would come in useful and the birds would do a bit of weeding and pest control. Biodynamic growers always try to have a few animals around and although Silvana had made it clear under her budget restrictions that I couldn't have a cow, she'd never said I couldn't have a chicken or two...

I walked back up to the village, leaving Daniel to dig the first furrows in his vegetable plot, took off my boots and set about lighting the fuel heater. This was more like it, I thought to myself. This was the kind of life I had wanted to lead. A bit of banter one morning with a friendly, neighbouring winegrower who does me a good turn with his tractor, leisurely lunches of fresh baguettes, French cheese, pâté and salad, with planning trips to a vegetable garden surrounded by ancient woodland

and with its own stream thrown in. And, to top it off, I would soon be able to rest my back against a warming fire, once I had got it lit of course. The main fire chamber seemed to be empty of fuel as none of the lit tapers I dropped in took. I opened the hinged metal front of the heater to fiddle with the lever that controlled the fuel flow, a bit like a manual choke on a car. I could see that some fuel had leaked onto the base plate, leaving a pool around one centimetre deep nearly the width of the heater. I wasn't worried as this appeared to be sealed off from the main chamber.

I have always loved fire, and have not always been a responsible fire lighter, as the scar on the right hand side of my head testifies. When my family moved house when I was ten, I offered to burn all the rubbish we threw out from the new house. This included piles of rubber carpet underlay. I worked out that by sticking garden stakes into the burning, molten rubber I could make an improvised torch. I decided it might be fun to hurl my torches into the night air as an improvised firework display. When the second burning stake-end landed on my cheek, just missing my eye, but burning my skin I ran into the house and hid under the dinner table for the rest of night, probably in shock. I knew that saying as little as possible was the best way to avoid uncomfortable questions, a tactic learnt from a previous fire disaster. When I was seven I accidentally set fire to a hay field at the back of our first house. I'd been playing with matches near a water trough surrounded by a thick mat of dried hay. This, of course, caught easily in the wind and despite my best efforts of peeing on the burning stubble, and trying to stamp out the flames with my little legs, was soon out of control. I ran home, dialled the emergency number and asked for the fire brigade, who within minutes had snuffed the fire out with flat rubber beaters on the end of long hand-held poles. The next day, in front of 900 pupils at school assembly, the headmaster and teachers (one of whom was my dad) asked for a standing ovation for my heroic efforts of the previous day. 'The fire was heading towards the school, until one of our pupils alerted the emergency services and avoided a disaster having seen smoke while out walking.' That had been my excuse when asked by the fire chief how I had come to spot the fire. 'I always go walking in the fields between our house and the school when school's finished.'

I agreed with myself to try one final attempt at lighting the fuel-burner before calling in Eric. I dropped a taper in and the whoosh made by the air being sucked in to feed the fire engulfing the fuel chamber and the heat pushed upwards by the fire itself made my heart jump in palpable fear. The fuel chamber been completely overfilled – the tapers I had been dropping had been going out before they hit the fuel level – causing a mini-inferno when a successfully lit taper did finally arrive. But, high winds pushing down the metal chimney-tube meant the flames were now being pushed onto the fuel-covered base plate. The fuel heater was alight, but it was also on fire. And the fuel reservoir chamber, that was full of about ten litres of fuel, was dangerously close to the blue flames coursing across the base plate. I didn't have a fire blanket to hand and I calculated that the time it would take me to find a container big enough to fill with water to hurl over the flames it would be too late. I didn't have a bucket and my biggest fruit bowl was still in a sealed box covered in bubble-wrap somewhere amongst 20-odd other boxes on the living room floor. I grabbed Harry and shuffled as fast as I could to Eric's house in my socks. Every time my feet landed on the cobbles they pushed my hips up into my spine, causing me to moan in desperate, breathless pain. With such a strong wind blowing I was convinced the fire brigade would never get here in time to save my house, let alone the two attached each side – one belonging to Eric's mother, the other to a married couple and their young daughter. 'It's on fire!' I yelled as I approached the mayor's office, around the corner from which was Eric's house. 'Fire, quick, help.' Screaming at someone's house did strike me as vaguely comic, especially as the wind was so strong someone only ten metres ahead of me would never had heard my bawling, plaintiff cries. Even if Eric was in he'd have no chance of hearing me through his thick front door and even thicker stone walls. And even if he was, what could we do if the house was alight by then?

Chapter 4

Anyone leaving the mayor's office that afternoon would have seen a sight worthy of a call to social services, or possibly even law enforcement, rather than the fire brigade: one tall man with a blond, Viking-style ponytail waddling rather than running due to a stiff lower back in a T-shirt, boxer shorts and socks despite the winter cold, accompanied by a shorter, darker haired man, also in socks and limping due to a stiff lower back and carrying a small dog. 'What are you trying to tell me?' asked Eric, white-faced. 'Has the stove caught fire or has the house caught fire as well?' He had unsurprisingly not fully understood what I had tried to explain in garbled, breathless French when he'd opened his front door which I'd almost broken down to attract the attention of anyone inside. Luckily, Eric was in having just finished a session fixing a tractor in his workshop.

'I don't know, but the stove is on fire for sure and I think the house might be on fire too,' I said as best I could, but was so out of breath the words would hardly come. Although it was only a short distance between my house and Eric's (less than a minute's walk) my back was so painfully stiff I couldn't keep up with Eric. He charged on ahead as best he could. When I finally caught up with Eric, the house was still perfectly in tact. He had cut the fuel supply to the main fire chamber that was now open. I thought he had damped the flames running across the base plate with some wet tea towels, but he hadn't had to do anything. That was why he was laughing, with relief more than joy. 'Monty, you can't light the fuel burner in such high winds with so much fuel in the system. You're asking for trouble, especially with this leaky fuel line. You're not very technical, are you?' That was a bit of an understatement, I had to admit. The fire on the base plate had burnt itself out due to a lack of oxygen while I was hobbling towards Eric's house. Had I left the main door to the base plate open to the air it might have been a different story, however, as Eric explained.

'I didn't realise the fuel chamber was so full. I've never used a heater like this before. I kept trying to get it to light, but I guess I overfilled it and panicked when I thought the whole lot was going to catch fire. Sorry, Eric. I am a bit of a maniac with fire to be honest. It's how I got these scars on the side of my head and cheek. But this has really shaken me up. You didn't look like you were having much fun trying to fix it the other day. The house still stinks of all the leaked fuel.' Even though Eric had disposed of all the paper tissues he had used to mop up spillages from the fuel line several days before, the central part of the house still smelled like a fuel depot. Even lighting a fire in a place that smelt of fuel seemed a bad idea, which at least showed me I had matured somewhat since my childhood. Eric didn't seem convinced that my fears were justified though. So I pressed on.

'I really don't feel so confident about this stove, especially if the fuel supply is so erratic and you can't really see how much fuel is active in the system. It's not as if you can stick your nose in there is it – well not with my sized nose anyway?' This last comment did at least elicit a laugh from Eric, whose forearm was covered in fine-black soot from trying to clean the inner fire chamber of debris, which he thought was partially blocking the fuel's arrival there. 'Maybe we could get a wood-burner instead?'

'If you use the fuel-burner correctly it works fine, Monty, honestly, I've had this thing for years,' said Eric. 'I think the previous tenants put some bad fuel in the system before they bunked off without paying the rent, to make it look like it was fuller than it was. We've never had a problem with it before. My father bought it about 30 years ago. If I can fix it... You don't want a wood-burner. It's much messier – you need to find the wood first of all, then after every couple of days or so you'll have to sweep the ashes out and take them away. The house will be much dustier and dirtier as a result, honestly.' As I couldn't fault Eric's reasoning, I knew I had to play what I hoped would be my trump card in an effort to convince him that a wood-burner was exactly what was needed. 'I see what you mean about the dust, but I can always compost that. Wood-ash is quite a good carbon source for compost microbes.'

'Okay, okay. Are all English boys so crazy for compost like you? I can certainly think of one thing that would bio-degrade quite easily, under the right circumstances!' Eric said, casting an obvious glance at Harry, who was sitting in the living room doorway at a safe distance from the noxious-smelling, non-functioning heater. 'Where are you going to get wood from? If you own woodland around here you have the right to cut a certain amount of your trees each year, but you don't own any woodland.'

'Finding wood won't be a problem,' I said confidently, hoping my ace was about to land face-up on the gaming table. 'I can collect all the dead wood lying around your vineyards on the plateau where my vineyard is. It's what, two days' work with a back like mine? Your vineyard guys are busy, and I have a bit of time until pruning starts, so...'

'What wood? From where I've been re-grafting, you mean?' asked Eric. I had noticed the first six rows of one of the vineyards near mine (that I knew belonged to Eric) were in the process of being re-grafted from one grape-type to another. Eric did this by first sawing off each vine trunk at ground level using a handsaw. Then into a small cleft he made in each stump he would insert a finger-length vine shoot from a different type of wine grape. The shoot would have one bud on it that would burst the following spring, eventually growing into a new vine complete with its own trunk, shoots, leaves and grapes. In this way a mature vineyard could be changed from one wine grape to another without needing to rip out the vineyard, and meant only one year's crop of grapes was lost. Ripping out a healthy vineyard to replant it entirely from scratch meant losing perhaps three or four years of grapes, and thus made no sense either environmentally or economically. Why spend time and money to lose the mature root-systems the vines had developed underground over the previous 20 years or so? It only made sense to rip out an old vineyard if the vines had been affected by a virus, for example – sometimes caused by soil microbes that poison the vines by their roots. As this wasn't the case for Eric, he was switching the vineyard from a red-wine grape,

Grenache Noir planted by his father to a white-wine grape, Grenache Gris. Eric thought Grenache Gris, which gives a rich, white wine with an agreeably buttery texture, would ripen earlier and more consistently on such a high, windy, exposed site. The only problem was that someone had to go through the vineyard and collect all of the cut vine-trunks so that they wouldn't hinder future tractor work by damaging disks on tractor-mounted ploughs, for example. I also saw another potential problem. 'Leaving all those dead vine-trunks lying around is the kind of thing that could cause you a major disease problem, Eric,' I suggested, thinking of a vine-wood disease called 'Esca'. This was normally a problem on badly pruned old-vines, where the woody parts either side of the top of the vine trunk were not getting enough sap flow, especially during hot summers. The lack of sap flow attracted the Esca spores, causing the woodiest vine parts to dry until the disease had taken over enough of the vine for it to have to be ripped out. 'Esca is attracted to decomposing vine wood, and you don't want to leave anything lying around that might encourage that, do you? If I collect the dead vine trunks and use them for heating the house here, we'll both benefit. Your vines will stay healthy and we can change this death-trap for a wood-burner, eh?' This was the first time that I think I could claim my organic 'prevention-rather-than-cure' philosophy in the vineyard had dovetailed so neatly with domestic arrangements in my new house. As part of the deal Eric said I'd have to help him find a wood-burner and help him carry it into the house, plus he said he'd want to keep a few vine trunks as barbecue wood for summer. French winegrowers never tire of telling anyone who'll listen that meat grilled on either old-vine trunks, or the thinner vine shoots pruned off each year in winter, tastes much better than meat grilled on ordinary wood, coal, or charcoal.

'Okay, Eric, you keep some of the wood for barbecues if you invite me along to eat with you, Paul and Corinne!'

'Deal,' said Eric, grinning. 'You English often burn the meat when you barbecue; you cook it too quickly by letting it get too close to the hot coals. You're going to trust a Frenchman to do a barbecue, are you? In France we like our meat nice and rare. *Bleu* we call it. I can't believe my ancestors didn't teach you lot how to cook meat properly when we invaded England in 1066.'

'So, you think you're a chef and I'm a pryomaniac – the deal is that I'll do the fire part of the barbecue if you do the cooking. Cook it however you want. I'll split the cost of the meat with you if you provide the wine. I'll handle the salad, bread and cheese. Deal?' We shook hands. I was learning that deal-making with Eric involved lots of give and take, and that he was disappointed if I didn't try to push him as hard as he he'd push me when discussing the finer points of the deal. So far, each deal we made – big or small – seemed to have left both parties highly satisfied, especially since Eric didn't eat cheese. 'For my waistline,' he commented.

Now all we had to do was find a wood-burner. So, the next day Eric and I drove to Perpignan to look around a few second-hand shops and showrooms on the outskirts of the city, near the rugby stadium, in an area called Haut-Vernet. I pointed out several wood-burners that looked aesthetically perfect for the house, but Eric had a more practical eye, observing that 'that one's too wide for the alcove in the house' or 'yes, that one looks nice but the back plate is rusty so not only will it not throw any heat, but it'll burn the walls of the house, too'. We ended up

pallet

buying a brand-new cast-iron wood-burner with a glass front
from a home supply depot – it was bulky, extremely heavy and
offered no easy places to grip it by hand. We only just managed
to lift it off its wooden palate onto Eric's van via the van's side
door. Lifting it up the house's short, narrow, spiral staircase
took us well over an hour. The staircase had marble tiles, so if
we dropped it not only would we smash our toes but the house's
original floor too. Corinne came to check out the new addition
to the house, but instead of offering moral support she just
laughed at 'two blokes, all arses and elbows, grunting away over
a piece of metal'. I picked up some dead wood I'd seen while
walking with Harry – an old wooden pylon left to rot. Eric,
Corinne and I were soon enjoying the heat both from the
vertical-glass-plate window that contained the fire chamber,
but also from the metal chimney that ran from the wood-burner
up and out through the roof. I'd be able to hang clothes off the
banisters to dry and could direct the heat into whichever room
I chose just by opening or closing a door. And, although the
chimney was made of a series of sometimes irregularly
interlocking pipes, that meant the house could get a little
smoky if there was a strong down-draft from the wind outside,
I much preferred the smell of wood-smoke to fuel.

I spent a couple of fruitful afternoons in the vineyards surrounding mine collecting dead-vine wood. It was just the kind of
light work I needed to try to regain a bit of fitness after
spending one entire month more or less lying horizontal and
then another month with severely restricted movement. The

tramontana wind was buffeting me from the west, causing the hood on my jacket to flap like a loose sail around my head, but its bracing, rather than chilly, nature made me feel alive after so much time spent convalescing indoors. I walked methodically up and down each vine row looking for winter fuel – some of which was hidden under quite thick mats of the wild grasses Eric had left to grow. Each vine trunk weighed only the same as an average bag of flour and had the same length and shape as a human arm. The only way I could collect them was by maintaining a perfectly straight body-shape, then bending my knees so that my backside almost touched the ground. I could then reach either side of me to grab the trunks. What I soon realised, however, was that my back was not yet flexible enough to make the body movements necessary for pruning. The vines in my vineyard each had ten branches on, with two branches or shoots growing off one of five thumb-like stubs – or spurs – left the previous winter by whoever had pruned the vineyard. One shoot would grow off one side of the thumb, say where the thumb joined the hand, and the other would be higher up and on the other side on the end of where the thumbnail would be. For my vines to be pruned properly I'd have to make around two cuts to create a new spur from last year's growth with the pruning scissors. The first cut would remove everything that had grown from last year's thumbnail. The second cut would remove all but the bottom two buds from the shoot that had grown from where the thumb joined the hand. These two buds would each produce a new shoot. Each shoot might produce two bunches. So, if both shoots from all five of the spurs on each vine produced two bunches of grapes, that made twenty bunches per vine, enough for two bottles, or 12,000 bottles in total. Eric had warned me though that as my vines were old, many shoots would not produce two bunches.

My problem was that I was unable to curve my back. To prune well you need to bend your back so you can see exactly where you are cutting with the scissors. Cutting off too much of last year's shoots would leave you without the two buds needed to grow this year's grapes. Leaving too many buds would produce too many grapes and too many shoots. The vine would become a tangle of leaves and shoots and bunches, and everything would get so cramped diseases like rot and mildew would surely strike. Not only could I not bend my back well enough to see where I was cutting, I was not able to make any pulling movements, to pull out pruned shoots from between the supporting wires. Pulling put so much stress on the muscles in my lower back that I could feel it start to spasm. The shoots needing to be pulled were around the same length as the vine trunks, but were much lighter being on pencil-thin rather than human-arm thick. The problem is that the vine is a creeping plant. In the wild it loves to grow up trees – that's why the ancient Greeks, the world's most artful winegrowers, used to let their vines grow up fruit and olive trees, getting two crops instead of just one from a single piece of land. To climb up trees vines put out tendrils: small and wispy hook-like shoots that curl around the branches of a tree or a metal wire in the case of a modern vineyard. These curly tendrils become very hard once they have hooked on to whatever they are climbing up. So, to pull vine shoots clinging by their tendrils to vineyard supporting wires requires not only strength but the ability to twist and also cut the tendrils with the pruning scissors. In my vineyard there were roughly 6,000 vines. With an imaginary pair of pruning scissors – the fore- and middle-finger of my right hand – I 'pruned' one vine.

I found it quite easy to prune the first two sets of shoots down to spurs for the coming year. They were at a good height for me to work without having to contort myself uncomfortably. They were also on my side of the supporting wires. Where I found it difficult was reaching and bending over and behind the supporting wires to the get to the six shoots on the three spurs on the far side. It was painful to reach them by poking my body through the supporting wires. In this situation the only alternative was to repeat and extend my wood-collecting position, by going down on my hands and knees with my back straight, to be able to reach under and behind the supporting wires. However, pieces of granite jarring into my kneecaps then resulted in involuntarily movements and this caused serious pincers of pain to flash up the base of my spine. Pruning the vineyard like this would take me around a month, instead of a week. When Eric appeared with his son Paul in his jeep later that afternoon I had no choice but to ask if I could hire two of his best pruning men, Dominque and Pascal, to do the job.

'You'll be pruning on the descending moon, right?' asked Eric, referring to the 13-day window of opportunity every four weeks when the moon's physical position in the sky becomes gradually lower*. I said that that was what I had intended, as pruning during the descending moon period kept the vines strong by allowing them to keep as much of their precious, food-rich sap in their roots rather than seeing it lost to vine shoots that were being cut off by the pruning scissors.

'The next descending moon period will be roughly during the first two weeks in February,' Eric said. 'Maybe I can get Pascal and Dominique to come at the end of the second week in February?'

* *The sun takes six months to reach its highest point in the sky at summer solstice and another six months to reach its lowest point at winter solstice. The moon rises and falls too, but it takes just 27.3 days rather than 365. This is called the ascending and descending moon cycle.* *(Continued over)*

Whereas I would take a few moments to think about exactly where I would cut the vines during pruning, Pascal and Dominique would do the job on autopilot, barely pausing before each vine. Pascal, whose wife Martine worked in the St-Martin mayoral office, had worked for Eric's family for twenty years. Eric had given him various nicknames, including 'Ton-Ton' or 'uncle' (even though they weren't related) and 'Wallace', as in the children's television characters *Wallace & Gromit*. It wasn't hard to see how Pascal's combination of short, curly hair, bobble-hat and round, effortlessly smiling face had earned him the second nickname.

'These vines were planted in the 1950s,' Pascal told me, cutting the smaller vine shoots with a pair of secateurs and the larger pieces closer to the vine trunk with a pair of hedge-trimmers that were wedged between his body and his belt when not in use. 'And in those days the vines would have been free-standing.'

'You mean there were no supporting wires?'

'No, they were put in during the 1970s or early 1980s, I think, before I started working. That was when the vineyard changed from being picked by hand to being machine picked. If you leave the vine shoots to grow in al directions they'll be snapped off by the machine picker as it passes over each vine. Then you're left with a real mess at pruning because if the shoots from last year have snapped off right to the trunk of the vine you won't be left with enough of a shoot from which to prune a spur on which to leave the two buds you need for this year's shoots.'

Bending the shoots up and between sets of supporting wires means that when the machine picker straddles the vines

When the moon is ascending plants send their sap upwards from the roots into the leaves, shoots, flowers or fruits. This is a good time to cut flowers – they'll last longer in the vase. But as sap flows downwards when the moon is descending this is a good time to prune vines because no valuable sap will be wasted by being discarded in the pruned wood being cut off. It all goes to the roots instead. This sap becomes a food-rich store ready for when the vine starts growing again to produce the following year's shoots, leaves and grapes.

each shoot is going vertically upwards and there's less risk of any shoots being snapped off.

'Like this, you mean?' as I put my arms out above my head to make a wide V-shape.

'Yes, a bit like that,' said Pascal. 'And it makes it easier for the grape bunches shaken off by the machine to fall downwards.' They wouldn't fall onto the ground, but onto the machine harvester's internal moving-carpet-type grape collector.'

'Is Carignan really a good grape to pick by machine?' I asked. There was no way I wanted to pick my vines by machine, but I was already starting to become nervous about my budget. I'd spent a lot of money on fuel for the house's now redundant heater and now I was paying Eric's two guys to prune vines. Machine picking was around 40 times quicker and so much cheaper than doing it by hand.

'Carignan's not the best grape to pick by machine to be honest,' said Pascal, 'because the grapes are stubborn and not easily shaken from the vine, even when they are ripe. Carignan is also a late and tricky ripener so you have to set the machine's vine-beaters quite hard.' These are the batons inside the machine that shake the vine's trunk and shoots to loosen the grapes. 'Machine picking too hard can really damage vines. When Eric took over from his dad he stopped using the machine harvester on his Carignan vines and went back to hand picking. But, he kept the posts and wires in place, because the wind here is so strong in spring and summer the young vine shoots can snap off. The wires help keep them in place.' The posts in the vineyard were an eclectic collection indeed. Some were made of wood, others of metal. The metal ones had little notches up each side where a supporting wire could be hung.

On the wooden posts, a couple of bent and rusty nails on either side of the post did the same job.

'When the shoots grow upwards in spring and summer,' explained Pascal, 'you simply move the two moveable wires up a few notches to hold the new-green growth in.' For pruning, the moveable wires either side of each post were allowed to dangle not far off the ground to make it easier to prune. The two permanent wires, one at vine trunk height to hold the vine in place and another running along the tops of the posts were never allowed to move. Support posts were spaced every five vines or so, with each vine around 1.5 metres apart. The distance between each row was around two metres. At the end of each row, the end-posts would be strained tight by a couple of wires that were either wrapped around a large stone or rock placed underground, or a metal peg with a hook. Even though I wasn't pruning I was having trouble even walking fast enough to keep up with Pascal who was. He made pruning look so effortless, making quick, clean cuts with the secateurs in his right hand, pulling away the pruned shoots and wood with his left. What's more, he never stopped smiling, despite the bitterness of the wind. It was so cold my bare fingers would almost stick to the metal supporting wires if I touched them without the barrier of my woollen gloves in between.

'But you don't just have Carignan in this vineyard,' said Pascal, pointing to a vine whose shoots were noticeably lighter brown in colour compared to its neighbours. 'That one is Grenache Noir, for example. In winter you can only really tell the difference between Carignan and Grenache Noir by the colour of the shoots. In spring and summer when the leaves appear it is much easier to tell which vine is which. Like trees, really. Except that vines are all the same shape, whereas the different shapes of an oak or an elm in winter make them easy to tell apart.'

'How much Grenache Noir do you reckon is in my vine-yard, then,' I asked Pascal, whose pace hadn't slacked and was pruning what looked to my uneducated eye to be another Carignan vine.

'Well, all I can say is around 80 per cent of the vines here are Carignan. Then you'll have around 20 per cent Grenache Noir and Syrah, two red grapes, plus a bit of the white grape Maccabeu, or what they call Viura or Biura the other side of the Pyrénées,' said Pascal, turning his shoulder to point his hedge-trimmers towards Spain.

'Carignan became popular in the late 1950s after the Algerian Civil War when French residents there came back to France and wanted a grape that gave high yields. The only trouble with Carignan is the higher the yield, the less ripe it is likely to be. Unripe Carignan is pretty tannic,' said Pascal, puckering his mouth to emphasise the point, 'so the old guys planted other, earlier ripening red and white grapes and would pick them and ferment them altogether. The white grapes give a good nip of acidity, while the Syrah and Grenache Noir bring a more fruity side to Carignan's typically leathery flavours. For them, a good way of softening the Carignan, and made for a more complex wine too.'

'A bit like a blackberry and apple pie?' I suggested, remembering the pies my maternal grandmother used to make me and my sister. 'You know, a mix of dark and light fruit each bringing different flavours and textures to the dish.'

'That's one way of putting it,' said Pascal. 'You'll find plenty of wild blackberries here, around the stone cabin,' pointing to his left, 'and along that wall running by the bottom of the vineyard,' pointing back towards Spain again. 'You'll need a long stick to pull the creepers to you as the brambles are so wild, though. We pick them as soon as the wine harvest is over normally, or during a quiet weekend near the end of harvest if harvest is late. But this year is looking like it'll be an early one. The winter has been so warm.' I watched Pascal continue pruning, and couldn't quite see where the Grenache Noir vines were dotted about the vineyard. Grenache Noir is one of the main red grapes used in red Châteauneuf-du-Pape – one of France's flagship wine regions, but often the source of oxidised, flabby, bitter and vinegary red. One of the reasons for this is that Grenache is a conundrum. The vines often grow to a huge size in the vineyard, but the wines they produce can be anything but mighty when made into normal red wines. This is because Grenache Noir's fruit flavours are fragile and more easily lost due to a lack of zip in the grape juice than those of more robust grapes such as Carignan or Cabernet Sauvignon. In the same way as a soft, juicy Golden Delicious apple won't last as long in the fruit bowl as a crisper, crunchier Granny Smith. The majority of winegrowers in Maury chose not to make their Grenache-based red wines like Châteauneuf-du-Pape, but to add in some brandy half through winemaking, which helps preserve the life of the wine for longer.

'Grenache doesn't have an especially deep colour,' continued Pascal, 'but, as Carignan has lots of colour it's not really a problem. Even just a bit of Grenache really helps soften Carignan's rougher edges, though.' I also knew that Syrah's elegant, classy qualities were just what the scruffier Carignan sometimes needed. If I wasn't convinced about Grenache-dominated Châteauneuf-du-Pape reds I was happy to agree that

France produced the world's best 100-per-cent-Syrah reds, with Hermitage and Côte-Rôtie from the northern Rhône valley top of the list. These wines had been undervalued for years until the recent wine boom sparked a renewed interest in them. In some ways they had become France's answer to the ripe, juicy reds that countries such as Australia, California and Chile had made popular with modern drinkers – even though vines had been growing at Hermitage and Côte-Rôtie since around the sixth century BC, at least 2,000 years before modern vineyards were planted in either America or the southern hemisphere. I asked Pascal about using the white grapes just to make a dry white wine. 'You could pick the white grapes separately to make a white wine, but you might only have enough juice for one barrel. I don't think you'd get two barrels out of the white-wine vines in this vineyard.' One barrel is 225 bottles, or 300 litres. 'That might be a nice idea,' I said to Pascal. 'It's not enough wine to sell commercially, but it might make enough for a picnic wine to drink at home or when friends come to stay in summer.'

'Yes, but to make just one barrel is much more work than it seems. And you'll have to find a barrel for a start; plus, you'll have to get your pickers up here once to pick the white grapes and then again, maybe three weeks later, to pick the reds. If you've got bottomless pockets.' To escape the cold my hands were stuffed firmly in my trouser pockets and they most certainly weren't bottomless, as I was only too happy to confirm to Pascal. 'Monty, stick to your plan if I was you. Get your bearings, make your first red wine and then you'll have an idea of what the vineyard and others in this zone are capable of. Don't get distracted from your original idea, that's my advice, especially with your back the way it is.'

'That's the kind of thing Silvana would say, Pascal!' and Pascal laughed. 'She'd be right, too, you know.'

Pascal and Dominique had come to the end of a row and I left them to work their way down the slope along the next row, Pascal pausing to sharpen his secateurs on a grey-green, oval-shaped whetstone he carried in one of the side-pockets of his fleece jacket. When I next popped up to the vineyard, at the beginning of the following week, it had been pruned and Pascal and Dominique were nowhere to be seen. I went to Eric's house to ask him if they had finished pruning for the year and he said that they hadn't. 'The latest ripening grape varieties such as Carignan and Cabernet Sauvignon are always pruned before the vines that tend to bud earliest, like white-wine grapes for example.'

'How does that make sense?' I asked.

'Well, if the earliest vines to bud and ripen are pruned last it minimises the risk of frost. In other words, late pruning delays, by a few days or weeks, the moment the vine bursts its buds. This can make the difference between having a normal crop of grapes, or losing all the crop through the frosting of the buds right at the start of the season. Late pruning is a delaying tactic if you like, to kid the vine into thinking it is still winter. If the buds burst too early and you get a frost you can go on holiday for the rest of the year. You simply won't have any grapes to pick.' I'd gone round to Eric's house partly to talk about the pruning, but also to show him the plan I had sketched out for the veg patch. We wandered down there together and I pointed out where I had planned to build a chicken run and where I wanted to dig a small water reservoir that could act as a pond or water bowl for geese, ducks, or chickens. I explained to Eric pretty much what I had already explained to Daniel a few weeks previously, about how worried I was at the lack of water in the village due to three essentially dry winters.

'That's not all you should be worried about,' said Eric, staring vacantly at a mulberry tree between the stream and the dry stone wall which prevented my allotment falling into the water. I had recently cleaned up this tree by removing the ivy that had already killed off one side of its trunk. 'This is not only the third dry winter we have had here, climatically it is easily the warmest, too. I don't know if you have noticed the almond trees on the road between your house and the wine cooperative?' Eric was referring to a small orchard of mature almond trees that Harry and I often walked past on our way to the village's recycling point. The high stone wall between the orchard and the road was too high for Harry, but I'd often thought how nice it would be to have a picnic there in summer.

'The almond trees always bud early, but already look as if they are about to burst, which would be about three weeks ahead of schedule. And with global warming the wine harvest is already creeping forward by an average of a few days or so a decade.' Although Eric was wearing a jacket, I was wearing only a T-shirt and a pullover, the light kind you'd wear if you were playing golf (I don't) rather than the thick, cable-knit kind you'd wear if you were mountaineering (I don't do that, either). It was unseasonably warm and had been for all but two of the last eight weeks; plus, winter hadn't really started until after Christmas, a relief in the sense that it had allowed me to get the compost spread on soil that had yet to freeze hard, but a danger because all the natural cycles were getting out of kilter.

'My grandfather and father often picked your Carignan vineyard as late as early November, but early to mid-October is usual. If we don't get some very cold weather we could be looking at picking it as early as late August.'

'Is that such a bad thing?' I asked, hurling a stone towards the stream at the bottom of the allotment, not entirely sure why we should be worried about a vineyard planted with one of the latest and hardest to ripen grapes, Carignan, ripening early for once.

'In one sense you could say early ripening is good for you, but, if we are picking Carignan in August then logically that'll mean picking the white grapes in July. That's crazy, the kind of thing that happens in north African or Greek vineyards, not here. But,' said Eric, scratching a circle in the groound with his boot, where he thought I would want my water reservoir to go, 'what you'll have to think about is,' Carignan needs time not just to ripen but to ripen well. It's all very well having Carignan grapes that have the right amount of sugar to produce a wine with the right amount of alcohol, but I don't think Carignan picked in August will have had the time to produce the right amount of flavours in its grape-skins and pulp to make an interesting tasting wine. Late-ripening grapes such as Carignan are always a challenge, that's true. But, part of the challenge is playing the waiting game to make sure they ripen their sugars as well as their flavours. What you can't do with these warm winters is leave Carignan with sugars that are ready in August to hang on the vine another month to ripen the flavours.'

'Why ever not?'

'Because, Monty, the grapes will shrivel and you'll end up making a really alcoholic wine tasting of jam, cooked fruit, raisins… I'm very uneasy about this weather. I can see budburst coming far too early, then a cold front coming in and destroying most of the crop, leaving me – and you – to farm what's left on the vine as if nothing has happened. You'll end up spending the same amount of money you normally spend knowing that at most you'd be getting only around ten per cent of your normal crop. Scary numbers, Monty. Scary numbers…' Eric was not the kind of person to dwell on bad news, least of all when the news was only potentially, and not yet actually, bad and especially when it was something out of his control – which the abnormally warm weather most definitely was. He turned away from me to climb onto the wall-come-path at the top of the allotment, to see exactly where the reservoir whose proposed site he had scratched in the ground would be. 'Your idea of a mini-reservoir for the garden is a good one,' he called across, lively again. 'Of course, you could save yourself the trouble digging with your bucket and spade and use the reservoir I made here when I was a kid.'

'I didn't know you'd dug a reservoir?' I said, following Eric who was moving towards the river.

'I haven't, for reasons you'll discover when you try to dig your own. There's a hard pan in the ground here, but you won't need to go very deep.' Eric pointed into the stream where the water slowed to a near stop, thanks to a barrier of large stones stretching the width of the stream. 'There's a readymade reservoir for you, right there. It'll be deep enough, even in summer, to dip your bucket into if you want to water by hand. But, you have to climb up and down the wall to do it. That tree root by the wall will act as a step to help you up and down. That wasn't there when I was a kid!'

The tree root belonged to the creeper I had stripped from the mulberry tree. I'd left the root in place as it acted as both a ladder to climb up into the tree when I was stripping it of green, creeping growth and as a step down to the riverbank as Eric had suggested. The readymade reservoir in the river was certainly an option I considered over the next couple of weeks as I carried the unused compost from the vineyard into the garden. French supermarkets no longer gave shoppers plastic bags to put their groceries into, but sold for minimal cost bigger, stronger, reusable canvas bags with comfortable cloth handles. With one in either hand I could carry a combined total of around 20 kg of compost at a time into the garden. With a bag on each arm I didn't seem to put my back in danger because I felt balanced. I must have made a hundred such trips in a couple of weeks, in fine, sunny weather more reminiscent of early summer than late winter. Every newspaper that seemed to come my way was full of reports not just of arctic ice shelves, known to have existed for millennia, melting in a matter of months, but of how migratory and breeding patterns of birds and animals were changing due to warmer springs. The last time *I* could remember snow in the UK around Christmas time was in 1984–5, when I was still at school. The 1985 winter was so cold most of Tuscany's olive trees got wiped out. It didn't seem that there had been any time for the few olive trees in and around St-Martin to have been pruned before spring was seemingly upon us. 'The vines,' Eric told me, one night over a beer in the *auberge,* 'are on a knife-edge. It's so warm that if we get a good dose of rain then *whooomf,* the vines will get the kick-start they need for budding. The rain will kick the roots into action, and they'll send all that food-rich sap up through the trunk and into the pruned spurs that will then allow the buds to push on out to make the first baby shoots. It's a nightmare. There's some cold weather on the way, but whether it'll be enough or not, I don't know.'

There was nothing to do except fear the worst while hoping for the best. One or two of the older villagers had mentioned in passing that colder weather was on the way, but I thought this was just a kind ploy on their part to keep my spirits up. Nothing I had seen on satellite photos gleaned from the internet suggested a cold snap was due. That's why I was the first among those half-dozen villagers who worked an allotment to start planting out transplants. When my elderly garden neighbour René Pastoret saw that I had planted out some baby butter lettuce transplants he almost thought his eyes were playing up. 'I haven't even started sowing seeds into flats, yet,' he confessed. 'The moon's wrong.' René, like most villagers, worked to just the full- to new-moon cycle sowing on a waxing moon (getting bigger). When I tried to explain I was sowing on a descending moon, René thought this was the same as a waning moon, even though the waning moon can be ascending or descending (because the full moon occurs every 29 days and a new ascending – descending moon cycle begins every 27.3 days).

'Your lettuce are going to have fun when the cold front comes in,' said René, laughing conspiratorially and wringing his (thumbless) left hand in the way the French do to signify something major is occurring. 'I'd cover them with a bit of straw if I was you,' he advised, 'to stop the leaves blackening in the freeze.'

'How do you know there'll be cold weather, René I've been working in a T-shirt the last fortnight.'

'Hmmm, I can just feel it in my bones,' he said simply, having checked the precise position and variety of the lettuce I had planted. 'You've done well to get your potatoes in though,' he said, although how he knew I'd planted them I don't know. 'What type did you put in, then?'

'It said "Spunta" on the side of the seed-potato box,' I said. 'They were certified organic.'

'Well, it won't do them any harm to be underground when it freezes,' said René. 'I normally wait until early April. I've got several hundred weight to sow.' Potatoes, I discovered, were one of René's favourite foods. He sowed nothing but potatoes (and maybe some broad beans) in a couple of disused vegetable plots every year he told me, because they kept well over winter and he and his wife Adeline loved eating them. For the next couple of days I carried on moving compost from the vineyard to the allotment, and began marking out where both my chicken run and the raised vegetable-growing beds I'd planned would be – now that all of the compost was in place. For this I used some wire and thin metal posts (builder's rebar in fact) Eric used to protect the vineyards from boar each autumn and which I'd liberated on semi-permanent loan from behind Eric's tractor shed. It was the end of the last week in March and I was still wearing only a T-shirt and shorts when the job of planning was completed in yet more crisp sunshine. I was wondering if René's sixth sense for cold weather was a bluff. 'I can feel it,' was the kind of vague, imprecise, sensuous, but unscientific, claptrap biodynamic acolytes like me tend to come out with. René was so convinced that what he was saying or 'feeling' about the weather was right it made me understand why sometimes people I met must think me barking mad when I described being biodynamic as being as much about what you feel as what you actually do. I'd even been talking about biodynamics with a phone engineer in Paris. For some reason, windy weather around a telecommunications-relay station near Perpignan had caused problems for quite a few landline phones in the village, and mine was no exception. I had worked out that the best time to call the phone company without waiting for upwards of half-an-hour in an electronic queue was late a night, when everyone else was either having dinner, watching television or sleeping.

It was past midnight three days after my last conversation with René, but I almost dropped the handset when I looked outside into a low, white sky. The bright fluorescent orange of the faulty streetlamp below my bedroom window was strangely muffled, and with each of its freeze-frame blinks I could see why. I strapped Harry into his walking harness and went for a walk outside where the air temperature was bitterly cold and the flagstones in my street were already covered in beardy snow, deep enough already for Harry's paws to make a lasting impression and for me to nearly lose my footing. The wind had picked up and the thick flakes had soon covered Harry's back, forcing him to squint his eyes up the street westwards to the mountains over which the snow was arriving. Snow had already starting banking up against Harry's favourite drainpipe as he lifted his leg to squeeze out what became a lemon-coloured, sorbet-like vertical stripe. By the time we returned home, half-an-hour later, the snow was over an inch thick in places. 'Well, my friend, looks like we're going to have to replant some lettuce,' I said to Harry in high spirits considering how late and cold it was. And then a thought hit me. If the vines had started to bud over the last few days, and as I hadn't been up to the vineyard for a few days as there was no compost left to move down from there, this snow would be a disaster rather than the natural check on vine growth I had wanted. Last time I had looked the vines were at the woolly bud stage, which means they are swelling and just about to burst as the sap has warmed up enough to push nearly the full bud out. The woolly bit is only gunk the size of a cigar match head that the un-swollen bud accumulates over winter. I wanted to drive up to the vineyard, but it was dark and the snow was clearly going to form drifts. I didn't fancy getting stuck in a car all night in the snow in seriously cold temperatures on a wind-blown mountain.

As Harry and I climbed into bed, him unusually inside rather than on top of the duvet, my head was spinning with both fear and excitement. Dawn would either see me revert to Plan B in the case of the vines being frosted into producing no grapes, leaving me to write a series of articles (on how global warming was screwing winegrowers) to earn enough quick cash to pay Eric while I divested myself of any idea of ever being a winegrower; or I'd stick to Plan A safe in the knowledge that the cold snap had put the vines and my first-ever winegrowing year back on track.

Chapter 5

EVERY ALARM CLOCK I HAVE EVER BOUGHT OR BEEN GIVEN AS A present has been lost, trodden on, or left behind in hotels during press trips. My last one – a silver digital pocket model bought in 2005 – ended up being hurled against a wall because it kept resetting itself to midnight, first of January 2000. I felt guilty enough to retrieve and recycle the battery from its wreckage, but seeing as this alarm clock's demise coincided with Harry's arrival from America I felt no need to go out and look for another one. Harry had become my *de facto* alarm clock, waking me up each morning with his 'if you aren't walking me outside within the next 20 minutes, I'll pee on the floor' face. He seemed especially keen to get outside on the morning of the snow, maybe because I had stayed up so late the previous night, mesmerised by the falling flakes that I had overslept. Harry slept on my bed each night and would only jump off into his basket if it was too hot or I was snoring too loudly. I'd been thoroughly briefed about Harry's habits by his previous owner, my school friend Dominic. In fact, I'd even met Harry just after Dominic had bought him as a puppy from a breeder in Santa Barbara, California. This was during a month-long trip I'd spent with Dominic at his house in Los Angeles' Hollywood Hills, a holiday I allowed myself after completing the first of my wine books. 'Harry has several foibles,' said Dominic on our way for my first walk with Harry. 'He seems stupid but Jack Russell Terriers are actually one of the most intelligent breeds. They have their own personality and won't just run and fetch a thrown stick over and over again like say a Golden Retriever. Harry will fetch it once and when you throw it again for him he'll basically give you the "get real, moron, fetch it yourself this time" look.' Harry's big weakness became obvious as soon as Dominic and I entered Dog Park: a small playing field for dog recreation sculpted out of the powdery hills behind the Hollywood sign. On the five-minute drive up to Dog Park Dominic would try to point out the houses or former houses of various screen actors, television stars, or sports idols over Harry's essentially unstoppable barking. 'He's not a great car passenger,' said Dominic, dryly, as Harry's slobber dripped onto the dashboard in front of the passenger seat whilst he tried to claw his way through the windscreen. 'Open your window a bit Mont, so he can stick his nose out but no more. Otherwise he'll try and leap out of the car.'

'Balls,' said Dominic. 'He has a real thing for balls.'

'You mean he is jealous about other male dogs who still have them?'

'No, not really. He's not so jealous of other dogs with their balls. He's grown up with a big, un-castrated dog.' This was Marlowe, Dominic's Ridgeback who was so docile you'd barely notice him. 'Harry's more into footballs, golf balls, tennis balls, balls you play games with. I wouldn't give him a tennis ball as he'll eat it and choke on the fur. You need to get him a ball somewhere in between a tennis ball and a soccer ball in size and he'll push it around the park until he wears himself out. For a dog with Harry's energy that can be highly desirable if you want the journey home in the car to be a quiet one, trust me.' When Dom became a father a few years later he began calling me from Los Angeles, worried about what to do with the now four-year-old Harry who, unlike Marlowe, had big issues with small children, probably, Dom suggested, because when he was a puppy (and before Dom got him) he was provoked by something a child had done. 'Put him up for adoption,' I said. 'That's what I am trying to do,' Dom replied, 'but I asked one guy I interviewed what he'd do with Harry if he had to leave the house for say a whole day and he'd said he just tie Harry on a lead to a post. No way.' This reminded me of a man I met at a farmers' market in northern California in 1999. I was selling apples from the biodynamic vineyard I was working on and complimented the man on his dog. 'Oh, we used to have two dogs, in fact, but one of 'em was a bit too rough,' the man said breezily, as he paused in front on my stall with his wife and two small kids. 'What happened to that dog?' I asked. 'Oh, he took a dirt nap,' came the reply – meaning the dog had been killed and buried. I'd had a Jack Russell called Pumpkin when I was a child so I knew what I was letting myself in for with Harry when I called Dom and told him (having cleared it first with Silvana) that if he organised Harry's flight from Los Angeles (via New York) to Rome and took care of all the paperwork, I'd keep Harry for life.

Harry's birthplace was the subject of the best wine movie I have ever seen, *Sideways*, in which the two main male characters enjoy a week of tasting Santa Barbara's Pinot Noir red wines before one of them gets married (the other having just been divorced). Pinot Noir is the world's fussiest, but potentially most enchanting red-wine grape. Its best red wines, from Burgundy in east-central France, are intensely perfumed and seductive offerings with velvety smooth textures that provide arguably wine's most sensuous tongue caressing experiences. The trouble with growing Pinot Noir anywhere in the world other than Burgundy is that Burgundy's sloping, chalky clay soils and peculiar climate of hot summers, freezing winters and languid springs and autumns are hard to replicate. Santa Barbara claims to produce California's finest Pinot Noirs, thanks to its location on the Pacific coast where cool fogs that regularly roll in from the sea are supposed to stop Pinot Noir from overheating – producing intense and juicy wines rather than unpleasantly hollow and jammy ones. On my only visit to the Santa Barbara vineyards (around 160 km north of Los Angeles) I saw lots of immature vines struggling on parched, dusty soils in front of expensive, modern, soulless wineries. I also spat out lots of jammy Pinot Noir reds with very ambitious prices that were presumably to help pay off the huge loans needed for all these new vineyards and wineries. Santa Barbara had turned to wine only recently, in the late 1960s after its oil fields had run dry and then its cattle ranching businesses became unprofitable. Even Dominic, a big fan of Pinot Noir, agreed that while the best wines could be good, they weren't great enough to match top red Burgundy.

'One reason is the actual type of Pinot Noir vines planted in Santa Barbara,' I explained to Dom over dinner one night at his house. 'This bottle,' I said, holding up a Santa Barbara Pinot with a lavish label depicting a winery designed quite possibly by the same team who had built Michael Jackson's Neverland, 'contains Pinot Noir from maybe one or two clones or strains of the Pinot Noir grape.'

'We're not talking Dolly the Sheep here, are we Mont?' asked Dominic, faking a Scottish accent in homage to both his and the world's first cloned sheep's Scottish ancestry.

'Yes and no. You make vine clones by going into the vineyard and cutting shoots from a few vines. If you go into the vineyard just before harvest you might be looking to take cuttings from one vine which seems to have produced a big yield of grapes, or one that has produced small, concentrated grapes, one that is disease-free, or one that has ripened nice and early. Pinot Noir is a tricky one to get ripe.'

'That all seems to make sense,' said Dominic, 'so what's the problem?'

'Well, there isn't one if you are planting a new Pinot Noir vineyard and want all your vines to be uniform so you can farm them cheaply from the back of a tractor to save money to pay off the loan on your brand new, Disney-style winery. But, you end up with boring wine. It's like all the pupils in a school class being the same height and all being good at algebra. Except, when you choose the kids' soccer team you don't have the tall kids you need to play in goal or in defence, or when you pick players for the school quiz team they might get all the mathematical questions right but do badly in history or languages. Burgundy is so great, irrespective of the fact that it has a great climate and the right soils for growing Pinot Noir, because the best vineyards contain a genetically diverse mix of Pinot Noir vines. In a old plot containing 5,000 Pinot Noir vines there might be around 1,000 vines with a unique genetic background. In a modern vineyard planted with clones you'll be lucky to find more than four genetically different Pinot Noir vines: a quarter the early ripening clone, a quarter the small-berried clone, a quarter the high-yielding clone and a quarter the frost- or disease-resistant clone.' I didn't have a bottle of Pinot Noir on me, but I had brought a bottle of northern California red wine made from the Zinfandel grape by a guy called Tony Coturri. It turned out to be one of the best wines I had ever drunk. 'It's organically farmed and comes from a genetically diverse mix of old vines grown in Sonoma County, planted originally by the old Italian families that congregated there during and after Prohibition in the 1920s and 1930s,' I told Dom, having been at the Coturri winery a few days before flying down to LA from San Francisco. 'If you think this wine has incredible texture, breadth and diversity of flavour, then maybe making wine from genetically diverse vines makes sense?'

I wasn't exactly sure of the genetic origins of my vineyard, except that its vines were genetically diverse having been planted from cuttings taken from various local vineyards rather than from clones. It was after lunch on the day after the snow had begun. We'd had to wait until early afternoon for the blizzard to have abated enough for us to see more than a few feet in front of us. I let Harry off the lead and tried to hit him with snowballs as he frolicked in the snow. I hadn't played snowballs in maybe 20 years (and never with a dog) but this wasn't the only reason why my mood was so light-hearted. It was immediately clear even from a distance that the vineyard was (as I had hoped it would be) like a black and white photo: black vines solemnly lined up against a carpet of white, with not a trace of green in sight. The vine buds were still firmly closed, with no green shoots and baby leaves poking out. When Harry and I returned to the village, Eric was trying to repair one of several rusty caterpillar tractors he owned. I could see a huge weight had been lifted off his shoulders. 'You're lucky, Monty. We all are in fact. Even if the snow melts tomorrow,' he said, prophetically as it turned out, as 36 hours later no trace of it remained, 'it will have chilled the vines, their sap and their growth hormones enough for them not to want to burst their buds for another couple of weeks at least. Then we'll get back to what a normal winegrowing season should be like.'

This was the window of opportunity I needed to get cracking on the allotment, currently a sight I was convinced was ugly enough for my gardening neighbours to want to ask me to abandon my dream of growing my own vegetables. True, there was greenery in the form of a few tiny lettuces, but these were now surrounded by mini-slagheaps of dark compost and the remains of a bonfire lit with the creeper I had ripped off the mulberry tree and a mass of fibrous roots I had already dug out of the topsoil. 'I think they are the roots of hops,' said René, 'planted by Eric's grandfather.' The boundary between our allotments was divided by a series of tall, oblong cement pillars as high as a basketball player. 'Eric's grandfather put those in to make a windbreak, as the wind blows from behind the main reservoir and across my plot. He hung some kind of blue canvas material there.' All that was left of this were some rags flapping in the morning's light breeze. René would never hang around for long on what became regular morning chats in the garden. He would pop around every few hours, spending time in at least three other plots located in various parts of the allotment area before returning – often to close off the water from the main reservoir if he had been flood irrigating. It was too early for watering – I was the only one seemingly to have planted anything – but when René returned after making his rounds, short-handled hoe in hand, I had bundled the remains of the blue canvas windbreak into a large plastic bin liner. It gave me a real sense of achievement to see René's eyes light up as his small, permanently hunched frame took in the new order. 'It'll be a bit brighter in my plot now,' he said, arching his arthritic arms as best he could to simulate the arc of the sun, whose rays anointed my plot before René's more westerly one. 'With that creeper covering the tree and now the canvas gone I'll be able to plant some tomatoes along the fence line this year.' He said he'd given up growing them because all the light was getting blocked.

I've always had a good rapport with old people, partly because my father was old (he was 44 when I was born) and when we went off to see the football together we'd go with a group of his friends, all of whom were, like him, from the same pre-Second World War generation. Old people had time on their hands that meant time for you, and were the best source of free, tried-and-tested knowledge around. I learnt more from these old guys than from most of my schoolteachers. I hoped that René and I would develop a real friendship, not just because I could talk to him about what it was like growing up in pre-war France (René was born in Paris in the late 1920s), but because he had a great sense of humour and was more dynamic, both mentally and physically, than the dull, dead-beat couch potatoes from my X-box generation. He was especially interested to see me preparing raised beds for my vegetables. 'It's a French system, René,' I explained, as I hilled-up topsoil to the height of an extended human hand and scraped it into oblong blocks half the width of the garden. I'd plant crops into where the topsoil had been hilled up, leaving where the soil had been scraped away as pathways. 'Some people call it the French-intensive system, but not because it resembles intensive farming in the battery-hen sense, but because with unusually deep fertile soil you can grow more crops in a smaller space. The idea is that the more space taken up by crops, the less space there is for weeds. So you spend your time making the crops grow rather than keeping the weeds down. And because you can water, weed, or pick each of your crops from either side of each planting block you never have to stand on the growing area and damage the soil by compacting it with your work boots.'

René may not have taken in everything I said as my French was far from perfect and he was sometimes a little hard of hearing, but he did come straight back at me with one of his usual pertinent questions. 'How are you going to keep the soil in place and keep your crops watered enough so they don't die in the summer?' I told René I was going to keep the backed-up soil in place by laying wooden planks along the side, bolstering the planks with small metal posts hammered into the ground. 'That'll make it easier to rake in all the compost I've brought down from the vineyard,' holding a handful of the crumbly, black gold in cupped palms for René to have a good sniff. His nose got so close he had a bit of compost left on it, leaving me in one of those embarrassing predicaments in front of people you don't know very well. Do you tell them a piece of food is stuck to their teeth, or ignore it? 'Are you going to take all my compost away on your nose René?' as I brushed it off with the back of a finger, leaving René unable to withhold one of his endearing, near toothless smiles.

'If my history is correct, the medieval French monks such as the Benedictines or the Cistercians (later) used to hill-up manure from their animals and grow crops on it. When my dad was small all the boys in his street would fight over who scooped up the manure left by the horses pulling the milk wagon every morning so their fathers could use it in the vegetable garden. I'm not the marrying type but in many traditional cultures a manure pile is a big part of bride's dowry. If you have manure you have animals and animals mean wealth.' If René was bored about being told stuff he already knew he was too polite to show it.

I measured out where my beds would go, and worked out what length of wooden planks I'd need. When my parents bought the family home I grew up in the previous owners', who had had some radical and frankly rather silly ideas on modernising the inside of what should have remained a very characterful suburban Edwardian house, had left a system of raised beds in the back garden. When I pictured this again in my mind's eye after all these years, I realised why some people called raised beds not just the French-intensive system, but a biodynamic system. With all that fertile, humus-rich topsoil banked up the beneficial forces that biodynamic growers see as enhancing healthy plant growth are supposed to optimised. If these forces coming to the earth down from the moon above or up from within the earth itself really do exist and really can work their way through the soil, into crops and thus as food into us, then having as much good soil as possible for them to grow in would seem to make biodynamic sense.

I ordered some wood from the only local DIY store in the village of Caudiès-de-Fenouillet – run by a French Tunisian who once worked as a magician's assistant but who now called himself 'Mr Brico' ('Mr Fix It'). Prices were a bit on the high side, but he had a captive market unless you wanted to drive all the way to the mega-DIY warehouses on the outskirts of Perpignan, which I didn't in my van. I had a dozen planks cut to size, enough to enclose three large, main raised beds but only eleven planks were still on board when I got home. I wondered why Serge, a larger-than-life shepherd from Fosse, the only hamlet between St-Martin and Caudiès, had waved so frantically at me as I drove past. He was trying to tell me the wood, which I had wedged on the back between the fuel tank and the top of the driver's cab, was slipping off. I had only recently met Serge. Eric had given me his name and address as simply, 'Fosse. Don't worry about the street names there. You'll find him, you can't miss him, in fact.' The first house I knocked at turned out to be Serge's brother-in-law. He pointed across Fosse's back-garden-sized main square to Serge's house. Serge invited me in to meet his wife Marie-Anne, his budgerigars and an orphaned baby lamb Anne-Marie was feeding with a milk bottle. It wasn't even lunchtime but Serge offered me a glass of wine. Serge had produced this by blending some half-fermented and so half-sweet musky white wine with some brandy. It was an ideal pick-me-up and just the encouragement I needed to come straight to the point and tell Serge why I come to see him: cow shit. 'I've got goats and sheep, but no cows. However, none of the local farmers will mind if you take the odd cow pat from the fields. Just don't go there with your dog, or he'll get shot.' How Serge knew I had a dog, I don't know. Harry wasn't in the van and I hadn't told him, but I guessed word got round pretty quick. I wondered how locals described the new Englishman in their midst: passable French speaker, childless, one dog, unmarried, girlfriend, weird ideas about winegrowing and gardening.

'I don't need too much manure, just a bucket or so. I am going to make some compost.'

'You won't make compost with only a bucketful,' laughed Serge, pouring me another glass of his deliciously sweet, strong wine.

'I only need a bit. I'm going to ferment it in a barrel. It's called barrel compost,' I said, almost laughing myself at how ridiculous it did sound. Serge could have said, 'you normally only ferment wine in barrels,' but he listened to my description of barrel compost and why I needed so little for my vineyard (less than a few hundred grams per hectare) before he asked me whether I knew anyone interested in taking on his small vineyard. This was the polite countryman's way of asking you if you wanted the vines without asking you directly. Serge told me he was due to retire and would either take money from the European Union to rip up the vines, or sell them. This was the vineyard I saw Serge waving at me from as I passed in my van, precariously loaded with the wood for the garden. The vineyard was right in the bottom of the valley and on what appeared to be quite heavy soil. The soil here had once formed the bottom of a lake but it wasn't this fact that made it a bad choice for red wine. After all, plenty of the world's best red-wine vineyards lie on soils that were once under water. The vineyards – Chianti in Tuscany, for example – grow on what was once seabed. If French wine producers ever made their own version of the movie *Jurassic Park*, the Jurassic being the geological era around 210–145 million years ago during which billions of tiny sea creatures such as corals and oysters were left by notably warm seas, leading roles would go to dry white wines such as Chablis (Chardonnay), Sancerre (Sauvignon Blanc) and any top red or white Burgundy you care to name. And, if you are wondering what happened to Bordeaux – the world's biggest fine wine region – it lies on a former seabed (the Aquitaine basin) that is covered almost entirely by smooth gravels mixed with sandy-clay that were washed there by rivers formed by glacial melt. The trick, though, is to plant vineyards on soils that are not too silty. It rains a lot in Bordeaux, but the soils have enough sand and gravel for the water to drain away quickly. The worst soils, in Bordeaux in particular and on Planet Wine in general, have too much silt in them. Too much silt means rain can't drain away from the roots and vines (as the old peasant wisdom goes) don't like wet feet. You'll get grapes from a badly drained, heavy vineyard soil but you'll never make a great wine from it.

Serge's vineyard suited his needs and although it made a lovely glass of wine for his dining table I wasn't convinced it would make a wine with flavours ripe and smooth enough for the kind of wine drinkers I was hoping to sell to. I said I'd let Serge know if I heard anyone was interested.

I had enough on my plate worrying about my own vineyard without taking another one on. Three weeks after the snow fell the vines began budding. It's not like green shoot-tips emerge on every bud on every spur on every vine at exactly the same time. Mother Nature doesn't work like that and more power to her I say, with bud-break especially uneven after warm winters such as the one my vineyard had experienced. That's one reason why you'll rarely hear farmers complain about cold winters that make spring growth more uniform and predictable. Cold winters can also help kill off potential pests, such as mites, that nest in the vine's flaky bark only to appear in spring to eat any tender, juicy green shoots that have started growing. The first few vines I'd check on my thrice-weekly visits to the vineyard were always those located in the lower part of the vineyard. I'd park the van just off the track running down between the cabin and the vineyard in case any other traffic appeared, most likely to be Eric's tractor as this whole plateau belonged to him. Harry would jump out and as he didn't appear to be really interested in winegrowing he'd run off to look for nests of mice or rats. These, Harry believed, were hidden either under gaps in the tiles on the roof, that he'd hop up onto via the stone water trough, or within the cabin itself among the accumulated mess of cracked and greying wooden support posts, metal ones squashed and twisted like a French bread baguette you'd accidentally sat down on, and the iron-and-wood carcasses of spike-toothed harrows and ploughs, abandoned with the animals who pulled them when the tractor era arrived.

In summer, Harry would burrow against the cabin's wall, vainly trying to dig through the cracks in the stone into which he'd seen small lizards disappear, bloodying both paws and stonework in the process. He'd be left to his own devices while

The stone cabin and my vineyard are
behind me, level with my upper right
arm between where the forest ends and
where the Corbières mountains begin.

I wonder if barrels half-buried in the
ground for barrel compost can also
double up as compost-toilets?

Using the nine biodynamic preparations is a must if you want to be considered biodynamic.

Stirring ('dynamising') biodynamic horn silica or '501'. Spraying it helps vines ripen their grapes.

Sulphur-dusting by hand requires old clothes and a pair of sturdy goggles.

Eric's anti-mildew sulphur spray arrives just in time before the weather – and disease – close in.

Eric prides himself on having one of the most modern tractor fleets in the French wine industry.

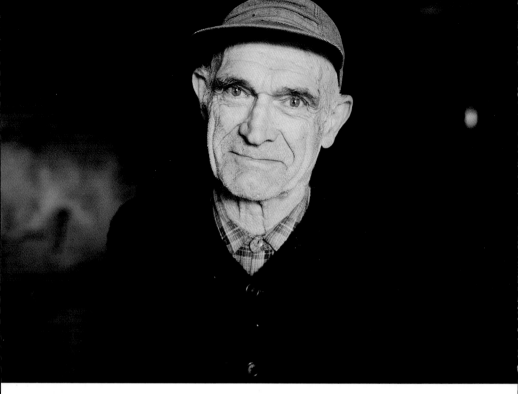

René Pastoret in his workshop where I would find him every morning on my way to open up the geese.

Silvana gears herself up for another budget discussion with me.

Back specialist Fred Py reassures me that as all winegrowers get bad backs I'm already ahead of the game.

St-Martin's mayor André Foulquier realises ordering the XXXXL ballot box for France's national elections was a waste of public funds.

Marinette Sire and the eggs she gave me for my biodynamic barrel compost (their shells block radioactivity).

Pascal Bozec (foreground, smiling) seems to have convinced Eric Laguerre (sitting in the tractor) that after twenty years' work it's time for a pay rise.

Mechanic Patrick da Silva tries to keep a straight face as my van turns up for another service.

Peter wets his vegetables with my biodynamic tea leaving John to wonder what potential biodynamic teas have as aphrodisiacs.

Serge wonders if there really is room for that last piece of dessert....

Overlooking vineyards on the hot Agly valley floor. Wouldn't you rather be up in the mountains?

A boar's view: this is the point in the forest from which the boar would crash into the vineyard.

I walked down the track. Where it became banana-shaped right at the bottom and over a bump in the ground I'd turn left and up into the vines. This was where the vine rows were longest and where the soil was at its darkest, heaviest and coolest. Even though the vines in this section hadn't begun to bud other vines further up the slope had. Vines, like humans, are pretty much in thrall to their hormones when it comes to getting stuff done, such as growing in order to reproduce, so when the soil in which the vine's roots grow and the air around the trunk warms up in spring the hormones get moving. The first sign of this movement and change on a vine comes when sap begins to weep from the cuts left by pruning last year's long shoots back to short spurs. It's just a sign that sap is pushing up from the warming roots and out through the only available exit points – the pruning cuts. Vines only bleed in spring if they were cut at some point the previous season and maybe this is where the legend of the donkey comes from with respect to the origin of pruning. A mythical winegrower, assumed to be St-Martin of the monastery at Tours in the Loire valley, left his donkey tethered too close to the vines one day in AD 345. When he returned to find the animal had gnawed off all the green shoots he was left believing that his fellow monks would get no grapes the following year. However, when in the following spring the ends of the gnawed vine shoots began to bleed sap and then produce a fruitful crop later that autumn the concept of pruning was born. Cutting off all (bar around ten per cent) of last year's green growth is the way to get the vines to produce grapes year in, year out.

I felt like a plumber about to deal with a leaky tap when I first stroked the drops of sap bleeding from a vine with my forefinger. Bleeding flushes out the vine's system before the green growth for the coming year's shoots and leaves emerges. The buds swell and the scaly-type husks that protect each dormant bud through winter are cast to the wind – no shortage of that in my vineyard, as tiny green shoot tips emerge like asparagus tops poking out of dark and tightly packed shopping bag. 'Another advantage of pruning late,' Eric had told me when we watched Dominique and Pascal prune my vineyard, 'is that when the warm weather arrives and the sap starts pushing no diseases can get into the pruning wound. In other words, the time between making the pruning cut exposing a naked wound to the elements and the moment the vine pushes its new, green shoot-tips out is relatively short. If you prune early, in autumn instead of winter, that wound becomes a target for fungus spores that bring disease. All the old guys around here go looking for wild mushrooms in autumn in the forest. The mushrooms appear if heavy rain is followed by a couple of days of drier, sunnier weather. Mushrooms are fungi, right? So, if you prune too early and get wet and warm weather (although you won't get edible mushrooms growing on your vines) you will get fungal diseases growing on the pruned vine shoots. Pruning late means if fungal-disease spores do settle on the pruning wounds it won't be long before the rising sap pushes them off and flushes them out.' As for the edible mushrooms, five months before I'd seen Eric go mushroom hunting not with a dog (he didn't have one) and a walking stick but from his blue jeep that he parked at the side of the road on his way back from showing me the vineyard for the first time. He'd only just finished pointing out some truffle oaks when he braked hard having seen what looked to be a particularly appetising mushroom growing in a ditch between the roadside and the edge of the forest. He disappeared behind the back of the jeep without saying a word and, having not seen the mushroom, I thought he'd gone for a pee. 'I love mushrooming,' he said as he climbed back in, placing a mushroom on my lap with the diameter of a dinner-plate and texture and thickness of a sponge cake, before carefully accelerating back to St-Martin. Eric didn't even bother replying to my 'What are we going to do with that?' question, but made me watch Corinne slice the mushroom and cook it in butter and garlic for lunch. 'I only wish I had more time for mushrooming,' Eric lamented. My lament was wishing I could keep that day's pungent, fresh earthy mushroom smell permanently on my hands and jeans. It reminded me both of the forest floor of my childhood and of the day I signed up to become a winegrower.

I hadn't signed up to become a vegetable gardener, in the sense that there was no formal contract, but I had signed a mental contract with myself to try to be as self-sufficient as possible in terms of growing my own herbs, vegetables and fruits. I didn't want a diet of shrink-wrapped vegetables flown in from all four corners of the earth at huge environmental cost when I could grow them myself for nothing. Nor did I want to buy eggs laid by birds who lived in a space smaller than the width of a lap-top computer. However, to have my own eggs I needed help, not just in the form of a laying flock but also a chicken house. As I'd never been much of a builder, I had called on the help of John and Pete, a British couple living in the nearby hamlet of Fosse. They'd moved to France from Harrogate in the north of England a few years previously, sailing from there to France in their own boat. Jasper, their miniature schnauzer, was on board during the four-month trip, with Jasper apparently coping better than Pete who was laid low by sea-sickness during rough weather crossing the Bay of Biscay. I'd first heard about John because he had been an osteopath in the UK and several people in St-Martin had told me he might be a good bet to treat my back. However, both John and Pete, a driving instructor, had given up their previous careers to run a holiday home or *gîte*. This had its own swimming pool and garden and formed part of the property in Fosse where John and Pete lived.

'We're a little bit tied up at the moment,' said John, whose faint accent picked up as a schoolboy in his native southern Scotland was barely noticeable on the phone, 'as we've just bought another house, or ruin I should say, in Le Vivier. There's a roof terrace at the top that we are re-doing as we work our way down the house, and we've already got our first guests coming in two months. We just don't have a lot of time, but we'd love to meet you. We made some wine last year and want you to try it. Maybe the best thing for you to get started is to contact a builder called Andy who lives up the road from us in Fenouillet. I know he's busy as well, but...' Andy, it turned out, had been augmenting John and Pete's building and renovation skills because he had so much work on himself. I met Andy over a beer at the Auberge Taïchac. His thin frame towered above me when he stood up to shake hands and his Midlands accent (Andy was born and bred in Birmingham) came through even when he spoke French at the bar. Andy had moved out to France several years before and was running a successful business renovating houses for mainly British ex-pats. 'I haven't built many chicken houses,' said Andy, in his tongue-in-cheek, laid-back manner, running a huge builder's hand through a wispy, greying but still full head of hair, 'but if you have some kind of design in mind it'll help.' I invited Andy and his (female) dog, Dinah, back to my house ('She'll be fine with Harry, no worries mate') to look at some pictures of chicken houses I had downloaded from the internet. 'Ideally I'd have a chicken house that I can move around the vineyard,' I said, explaining to Andy how important I thought it was from a biodynamic point of view to get living creatures in the vineyard.

'You might be biting off more than you can chew there, mate, to be honest,' said Andy, pushing his chair back from the dining-table-come-desk, to give his extensive legs more room. 'For the time and money you are going to spend on designing and building a mobile chicken house, plus the time and money you are going to spend getting up and down to the vineyard every day... I mean, I've never kept chickens but from what you've told me,' he said pointing to a design I had sketched in pencil on the back of a bank statement whereby rainwater falling on the coop's roof would be directed into a water trough, 'they need a lot of fresh water. It's pretty dry here in the summer, Monty,' said Andy, breaking out into the kind of ironic, rather than sarcastic, smile a wise father would reserve for a son with over-ambitious plans. 'And, if you can't make it up to check the water situation because your back has gone, it would be a real shame for the chickens. Wouldn't it? Sorry mate, I'd love to help but I think you'd be wasting your money. I mean, I can do the job for you, but why don't you just buy a ready-made garden shed and convert it into a chicken house. You could stick it in your allotment and that would be easier for you to get to. Plus, you could keep your garden tools in there.' Andy hadn't even seen my allotment, but there was plenty of space there. 'And it'd be a lot cheaper for you, too.' When *de facto* builder John gave me the same prognosis it made me think that whereas the Spanish Conquistadores brought beans, potatoes and tomatoes from the New World and the Norman Conquest had brought fallow deer, rabbit and pheasant to the UK, modern-day Brits were bringing something equally valuable and hopefully as enduring to the continent: honest building appraisals. Andy told me where in Perpignan I could get a self-assembly garden shed from on our way down to the allotment. 'If you're going to use those old wooden vine posts,' said Andy, pointing to the pile near the wall-come-pathway, 'next time you have a bonfire just temper the base of the posts in the fire, just until they start smoking but before they start burning. If you do that they'll not rot so quickly when you put them in the ground.' This was a great tip, especially as Andy pointed out that these vineyard posts had already and quite clearly suffered some damage when they'd been part-buried in the vineyard. 'There are lots of foxes around, too, so I'd dig a trench for your wire fence. Part-bury it in the ground. That'll stop foxes, stoats, ferrets and other vermin getting in. It's quite a bit of work, but there's no point you paying me to do it when you can do it yourself.'

Andy was the kind of guy I could easily relate to because he didn't like wasting time or money and he kept things simple. I began marking my trench-line out the next day, a pretty un-ambitious oblong shape, and felt as if nothing was going to hold me back. I knew my garden looked a mess, with piles of compost and soil, fence posts and planks everywhere and the ugly scar of a bonfire now joined by a trench, but I did my best to explain to the puzzled locals what my goals were. A few days later, I had slightly more trouble explaining to the Perignan police why I was driving around in a non-road worthy vehicle looking for a chicken shed (*see* Prologue). It turned out, after my brush with the law, the chicken shed was way too heavy to be transported on the back of my van anyway. When Andy heard about my dilemma he called me up to check exactly which model of shed I wanted, and appeared with it the very next morning. 'I'm often in Perpignan picking up stuff for my building business and John and Pete lent me their trailer so I could pick stuff up for them as well. I'll help you put the thing up tomorrow morning if you like and John says he'd like to come along and meet you finally.' Andy asked me if I could move the flat-packed shed off its palate and into the garden by the time he came back. There were around 100 pieces of wood to move, mainly the thin, light planks that formed the sides by interlocking without any need for nails, and other bigger, heavier ones for the gabled roof and front door that I could only just lift on my own. René inevitably appeared almost as soon as Andy had driven off, but I absolutely refused his help moving the heavier pieces. 'I'm only going to let you carry the smaller bits René,' I insisted, René being slightly offended that I had refused his offer as if he was an energetic teenager rather than an octogenarian. 'The only thing I want you to carry René is some eggs home to Adeline, that's if it all works out and we get some eggs.' Putting the shed up the following morning was easy, especially under Andy's watchful eye. 'The main thing with these self-assembly things is making sure that you get everything level, but I've left my spirit level on another project…' I made my way up to the house to get my spirit level and to fetch some hot coffee and biscuits that I thought Andy would appreciate. When I arrived back in the allotment 15 minutes later Andy had already levelled off some soil and placed four grey breezeblocks underneath where he thought the corners of the chicken shed would go. 'Years of practice, mate,' said Andy, slurping on some coffee, biscuit in hand, smiling broadly when I revealed that my spirit level told me each block was dead level. 'As a builder you just get an eye for what's straight and what isn't,' said Andy, his hand momentarily stuck so far into the packet of biscuits it was half-way up his jumper.

'Gotta go,' Andy said, as soon as John arrived, dressed in sweatshirt and shorts in keeping with the warm spring weather, and carrying a heavy tool box complete with a drill and power generator for driving the 100-or-so deep screws in that would make the shed structure safe. 'I'm renovating this barn, mate, and I'm due to cement the floor for it, but I'll catch up with you when the chickens have arrived, alright?' I asked John if Andy was getting horses or cows for his barn and John laughed and said 'Noooooo, Monty, he's going to live in it. Lots of old barns round here are getting renovated. They're popular because they are relatively good value to buy and you can lay the interior of them out exactly how you want. With an existing house it's much harder to move things like staircases, kitchens and bathrooms.' John and I had each other in stitches, swapping stories about our schooldays: me in a non-conformist, permissive, sex, drugs and rock 'n' roll girls-and-boys boarding school in soft southern England; John in a hard-core Protestant, strict, boys-only hellhole located on the bleak Scottish borders and full of bullies who'd bend you over and whack you with a gym-shoe for no apparent reason apart from it being 'your turn'. When the shed had been assembled, apart from putting the front door on (which was for human use only) and making a hole in a side wall for the hens to get in to the house to lay and sleep, John packed his tools away. 'Just one thing. I'll leave a pot of wood varnish in your basement next time I am in St-Martin. It's left over from the boat that we've decided to sell. We're getting a barge so people who stay in the holiday homes can go on canal trips on the Canal du Midi. I'll be the skipper and Pete'll lap dance as ship's entertainment.' I can be very gullible and was almost taken in by this. 'No, Monty, you've not met Pete yet but he's Yorkshire born-and-bred – not the type to lap-dance! Anyway, you'll need this varnish to protect the wood. It's not at all noxious and you'll only have to paint the outside, so it won't affect the chickens. Oh, and before I forget, your shed is so light that I'd baton it down with guy ropes like you would do a tent, but metal rather than twine if you've got it. If it blows away in the wind it'll make a great spectacle, but I can't see your neighbours being too thrilled having your shed end up on their crops.' I'm a terrible one for leaving jobs half done and the dramatic changes in St-Martin's weather were already catching me out. If the wind blew from the Mediterranean the village could feel either warm and sticky or unbearably hot and dry, or salty rain might fall for days on end. If the wind blew across the mountains from the Atlantic it might be cold, or wet, or both, or neither. If cloud-cover was low the village would be shrouded in fog. If cloud-cover was high it might just be a normal day.

When I had torn down the blue-canvas windbreak in the allotment, I made the mistake of leaving the plastic bin-liner I'd stuffed the canvas into there. It seemed a waste to throw away a large plastic bag that was only half full. Banning the use of small plastic bags in supermarkets is a good thing I think, but it might see more people who used to use these for their rubbish chucking small amounts of rubbish away in over-sized bin-liners. The wind had blown my bag and its contents halfway across the neighbouring allotments, leaving me to spend an hour picking up the pieces. I'd lost count of the number of times I'd left the driver's window on the van open after a trip on a dry and sunny day (having the engine right under the cab meant for a hot, airless journeys otherwise) only to find the driver's seat soaked the next day from a torrential downpour. And, in the first month of using the wood-burner in the house I'd never managed to regulate the indoor temperature as I wanted it for more than a day or two, it being either bitterly cold or unseasonably warm. The wind was a constant menace. I'd seen my shopping blown away twice when unloading it. The village's phone lines were down on average one week per month between winter and spring due to wind damaging local communications aerials. The gap between the bottom of my garage-width front door and the road outside meant the basement was covered with leaves and wind-blown dust almost daily. The potatoes in the allotment were safely underground but the leaves of the lettuces above were getting shredded, even though they were so close to the ground. I'd initially treated the blue-canvas windbreak as an excess – surely the wind couldn't be that strong? Likewise, John's warning about the shed blowing away. If anyone was going to know about wind then people like Eric's grandfather who'd lived in St-Martin all his life, and John, a sailor, would. I had to learn to observe and listen more if I was not to waste time re-doing jobs I'd already done.

Thank goodness the shed didn't budge when for three of the first four weeks of its life in St-Martin the *tramontana* wind blew hard enough to almost knock you over. The shed didn't budge, not because I had made it safer with guy ropes – I hadn't – but because it was fairly sheltered in the far, riverside corner of the garden in the lee of the oak forest, and I had weighted it down from the inside by installing a heavy wooden floor partly weighed down by rocks. I protected the lettuce as best I could by placing shovelfuls of compost on the windward side as a windbreak, but there was nothing to be done in the vineyard. The pine trees Eric had planted were still too small to have any major buffering effect. The vines' attempt at pushing tender little shoots and tiny leaflets into near-gale-force conditions were about as sensible as setting sail in a dingy in the typhoon season. The battering the shoots and leaves were taking – being whipped against the supporting wires – meant shoots were being bent or snapped and the first couple of leaves on each shoot-tip looked as if they'd been shot by someone with a pump-action air-rifle (should such a thing exist). The vines weren't going to stop growing because of the wind because the warming spring temperatures meant that they were completely in thrall to their hormones – and I, unfortunately, was in thrall to the wind.

Chapter 6

E RIC WAS REMARKABLY RELAXED WHEN I DRAGGED HIM UP TO THE vineyard to inspect the leaves and shoots for wind damage. He offered to drive, taking his small white van instead of his Land Cruiser. This was usually reserved for when he had his son Paul on board, or for trips requiring four-wheel drive. 'If we go to the vineyard in your "onion",' as he called my rickety van, 'we might not be back in time for lunch.' He parked at the top of the vineyard where the compost had been delivered. I began striding off towards the centre of the vineyard, convinced this was the best place to check for wind damage but Eric called me back. 'Eh, Waldino,' he laughed. As Silvana was due to arrive soon from Italy for a long weekend Eric had begun calling me 'Waldino', his Italianate version of my surname. 'You only need to look at the top few vines in any row,' he said, twiddling a few shoots and leaves in his fingers. 'You don't need to walk all the way to Spain!' he said, pointing across the vineyard and towards the Pyrénées where the Canigou was shimmering in dappled sunlight below high, puffy, fast-moving clouds. I bumbled back up the hill to join him.

'Okay, so the wind has broken off a few shoots, but the shoots you've lost are the ones you're always likely to lose anyway, off the weaker pruning spurs on a few of the weakest vines. They wouldn't have given you grapes worth having. This is an old vineyard, remember,' was Eric's prognosis.

'But what about the leaves? You know "the leaf is the sugar factory of the vine" all the wine books say. No leaves means no sugar in the grapes come harvest, right?' I said.

'Right and wrong, Waldino. Ahhhh, you wine writers. The wine has battered the top couple of leaves on the shoots, but how many leaves will have formed on each shoot when the shoots have reached their full length?'

'Um.' I could feel Eric about to add the word 'cretino' to make 'Waldino cretino' if I got this one wrong. 'Anywhere between eight and, say, 12?' My tone was hopeful rather than stonewall confident.

'Around 12. And how many leaves have you lost off each shoot?'

'Um, no more than three?'

'No,' said Eric, firmly. 'First, you haven't lost any leaves. They haven't been blown away in the wind. That only happens in autumn, not spring. The first couple of leaves to emerge from this year's buds have suffered some puncturing, that's all. So, you've lost a smallish percentage of whatever 12 divided by two is.' I calculated that this meant one sixth of the leaves had suffered some damage. It still made me nervous, which Eric sensed. 'Monty, listen, it's pluses and minuses. Just because there's a bit of wind it doesn't mean the shoots will stop growing. They will still extend themselves up to the sun, but both the shoots and the leaves growing on them will get stronger and more wind-resistant. It's like a baby coming out of the womb. It's small and fragile when it pops out then gets stronger in time and bigger, too,' said Eric, making an effort to pat my middle-aged spread. 'The leaves at the tips of the upward-growing shoots that got a bit bruised will still capture enough sunlight.' Vines need sunlight for photosynthesis. Chlorophyll in the leaves converts carbon dioxide and water into sugar and oxygen. Some of this sugar the vine uses to feed itself and the rest goes into the grapes. 'If you were pushing your vines hard to produce large quantities of grapes with fertilizers and irrigation then you could worry you wouldn't have enough leaves for photosynthesis. But that isn't the case, is it, Waldino? You've got yourself a vineyard on the top of a mountain in a hot, sunny spot with naturally drying winds. Trust me. This kind of wind thing often happens in spring. Yields of grapes here are naturally small enough for you to lose a tiny bit off a couple of leaves with no ill effect on the wine. Even if the wind blows hard for the rest of spring and summer, which it won't, the vine shoots will grow strong and hard enough for the wind not to be a problem. Then you'll be glad that the wind keeps the vines free of diseases, such as grey rot, by drying them quickly if and when the rain comes.'

Eric began walking back to his van across the bumpy track that separates the vines from scrub and forest bearing the demeanour of a man in the middle of just-another-day-at-the-office. I lagged behind, trying naively to work out from the clouds' movements exactly where the wind was coming from and when it would calm. Even though I had been sailing a few times it had always perplexed me how boats with their sails up could make progress sailing against the wind. So I resigned myself to waiting for a calm period during which time I could apply my first vineyard spray – horn manure. This spray would go directly onto the soil rather than onto the vines. Silvana, who was planning her latest trip to see me in France from her family home in Tuscany, received regular weather updates from me by phone. Long-distance relationships are never easy at the best of times, but Silvana and I seemed to cope with the situation pretty well. Silvana's distance from the drama of France meant she had more of a perspective than me when things seemed not to be going according to plan. 'Don't let the wind worry you too much Mont, I'm coming by bus to France, not by aeroplane,' she teased. 'And it's not as if horn manure has to go onto the soil as a fine spray which would be a problem if it is as windy as you say. Horn manure should be sprayed like big rain drops instead – or in large droplets, to be precise. That's what you said about it in your biodynamic wines book anyway.' I'd foolishly given Silvana a copy of this book as a present and her near-photographic memory meant the contents of its 500-or-so pages were memorised and filed securely away in the huge brain that was somehow squeezed into her pretty little head.

Horn manure (or '500' as it is also known) is a pillar of biodynamics. If you don't spray it on the soil at regular six-month intervals you can't be biodynamic. Horn manure is simply cow manure stuffed in a cow horn that is buried underground for six months between autumn and spring. During this time the manure changes from a moist, lightish brown and obviously manure-smelling substance to something drier, more earthy and much darker brown in colour. Once dug up the horn's contents (not the horn, that can be re-used to make more horn manure the following season) are diluted with warmish water. You need around 60–120 grams per hectare, roughly the contents of one horn. You spray it on the soil in autumn and spring. To make the spray: crumble the horn manure into the water and stir the mixture back and forth for one hour. This aerates the millions of beneficial microbes the horn manure contains, activating them for when they go onto the soil. In my case, I wanted these microbes to help break down the compost that had been spread. This would build-up the level of humus in the soil, humus being the 'earth within the earth' so to speak. In humus-rich soil crops can grow stronger, thicker, deeper roots; so the horn manure and compost combination is just like giving the house you're going to build a decent foundation to stand on. Also, my taste buds consistently told me that wines grown on biodynamic soil had more of a unique 'this-wine-can't-come-from-anywhere-else' taste, and that's what I wanted from my wine.

'You're convinced biodynamics works, Monty, but don't be surprised if some of the locals you meet in France take a bit of persuading,' said Silvana, who'd heard many times my spiel about how horn manure would be good not only for my wine but also could work as a potential cure for the ills of climate change meaning the soil would resist erosion in hot weather and flash flooding in wet weather after a dose of horn manure. 'People have to be ready for something as radical as biodynamics. You've seen how the farmers in Tuscany have had it too good for too long. Rich foreigners have spent the last 30 years paying them over the odds for ruined farmhouses that can't be redesigned due to strict planning laws. They look good after restructuring, true, but they usually remain draughty and badly insulated,' said Silvana. She was right. Tuscan open-fireplaces, I had noted, looked great but burnt vast amounts of wood and gave precious little heat. Craning my neck from the dining table I could see the wood-burning stove that Eric had installed in my house. It was not a thing of beauty but at least it and its black-metal chimney pipe did throw out lots of heat for the small amount of wood it burnt. Silvana considered herself a southerner even though she was born in Tuscany because both her parents were from the south; but she described herself as being '*né carne, né pesce*', which translates as being 'neither meat nor fish'. Southern Italians consider her a Tuscan, while Tuscans and Silvana herself consider her a southerner. Silvana never held back when expressing an opinion on Tuscany, however.

'Many Tuscan wines have sold for unjustifiably high prices because they've been overrated by wine writers, especially the Americans, who've fallen for the romance of Tuscany. Some of the margins these wines sell for are unbelievably high – and I should know because I see the books. And then you come along, Monty, with your baby face, and from a country that doesn't even produce wine, and tell them they need to become biodynamic if they want to preserve their heritage, their soils and so on. Their attitude is, "What can this guy teach me that I don't already know?" The answer is nothing. They're not ready for biodynamics, which seems completely unnecessary to them. Once they see it in action, however, and see how it works and that it works, then they'll start to listen. But, it doesn't happen overnight. I suspect it's the same in any agricultural community,

French or otherwise. Tradition rules, and change however logical and necessary is resisted.'

When Silvana and I next spoke, a couple of days later, I could tell her that despite what were still blustery conditions, and using the back sprayer, I'd finally managed to spray the biodynamic horn manure on the vineyard soil. However, I didn't tell Silvana about how I had tried explaining the finer points of the biodynamic horn manure to one middle-aged woman in the allotment area. She tended to do her gardening very early in the morning, possibly to avoid having to talk with anyone else, and was known as a difficult character. Due to yet another dry winter she had already begun watering the lawn of her house in the village nearly every lunchtime with a long yellow hose. A biodynamic lawn, I guessed, might need water once a fortnight, if at all, and then would only be watered in the late afternoon or evening to minimise water being wasted through evaporation.

'There are lots of vineyards around here that are biodynamic,' she said, when we first met. She didn't beat about the bush saying, 'You must be Monty,' then asking why I had moved to St-Martin. I figured that if someone had told her my name they must already have told her about my biodynamic vineyard. I had no hesitation correcting her straight off by saying that she was making the common mistake of confusing organics with biodynamics.

'What's the difference, then?' she asked.

'Well, you have to use nine so-called biodynamic preparations to be biodynamic. Organics is all about using organic substances, like organic fertiliser, whereas biodynamics is about forces as well as substances. If your plants can harness so-called life or growth forces through biodynamics the idea is that they will be inherently stronger.'

'You mean working with the moon,' she said curtly, placing her watering can filled, bizarrely, with weeds she had just pulled, rather than water, on the pathway between me and my garden, effectively blocking my route. I knew I'd probably be wasting my time explaining biodynamic thinking to her, in the sense that she'd never ever become biodynamic herself, but at least I'd be able to show her I knew what I was talking about. I thought I'd give her the full Monty, so to speak, about the horn manure preparation as an example of biodynamic thinking.

'Basically, most people agree cows produce great manure, right? Worms are attracted to cow pats in fields almost immediately, as you can see by lifting one up with your foot the next day. Well, the reason cows produce such great manure, according to Rudolf Steiner who invented horn manure back in the 1920s, is that they have horns and hooves.'

'Do all cows have horns?'

'Well, cows do have horns, but most cows are de-horned when they're young. Biodynamic farmers are not allowed to de-horn their cows. The reason is the energy released when the cow digests her food is so great she can't use it all for her own needs that are more physical than mental, unlike humans, for example, who use a lot of energy thinking and talking. Rudolf Steiner said that this energy is not lost, but stays inside the cow because it bounces back into the cow off her hooves and horns. The manure becomes even more potent when stuffed in the cow horns themselves. The logic is that if the horn has the power to block energy, or "cow power" you could say, by not allowing this digestive energy to escape from the cow, then the horn can be seen as an energy capturing sheath. Most cow manure is good to use on your allotment and is certainly better than chemical fertiliser. But, biodynamic cow-manure is best because of the horn thing.'

'I've heard of Steiner, I think, as in Steiner schools,' said my interlocutor, who turned out to be a retired schoolteacher.

'Steiner founded what became the Steiner Waldorf school movement in 1919. Steiner said the aim of schooling should be 'to develop free human beings who are able of themselves to import purpose and direction to their lives'. I suppose you could say biodynamics is a way of getting plants to think for themselves, the idea being, as Steiner said, that there was no matter without spirit, and no spirit without matter.'

'And you attended a Steiner school I suppose?'

'Er, no, actually, I'd never even heard of them by the time I left school. But, I did go to a school where if you were not very academic you weren't punished for it. The teachers would encourage you to develop music, sport, even gardening skills. Everyone has a talent, after all.'

'There no scientific proof of all this, though, is there?'

'Well, conventional science isn't very good at measuring life forces. But, if you stick some horn manure under a microscope you'll see it has noticeably more microbes than simple manure. If you bury cow manure in a glass bottle, an aluminium drinks can, an old shoe, a porcelain or clay pot, or a cow horn, even your watering can, only the manure buried in the horn will turn into what horn manure is supposed to be. And that is a really humus-rich substance. It's as if the grass the cow had eaten had been turned back into the earth from which it grew, but with added cow power. Manure in the others will go stinky and turn green as if the grass is, er, turning back into the grass in the cow pasture.'

'So why do you have to bury the horn for six months?'

'The idea is that by burying it for six months between autumn and spring this allows the manure to capture lots of vitalising energy from the earth. This is the moment the earth breathes in, if you like, and plant roots and worms and everything else underground becomes active. This is the opposite of what happens from spring to summer when you can see the earth breathing out as everything above ground, such as flowers, shoots and leaves, is growing. And, as biodynamics is all about forces as well as substances you have to stir the solid horn manure into the water first before spraying it. The water acts as a carrier for these forces when you spray the horn manure on the soil. You always spray horn manure in the afternoon, when it is starting to get dark and so-called earth forces are dominant, rather than under the midday sun when bright, solar forces are dominant.' The old lady began moving off, directing a forced smile my way. I never had another conversation with her apart from the odd 'good morning' or 'good afternoon' greeting, made usually from a distance, as I never crossed her on that path again, despite the fact that we both used it for access to our plots and to get to the water reservoir. More usually, she'd pretend to be so immersed in her vegetables when I passed that she would ignore me.

One elderly lady in the village I was always pleased to see was Marinette. I'd have to walk past her veg patch to get to mine and would often pass the time of day, although I would try not to linger long as she was always busy and seemed much more shy than the extrovert René. 'Are those flowers for the table?' I asked her once in early spring as she was furrowing out a line of soil into which she was dropping large flower bulbs. To make the furrow she was using a combination of a long-handled hoe and her feet. Despite having a tough job working nights in a local old people's home Marinette's daughter, Christine, often helped her mother in their patch. Christine said that her mother was putting the flowers in to stop the moles. 'They don't like the smell of the flowers' roots, it seems. The moles seem to be much more of a problem down this end of the vegetable area than at your end,' she said, as her mother gently covered each bulb with fresh soil, working in that quick, efficient way that comes so naturally to old people. Marinette would collect nearly ripened walnuts in late summer and marinade them in brandy to make a delicious walnut liqueur. The bottle she and Christine gave me for me for my birthday was probably my favourite present. There were other ways of deterring moles. Daniel, I had noticed, had installed a battery-powered element the size of a mobile phone that was supposed to keep the moles out of his garden by beeping in a frequency they couldn't abide. The noise it made was barely audible for humans. Not so the noise of my cock crowing every morning, although it took him a couple of weeks to find his crowing voice once he had arrived with several Rhode Island Red hens for company. You could just about hear him in the village square on a quiet day and with no traffic passing through. All my birds had come from the region's largest egg producer, located on the quite intensively agricultural flat plain of the Têt valley west of Perpignan. The cock arrived with a bent foot, and both cock and hens seemed to suffer a bout of agoraphobia, perhaps because they had never been allowed out of their batteries into the Great Outdoors.

To get them certified organic chicken food I had to drive into the foothills of the Canigou to a place called Los Masos. Eric saw me preparing the van early in the morning by loading the driver's cab with half a dozen plastic bottles filled with tap water to cope with a leak in the cooling system. 'You're mad, Waldino,' he said when I told him where I was going. 'You've never done that journey before. You'll have to cross one mountain range to go through the Têt valley, then you've got to get up onto the Canigou mountain itself. Even with a normal car it's a tough one. You'll never do it in your van, unless you're planning to camp a night out either on the way there or on the way back. If you break down I'm not coming to get you.' It wasn't a particularly hot day. In fact it was overcast and cool as I set off through the villages of Prats-de-Sournia with its cliff-like vegetable gardens seemingly hanging off the side of the road, and the bleaker Sournia itself, towards the large town of Prades on the Têt valley floor. My destination, Los Masos, lay beyond on the Canigou itself. The weather meant I wasn't too worried about the cooling system, nor was I was in a hurry. How could I have been with a van like mine? However, the van did seem to be leaking more water than I had thought, but by the time I got to Prades and pulled over in a lay-by to let things cool down a bit I'd used less than a quarter of my water, and Los Masos was only a few kilometres away on the map. To find the organic chicken farm, however, proved almost impossible on the narrow, slippy, un-surfaced mountain tracks surrounded by thick forest. I thought I had found the right place, a house surrounded by chicken sheds, but the only person who came out to greet me was a very small boy chewing a piece of chocolate bread almost as big as his head. 'Watch out for foxes,' he warned, assuming perhaps that I was looking for chickens rather than chicken food.

I'd almost given up, and was looking for a place to make my final U-turn when I saw a house, half hidden in the forest, with an old man wearing a very smart panama hat out front mowing his lawn. I introduced myself in French and he responded in perfect, public-school English. Mr Bramley, as he was called, very kindly let me use his phone to call the chicken-food supplier whose initial directions, now that I had seen the local terrain, had proved vague in the extreme. 'I used to work in Kenya,' said Mr Bramley, 'in agro-chemicals, although originally I am from Sussex.' I pictured a thatched cottage, smoke gently rising from the chimney stack on an autumn day, with apples (bramley of course) gently ripening out front ready for a home-baked pie sprinkled with brown sugar and served with lashings of steaming custard. 'I'm quite proud of my organic garden now, though,' he said, as he returned to his mowing and I finally made my U-turn.

My organic-chicken-feed supplier, a guy called Maurice Picco, was as happy to speak French to me as Italian, having originated from Friuli in northeast Italy. It was easy to see how Picco with his wispy white hair and intense, energetic manner had become one of the main movers and shakers in the organic movement in France. He'd chaired various committees and lobby groups and was currently busy opposing more trials for

GMO crops in Roussillon. His several hundred chickens made him the largest producer of organic eggs in the region. He and an assistant were marking with an ink stamp each egg from that day's lay for traceability purposes. We loaded three 50 kg sacks of feed onto the van, I paid the bill but the van wouldn't start as I set off. Had Eric booby-trapped it to teach me a lesson about not taking risks? Would I have to bribe him to come and get me with a month's supply of eggs. It took me a while to work out that one of the cables connecting the battery to the ignition system, that was worn anyway, had finally snapped due to the jolting caused by the sacks of feed being dropped onto the back where the battery was positioned. It wasn't difficult to fix, but took an hour of fiddling. The extra weight of feed on the back, plus the fact that the sun was getting higher and hotter in the sky than I had hoped, meant that I was having to stop the van more and more frequently to keep the system topped up with water. On the penultimate mountain climb, towards Sournia, I was overtaken by an eight-strong group of guys on modern motorbikes with British number plates. I waved them past and then passed them when they stopped to take photos. This overtake-and-be-overtaken game must have happened at least three times until I heard a sizzling sound from within the cab. The engine seemed about to blow and I had only one more bottle of water left. As the bikers past me I tried to wave them down, but they must have thought that that friendly chap in the clapped-out French van was simply saying hello again and waved politely as they sped past. I waited a good half-an-hour for the engine to cool, topped it up, and drove as slowly as I dared, limping into St-Martin mid-afternoon. A big lorry was blocking the road in front of the wine cooperative and Eric was unloading a tractor he'd had to repair when he cracked its axle. 'You look white, Waldino. I didn't think we'd see you back in St-Martin for at least a couple of days.'

'I thought I was gone for good at one point,' I explained, as I helped him get his tractor off the trailer 'but it'll all be worth it, Eric, once you taste the eggs.' The chickens seemed to like their new food, but didn't lay for a few weeks whilst they de-stressed and got their bearings.

When John came to drill an opening in the side of the shed as a separate doorway for the hens he took one look at my posture and said, 'Hmmm, you're still not 100 per cent right on the back front, are you?' He'd say this every time I saw him throughout the rest of year, in fact. John had brought Pete with him, and even a small generator to power the drill. 'The house we're renovating in Le Vivier to let had no water or power when we bought it, so we needed a generator to start work on it,' John explained. He was putting an entrance for the hens in the side of the shed so that I could enter it via the main door when collecting eggs, grabbing garden tools, or cleaning out the droppings; and the hens would have their own entrance to their wide, high-wire pen, that was there to protect them from foxes and other vermin. Pete was physically smaller and less extrovert than John and as attached to Jasper as I was to Harry who was too unpredictable to be allowed unsupervised in the allotment, especially with chickens around. Pete had immediately spotted the oak barrel I had half-buried in the garden for my biodynamic barrel compost.

'Barrel compost being normal compost made in a barrel, I suppose?' asked John.

'Um, yes and no. It's a quick compost as the compost I used on the vineyard was only organic and not biodynamic because it didn't contain six specially prepared medicinal plants or compost preparations. These are yarrow, chamomile and dandelion flowers, whole stinging nettles minus the roots, oak bark and a liquid extract made from crushed valerian flowers. These six biodynamic compost preparations carry life forces into the compost.'

'Life forces? How does that work then? As in *Star Wars* and "may be the force be with you" type thing?' Despite being a film lover I had never seen *Star Wars*, a fact I was too embarrassed to admit, especially to John who was a similar age to me and who as a pre-teen like me had attended an all-boys, 'wear-shorts-even-in-the-freezing-cold' preparatory school for boarders. At this time films like *Star Wars* and *Grease* (which I had also never seen) were all the rage among my school friends. I first explained to John and Pete how horn manure was made, how biodynamics was as much about substances as well as forces and how cow horns radiated forces back into the horn manure to make it special.

'You prepare some of the six compost preparations a bit like the horn manure, using an animal organ as a sheath. You use a stag's bladder for the yarrow flowers, a cow intestine for the chamomile flowers, a cow skull for the oak bark and a cow's mesentery for the dandelion flowers.'

'A mesen...what? As in the bit that holds the internal organs in?' asked John, whose osteopathic training meant he was pretty familiar with body parts. 'Isn't it a bit of a problem having all these animal bits in your compost, what with mad cow disease?'

'The animal parts don't actually go in the compost. They're just used as sheaths when you make the preparations. It's ironic that the farming system that caused mad-cow disease by allowing farmers to turn herbivore cows not just into carnivores but cannibals is now trying to give biodynamic growers a hard time about using a cow's intestine as a sheath when no biodynamic cow has ever suffered from mad-cow disease. I used my mum's wooden-framed tennis racket that had cat gut for strings at school and no one seemed to mind. And some home butchers I know still use real animal intestines for their sausages. It's quite fun making sausages filled with chamomile flowers.'

'Depends on you definition of fun, I suppose,' said Pete, all mock-horror.

'You must get a lot of people thinking you are away with the fairies when you talk about biodynamics,' said John. 'Some of it just sounds bonkers.'

'Don't give Monty too hard a time,' said Pete. 'We might be drinking some of his biodynamic wine day.'

'The proof of biodynamics is in the pudding.' I said. 'The idea behind using the animal parts as sheaths is to enhance the beneficial, or healing, effect that each of the plants used in the compost preparations have. Take chamomile, for example. You drink chamomile tea to relieve stomach ache – when you feel blocked up. The cow's intestine is pretty important in keeping the cow's busy digestion system from staying unblocked. Stuffing chamomile flowers into cow intestines provides the flowers with the right forces to help the compost to break down fully and in the right way.'

'Sounds a bit weird to me, almost like witchcraft, what with cow skulls and everything,' said Pete while passing another bit for the power drill to John, who already had one drill bit in his mouth and another smaller one behind his ear. The other ear held the pencil John was using to mark where he was about to cut the hen hatch in the shed's wooden panels.

'It is a bit of a leap of faith, I'll admit,' I said, 'but even peer-reviewed scientific research now suggests that a compost pile infused with the six biodynamic compost preparations will ferment better than one without the preps in.'

'What do you mean by better?' asked John.

'What you want when a compost pile is fermenting is for things like weed-seeds and bad microbes to be killed off, so the pile needs to heat up to a certain temperature and stay hot for weeks or even months. And, you want finished compost that contains the right kind of food for the soil. If the pile gets too hot all the weed-seeds will be dead but all the food for the soil will have been burnt off as steam. If the compost ferments too cold you might get some good soil food, but when you spread it the weed-seeds (from weeds you've pulled or weeds that the cow ate and ended up in her manure) will be able to reproduce and take over the land you wanted for your crops.'

I then tried explaining to John and Pete about why the yarrow flowers are aged in a stag's bladder, the bladder being a very sensitive organ because we pee when our senses are heightened by excitement or fear, and how yarrow's tiny little flowers were seen to be so sensitive by the ancients that they called yarrow a Venus plant.

'As two blokes living together we're maybe more into Mars plants, if there are any of those....' said Pete, trying not to laugh himself but making me laugh out loud instead. It was a shame John and Pete didn't have the chance to see the barrel compost being made. This involves mixing together cow manure and some eggshells for one hour. The calcium in the eggshells is supposed to diffuse background radiation. Once mixed, the manure is placed in the bottom of the barrel and a little of the biodynamic yarrow, chamomile, stinging nettle, oak bark and dandelion compost preparations are sprinkled on. These are dark and crumbly whereas the extract made from the squashed valerian flowers goes on as droplets. Valerian's role is to act like a kind of heat blanket, preserving all the benefits of the other five preps within the compost. Burying the barrel half in the soil and half above ground is said to allow the barrel compost to fill up with both earthy and cosmic forces.

The next time my doorbell rang, Harry yelped and ran downstairs to find John and Pete. They had brought some melon, cucumber and tomato transplants. 'We've been spying on your garden, Mr Waldin,' John said. 'It's really starting to come together.'

'Okay,' I said. 'All these compliments and gifts mean you guys need something,' I said, inviting them, and Jasper (whom Harry adored), in for a coffee. It turned out that John and Pete had once made a few experimental bottles of red wine from the same type of grape as I was using, the troublesome Carignan. 'Wow,' I exclaimed, as I spat out one of the harshest, most burnt, rubbery-tasting reds I had tasted in a long while. 'Did you make that in the bath or something?' I said, rather unkindly even though my guess turned out to be pretty close to the truth. John and Pete took my comments in good spirit. I always try to see the positives in a wine. 'My advice to you for next time is to pick the Carignan when it is ripe. This wine has been picked too early which is why it is so harsh and has these dominant rubber and banana flavours,' I said. It was those types of flavours that had given the Carignan its bad name.

'How do you know when it's ripe, then,' asked Pete. 'By tasting the grapes regularly, and checking if the seeds or pips inside are still green or are getting brown. The browner the better as the chances are that the watery, sugary pulp protecting the pips will taste more sweet than acid. Don't forget that the vine is tempting birds or animals such as wild boar to eat its grapes by making them sweet. Once the pips exit the digestive system of whichever animal has eaten them they can grow into new vines – this is how vines reproduce in the wild.'

'Why is it then that some Chardonnays I like taste ripe and juicy but quite tart at the same time?' asked Pete.

'I guess, Pete, you're referring to wines from places like Chile or Australia?'

'Why do you ask?'

'Because Chile, Australia, New Zealand and California all label their Chardonnay as Chardonnay. France is still stuck in a time-warp when it comes to labelling their best Chardonnays, which must carry the name of the region the wine came from, such as Chablis, Pouilly-Fuissé, or Macon-Villages, rather than the grape it was made from. I once had a chap come into a wine shop I was working in and when I offered him a Chardonnay he said "I don't like Chardonnay. Got any Chablis?" I had to tell him that Chablis is in fact a 100 per cent Chardonnay wine.'

'No wonder people get confused about wine,' said John, who was scanning my bookshelf vainly for helpful wine books.

'Anyway,' I continued, 'to answer your point about why New World Chardonnay can taste both ripe and tart: it is because Chardonnay grapes ripen so quickly, especially in hot climates, and some growers start picking deliberately early, when it is still slightly unripe. This gives the tart edge to the wine that you picked up on. The next lot of grapes will be picked perfectly ripe, but by the time the last grapes are harvested the Chardonnay will be over-ripe, a bit like marmalade. Blending the unripe, ripe and over-ripe grapes produces a more interesting wine, one that's ripe, mouth-filling and mouth-watering at the same time. It's a bit like making an apple pie from fallen apples: some are on-the-button ripe, others are a bit hard and green and some are yellow and starting to get wrinkly skin. But, they all go in the pot just the same and the pie is no worse for it.'

'And the apples will probably taste better because they're from your own garden and *de facto* organic,' Pete said, 'just like our wine. We didn't spray the vines at all.' The vines they were renting belonged to Serge the shepherd. 'We know you are supposed to spray it with sulphur to keep the mildew off, but we never bothered.' I replied that if I could help them with this year's wine I would, but I reminded them that I was still very much on a learning curve with Carignan myself.

This became apparent when Silvana arrived soon after for the weekend of her thirtieth birthday. I was struggling to work out the key dates in the vineyard calendar: when I would have to start spraying the vines against the powdery mildew John and Pete had mentioned; when the vines would flower and when the grapes would be ripe. 'Your vines budded last week, the third week of April. They should flower about eight to ten weeks later,' said Silvana, 'depending on how warm and dry it is.'

'How did you know that?' I asked. 'You're an accounting expert, not a winegrower?'

'I've been reading your winegrowing books, Monty.' I'd recently bought Silvana some books on turtles, her favourite animal (after Harry), precisely to keep her inquisitive little nose out of my wine books. Silvana was a polymath, capable of learning about anything. 'The educational books on winegrowing by the Australian universities you have aren't too difficult for me to understand. I find them easier than the French winegrowing books, to be honest, because the approach is more scientific, with statistics, numbers and facts rather than boring stories about what used to happen when great-grandad was alive. Your vines should flower around mid-summer, the third week in June.' In the northern hemisphere the third week in June gives us the longest day. The wine books say that the grapes are usually ripe 100 days after flowering, but this exactitude is somewhat spurious bearing in mind early and late-ripening grapes ripen at different speeds and flowering usually lasts a minimum of one week and sometimes nearly as long as two. So, the precise day of harvesting can be anywhere between 90 and 110 days, or even longer. Under the 100-day rule I'd be picking in mid-September, but Eric had sometimes picked my vineyard as late as November. Silvana's arrival was also the moment for the biodynamic barrel compost to be sprayed on the soil. As barrel compost is an earth remedy it is made when the moon is in front of an earth constellation, with Virgo being seen as better than either of the other two earth constellations, Taurus and Capricorn. The barrel compost is removed from the barrel 27 days later when the moon is back in front of Virgo (whereas it takes the the sun one year to pass in front of the belt of 12 astronomical constellations of the zodiac lying behind its path on the ecliptic, it only takes the moon 27.3 days to complete the same circuit).

I took some barrel compost round to John and Pete's place in Fosse, having first mixed it with a stinging-nettle liquid-manure that I'd had prepared by soaking some nettle leaves for a couple of weeks in a porcelain crock in the basement of the house. That part of the house now stank like cow sheds and old drains, but the liquid concentrate would be a great pick-me-up for John and Pete's plants, as well as for the soil around them. Their allotment was at the bottom of the village, away from their house whose massive front garden was given to lawn for Jasper to play on, plus lawn and private swimming pool for the guests staying in their holiday cabin. Getting out of St-Martin made me more confident about asking John to fill me in on the hot, local political issues and how important being friends with the local mayor was. 'There is a "clean-up Fosse" day each year, organised by our mayor with the rest of the village. Pete and I volunteer for the worst job.'

'Which is?'

'Cleaning out the open-air, public swimming pool. We don't use the pool ourselves as we have our own, but we figured that as most people who use it are foreigners, especially British, if we cleaned it out it might go down well with our fellow villagers.

The pool is unheated and deemed too cold for the locals who go to the one in Prats-de-Sournia up the road when they want a swim. You'd never believe how many leaves, dead rats and birds you find in that pool.'

John and Pete weren't married, but under French law could become a legally recognised couple under a civil partnership. I'd heard that one local couple – a French lady and her Moroccan boyfriend – had had a lot of trouble with a local, female mayor who refused to let them marry in her commune, allegedly because she was anti-Moroccan. The French lady's brother was then taken to court by the same mayor due to an eco-home he had built, even though the mayor was approving building permits left, right and centre for her many local pals.

'French mayors have a lot of power,' said John, 'so you wouldn't want to buy a house without making yourself known to the mayor first, just to see the lie of the land.' The mayor of St-Martin, André Foulquier, was known to all and sundry as clever, nice, go-ahead, fair-minded and pro anyone coming to St-Martin to live or work. He'd successfully reversed the national trend of a declining population for a village of St-Martin's size. André was the one who had essentially given me a working (albeit old) van for next to nothing and for the last few years had made sure no one in the village lacked drinking water by rationing the village's own supply (from a mountain spring) in high summer while buying water in by the tanker load. Three dry winters and a possible leak in the water-pumping system had meant the village's water reservoir was low from late July onwards. André had served 20 years as St-Martin's mayor, but was due to retire soon which meant there was jockeying between various groups in the village to succeed him. 'I suppose the biggest local issue is wind-farms,' said John, which seemed odd somehow on such a quiet, windless evening in the calm of John and Pete's veg patch. The hills around St-Martin had been earmarked as a site for wind-turbines to provide eco-energy. The feldspar quarry in the nearby village of St-Arnac was part wind-powered, but the thought of having several more, much larger wind-turbines was too much for some locals who had organised protest groups. No one doubted, however, that locally the wind was so strong that the area was a prime one to be considered for wind power. John and Pete diluted the liquid concentrate I had brought and began sprinkling it on their vegetables. Pete had been worried about some sickly looking basil plants. 'Wet the leaves and the soil around the plants,' I said.

'How much of these biodynamic preparations do you need for a garden our size,' asked Pete, whose jeans-cut-off-at-the-knee, rather than overalls and beret, marked him out as a typical Brit. 'You can take the Englishman out of England, but you can't take England out of the Englishman,' I remarked *sotto voce* to John who was watching his partner from the water butt.

'A teaspoon's worth of each of the six biodynamic-compost preps is easily enough for your garden,' I said. The garden was overhalf the size of a soccer pitch. 'I know a teaspoon's worth does sound a ridiculously small amount, but it begins to make sense if you can think of the compost preps as carrying beneficial forces into your garden. Biodynamics isn't about adding tonnes and tonnes of stuff to your plants. That's how conventional farming works – or rather fails. Biodynamics is a bit more subtle because it guides plants to find their own rhythms and balances. Conventional farming seems designed to do the opposite – throwing so much stuff on which then throws everything out of balance. Anyway, I'll get off my soap-box now. Just remember to spray the garden again in a week's time, like today, in the late afternoon or evening,' I advised.

I was starting to get enough food from my own garden to prepare Silvana a special birthday meal. Salad made from two types of lettuce (butter and lollo rosso), radishes, baby carrots – thinned from the furrows to leave the remaining carrots extra space to grow bigger – and rocket leaves. 'In Italy we can't believe how something as humble as rocket is so trendy and expensive in London,' Silvana said. Silvana's previous job working for a famous Italian winery combined with her excellent language skills meant she had often gone to London on sales trips and had eaten in London's top Italian eateries. I doubted she had eaten rocket salad surrounded by the kind of vomit-coloured 1970s-style wallpaper that the walls of my house in France had and which I had never got around to redecorating. Silvana was usually so exhausted from the overnight journey from Italy that she preferred just a salad, rather than heavy pasta dish as well. However, as I had wanted to surprise her I had cooked *Spaghetti a la puttanesca*, or 'whore's spaghetti', a southern Italian dish that her mother had taught me to cook and that contained anchovies. These were a speciality of the nearby Mediterranean port of Collioure. You warm some olive oil, anchovies and garlic in a pan, add in some capers and pitted olives, then some chopped tomatoes and simmer until everything is soft and all the different flavours have melded before serving it onto spaghetti. I sprinkled on some chopped, fresh parsley from the garden (we had plenty of herbs such as rosemary, parsley, basil and sage, some of which Silvana and I had planted out from cuttings from Silvana's mother's garden in Tuscany.) 'Not bad Mont,' was Silvana's verdict, 'although in Italy we never mix olive oil with butter.' I had added a bit of butter, a tip from Silvana's father who said it gave the sauce extra texture. I'm not sure many of my wine-tasting-expert friends would have picked up the presence of the butter.

When John telephoned soon afterwards next day to say, 'I don't know how it works, this biodynamic stuff, but the weaker plants just look a bit stronger to my uneducated eye,' I felt a bit like a doctor who had cured a sick patient. Real hard-core biodynamic growers always talk about using the biodynamic preparations to 'heal the earth'. I wasn't sure biodynamics would ever be able to do that, but if it had helped put John and Pete's basil back on track then that couldn't be such a bad thing, could it?

Chapter 7

SPRING IS ALWAYS THE TIME OF THE YEAR WHEN WINEGROWERS become especially anxious. They worry about what exactly the coming season will bring in terms of grape yields, wine quality and then profit or loss. This year, however, was an exception because some local winegrowers were so agitated about the state of the wine market that they had resorted to terrorist tactics.

'Did you hear about the bombs?' said Eric, as he came round to my house for his now daily morning coffee.

'What bombs?' I replied, thinking that the only thing odder-sounding than a wine terrorist might be a vegetarian beef farmer, or an illiterate librarian.

'It's CRAV again,' said Eric. 'They've been causing trouble around supermarkets down on the coast.' CRAV was the Comité Regional d'Action Viticole (or Local Wine Action Group) – made up of balaclava-clad, militant winegrowers. It intimidates local supermarkets, wine merchants and wine importers it accuses of importing cheaper wines, putting local winegrowers out of business. CRAV's tactics range from plastering graffiti on buildings (like agricultural banks) to pouring imported wines direct from the (usually Spanish) road tankers they arrived on down street drains to exploding homemade devices outside supermarkets stocking imported wines that undercut locally produced ones. CRAV had attacked supermarkets in the Mediterranean port city of Nîmes that morning and from his tone I could see that Eric was ashamed. 'You should always be able to find a market for your wine if it is good enough,' he said, leaning back in his chair so the steam rising off his coffee no longer went straight up his nose. 'We live in a free market so you must accept there'll be other winemakers from outside France, and outside Europe even, in competition with you. In Europe we've become too addicted to government subsidies. Paying us to produce a lake-full of wine that is then distilled into industrial alcohol, or even fuel, because no one wants to drink is madness.' As Eric's vineyards were naturally low-yielding he never produced more wine than he could sell, so never received the kind of subsidies that CRAV aimed to preserve. CRAV's latest bout of militancy was timed to coincide with the announcement by the European Union of plans to remove many agricultural subsidies, and those paid to winegrowers in particular. The original idea behind the subsidies was that while it was fair to assume that industrial factories may come and go agricultural enterprises such as vineyards must be preserved for the jobs they created and to maintain the way of life rural vineyard communities.

'Do you think that when winegrowers pour wine down the drain it's just an insurance scam to get rebates for their own wines that they know are unsellable against foreign competition?' I asked Eric, as he placed one foot on the top of the stairs, while with the other he blocked Harry from exiting the house with him.

'That's what some people say, for sure,' he said. 'And you'll be tipping your wine down the drain unless you get those vines sprayed soon,' he warned me as he disappeared.

Eric and other winegrowers in the St-Martin area had been getting very nervous because a constant stream of wet and windy springtime weather had meant that no one had yet been able to do the first sulphur spray to prevent powdery mildew. All winegrowers spray their vines with sulphur. It is approved for winegrowers who are certified organic or biodynamic because it is naturally occurring and doesn't leave a residue in the vines or the wine. But, spraying vines when it is wet is essentially a waste of time. The spray will simply wash off and the tractor will get stuck in the mud. It's also worthless spraying when it is windy because it is tricky directing the sulphur spray precisely enough for it to land where it is needed on the vines.

'You can spray the vines by hand, Monty, but it'll take you at least a couple of days, probably even more with your back,' said Eric, despite knowing that I had managed to spray the vineyard with biodynamic horn manure using the back sprayer in a single long afternoon. However, horn manure was sprayed on the soil rather than on each vine, so it is possible to spray three rows more or less at once: one to your left, the ground in front of you, and the row to your right. But, this type of three-for-the-price-of-one spraying was not possible with sulphur. It had to go directly onto the vines and row by row. 'With a back sprayer you'll have to spray the row from both sides,' said Eric, 'to get full coverage. If you only spray from one side you'll only cover half or one side of the baby grape bunches and only one side of the shoots and leaves.' In other words I'd have to walk up and down each row twice, which would slow me down enormously because I'd have to keep filling up the back sprayer (which only held around 20 litres) up to 15 times.

'And if you manage only to spray half the vineyard and then bad weather sets in for a few days the vineyard will be out of kilter, which is not good. Only the half that you sprayed would likely stay disease-free. And if the half that you didn't manage to spray does get powdery mildew you might as well write off the other half, too,' Eric warned.

The next ten days was a tortuous wait, as Eric and I conferred daily under grey, wet or windy skies. Eventually I had to drag Eric away from his lunch to spray my vineyard with sulphur using his recently repaired tractor. It was a public holiday in France and should have been a day off for Eric to spend with Corinne and Paul. It was cold and very blustery, hardly ideal conditions to spray the vines, but Eric said that there was no choice. 'It can't wait any longer. I've seen spots of powdery mildew in neighbouring vines and you can be sure with the kind of year we're having your vineyard will catch it big-time. I'll spray your vineyard by tractor – it'll take me one hour. If you don't get this right you'll lose all your grapes because the powdery mildew will damage the baby grape clusters.' The clusters were already visible on the shoots that were now about twice the length of a long pencil. Each grape cluster (called an inflorescence) was about the same size as a human thumb. I helped Eric mix the sulphur powder in water, my heart pounding with excitement, fear and breathlessness caused by running after his tractor from his tractor shed across the village. Eric had a key to the door of the water pump by the side of the road in St-Paul. Inside a number of taps, each with the name of someone from the village, were also sealed with combination padlocks. Eric entered his code to release the tap and began filling his tractor sprayer with water. I emptied sacks of powdered sulphur into the spray tank while Eric turned on a mixing pump inside the sprayer using a lever in the tractor cab, so the sulphur would be mixed properly.

'When the shoots are so small you get better coverage spraying sulphur in solution rather than just powder,' he said. 'When the shoots are longer and there are more leaves on the vines you can spray with powdered sulphur. But, early in the morning or late at night and never during the heat of the day with dry sulphur power or you'll burn the vines.'

Eric added, 'You've helped me a lot this last week or two, Monty, so I owe you one,' as we shook hands and he drove off to the vines in his tractor, me following with Harry in the van to make sure Eric didn't miss a row (as if he would have). During the previous week of waiting to spray the vineyard I'd helped Eric with a number of tasks. He was renovating part of his house and I'd spent a dusty morning loading a tractor trailer with rubble taken from what was going to be Paul's new bedroom. Eric had been having serious problems with his back and was never going to be able to move all the rubble, especially the bigger pieces of stone, all on his own. In one of the walls Eric knocked down we found it had been insulated using newspaper and fleeces of sheep's wool. 'That's how they did it in my grandfather's time,' explained Eric, 'and more to the point it's a system that works.'

Eric was very practical when it came to home renovation and vineyard work, but pretty hopeless at modern inventions such as email. As he did not speak much English I'd helped him translate emails from English and American companies who imported his wine, and I wrote a short description in English of Domaine Laguerre, Eric and Corinne's wine business, to be used as a fact sheet for anyone who called at the winery. When Eric was tied up on his home extension I covered for him in the winery by topping up his 60 or so wine barrels. This entailed replacing wine that had evaporated through the wooden staves with a wine-filled watering can. If an air gap forms in the barrel the wine soon turns to vinegar. That's why vinegar barrels are never fully topped, but wine barrels are. I'd also go in to St-Paul to shop for the picnic lunch that Eric provided for his seven-man crew that had come in to bottle, label and box-up the previous year's wine. Time, I had worked out, was the most valuable currency I had to give, a point I understood when I offered Eric money for the fuel he had used when spraying my vines. 'I owe you, all the hours you've put in, not the other way around,' he said. 'Silvana is spot on when she says you don't have a head for numbers, Waldino!'

The most interesting and fun job Eric asked me to help him with involved spending a long afternoon towing a caterpillar tractor that he needed to fix. Eric had abandoned the caterpillar tractor's rusting hulk in a clearing in the forest over a year before after it had broken down on its way back from claw-ploughing the steepest vineyard Eric owned. He simply hadn't had the time to tow it back home using a normal tractor (one with rubber wheels). Caterpillar tractors were a much better and safer choice in the very steepest vineyards than tyre-mounted tractors, especially for heavy work like ploughing. They caused less soil compaction, too, because the weight of the tractor was more evenly spread.

'You can't tow a caterpillar tractor on the roads, Monty, because the metal teeth of the caterpillar tracks will damage the road surface.' So we had to take a circuitous route over the mountains: Eric in front laughing at me from his tractor cab and me behind with no protection from the bitter wind steering the caterpillar tracks by pulling or braking on two levers or pedals either side of me. I had to grip the levers so hard my fists almost froze to the metal. The noise was excruciating, both from Eric's tractor ahead of me and from the rusty, inert beast I was sitting on. Eric thought it wildly funny, but he made sure to stop every so often on the mountain, pointing out the best views, hunting tracks his grandfather used to follow and the local geology. It was easy to see why men like Pascal and Dominique, and Pascal's brother, liked working with Eric. He told you what he wanted you to do, would never ask you to do something beyond your capabilities and made the work fun by sharing his knowledge in a way that enriched rather than belittled you. The most amazing thing was that when Eric started to fiddle with his tractor, once we had got it back to his garage, I watched what he was doing and then made a suggestion as to how he might solve his problem – and my suggestion worked! I have never, ever had *any* gift for engines or mechanics. I suppose that being around someone like Eric made me come out of my shell a bit more and try things I always thought were beyond me. When Eric finally got his tractor started I'd never seen him so happy. 'If I can help you again, like getting you to change those ghastly orange overalls for example, you know where to find me...' I said as my parting shot, wondering how Corinne could let her husband cavort in such visually challenging attire.

'I think Eric looks nice in his orange overalls,' said Silvana, probably to annoy me, when I told her how proud I was at finally developing some potential skills as a tractor mechanic. 'You know, in Italy we like bright colours. You English are so grey, so conservative.' I wondered whether I'd be able to hide the grey pullover I was about to put on, as Silvana and I readied Harry for a trip to the vines. I held Harry while Silvana jumped in the cab and used my waterproof canvas jacket to cover her knees against Harry's spittle, then I fired up the van, Harry barked madly and we were on our way. 'What are you going to do about the weeds, Mont?' Silvana asked when she saw the state of the vineyard. I knew I'd have to plough the weeds away at some point, but I only wanted to plough away the weeds closest to the vines. This would leave enough grass cover over the soil in the middle of the row for it to be protected from erosion. The effect of turning the soil would bring air into the soil. The aeration would release food from the soil to the vines because it would stimulated a chain reaction in the soil: some microbes would reproduce like yeast in a dough mix, thanks to the influx of air the ploughing would provide, while others would die. These would decompose into food that vines could use. This food would be created exactly where it was most needed, in the zone close to the vines where most of the vine's feeder roots grew. Flowering is a stressful process for vines. Vines in flower are not as pretty to look at as say an apple or cherry tree in blossom, but the results of successful flowering or blossoming are the same: fruit.

By mid-summer each baby grape bunch growing on the emerging vine shoots had produced tiny flowers. Each flower can become a single grape if the flowers are pollinated successfully. Lots of plants need insects like bees to transport pollen to the flowers, but vines can self-pollinate because vine flowers usually contain both male (stamens) and female (a pistil-containing ovary) parts. A fertilised flower will produce a grape with a pip (the vine's seed). If I had ignored Eric's offer of spraying the vines and powdery mildew had struck, any grapes that did grow from successfully fertilised flowers would have been left partially split or with protruding pips because the grape tissues would have been permanently damaged. When Eric told me the vines looked healthy enough and that, all being well with the weather at flowering, I could get a normal yield I felt a lot more confident about organising the weeds to be ploughed away by horse, as this was one of the most expensive operations I had planned.

The only potential problem was that Viviane, the lady who would drive the horses, had just had a baby girl and would only be able to spend the day and a half required to plough the vines during a weekend, when her husband, Arnaud, would be able to look after the baby. Arnaud was a woodcutter and as he was either delivering wood or cutting joists and such-like for roofing he was tied up with building jobs during the week. As Viviane and Arnaud kept their horses in Fosse the journey from there to my vineyard was a short, flat one. Viviane brought two horses and both were Percherons. One, a bay gelding, pulled Viviane and a trailer on which the harnesses and ploughs needed for the work were carried. The other, a white horse called Cajolle, was destined to do the ploughing. Cajolle tagged along bareback behind the trailer so as not to arrive for work too tired. I helped Viviane as best I could to harness up Cajolle and strap her to the plough. First we put a thick leather collar with a warm, tan smell around her neck, then the bridle went around her head and the bit between her teeth. Finally, a pad with a series of leather straps was placed over her back. These held two shafts on either side that held the plough in place behind her. I checked that the edge of plough was nice and sharp, remembering that a blacksmith had once told me, 'ploughing is like sewing a garment for the plants in the soil'. A sharp plough meant that Cajolle's work would therefore be almost pleasurable. I did have one query, however.

'Why are these shafts made from metal and not wood?' I asked Arnaud. I had seen some old ploughing implements made of wood quietly decomposing in the vineyard's stone cabin.

'It's easier for the horse because it weighs less,' Arnaud explained in his native Italian, the morning sun brightening the dark stubble on his chin. 'Just because we're into the traditional ways of farming doesn't mean we're blind to technology.' Arnaud explained how he and Viviane would use the horses for different jobs during the year: ploughing furrows for vegetable growers in late winter and early spring, ploughing weeds in vineyards in late spring and dragging fallen or cut trees from forests for the rest of the year.

'It's much kinder to the soil to work in the forests with horses rather than tractors,' said Arnaud.

'And quieter too, I bet,' I added, thinking that Arnaud and Viviane's baby was yet to make a sound and was fast asleep in the pick-up truck Arnaud used as transport from one building job to another. Viviane and I confirmed how the work would be done before she began her first row.

'I could plough-out all the weeds in the row,' said Viviane, 'but I'd have to go up and down each row around eight times.' The space between each row was nearly three-metres wide, and each pass with the plough knocked out weeds in a strip no more than 30 cm wide. Removing all the weeds like that would be very slow and consequently very expensive, and way beyond my budget. Weeds, for some reason, are defined as plants growing in the wrong place. I didn't want Viviane to plough-out the weeds growing in the middle of each row, because as native plants they attracted the right kind of beneficial insects into the vineyard, maintaining more of a natural balance than if I had sown seeds of non-native plants instead. I asked Viviane to only plough-out only weeds growing close to the vines: a strip about 50 cm wide.

'If you want me to plough-out weeds close to the vines you'll lose a few vine shoots, you know that don't you?' Viviane called to me over her shoulder as she began the work, coaxing Cajolle into action by speaking key words in a particular tone of voice. She meant the horse, which was wider than the plough she pulled, would knock off any vine shoots growing at an angle rather than upright. And, each shoot that was snapped off was potentially a bottle of wine thrown on the ground.

'Don't worry,' I said, trying to sound calm. It was too late to change plan and, besides, the pain of losing a few shoots was worth the gain of weeding by horse instead of by tractor. Ploughing by horse meant I could direct exactly where I wanted weeds to be removed, turning and aerating the soil in the gentlest way possible stimulating soil-microorganisms to release a bit of food to the vines just when they needed it.

'I won't be able to get to the weeds in between each vine along the row,' said Viviane, as I followed her gently down the slope. Her baby had been born just ten days before, but she looked radiant, despite wearing only a well-worn T-shirt and pair of shorts. I couldn't imagine some of my female friends with office jobs in London doing the work Viviane was doing, and it was inconceivable (if you'll excuse the pun) that they'd do it so soon after giving birth.

'I'll pull out weeds under the vines by hand when I remove the suckers from the vine trunks,' I said. I spent the rest of day running ahead of Viviane, and Arnaud when he took over so Viviane could breast-feed, tucking in straggling vine shoots between the vineyard supporting wires, to minimise any being snapped off by Cajolle. It was a beautifully warm, clear, sunny day, not too hot for horses or humans. Viviane led the horses down to the water trough at the side of the cabin for a long drink at lunchtime, then she roped off a small paddock for them at the top of the vineyard with some stakes and twine from the trailer. The horses mumbled what grass they could find there, while Viviane, Arnaud and their baby drove home to Fosse for a siesta, before returning for a few more hours work in the late afternoon when the sun's rays were less intense. The soil Cajolle had turned was dark and cool to the touch in my palms. It was clear that the level of all-important humus was high, helped by the compost that had been spread four months previously. I was reassured that even if summer turned out to be a hot and dry one, there seemed to be enough moisture in the soil for the vines not to become dangerously stressed. If they did, the grapes would shrivel and raisin and I'd end up making a red wine that tasted of Christmas cake and currants, when instead what I wanted was a red wine tasting of freshly crushed, juicy red fruits.

Although moisture levels in the vineyard appeared good, water levels in the village were another matter altogether. Some local villages were already gearing up for water rationing and it looked like St-Martin would soon be doing the same. The mayor had organised for holes to be dug at strategic points in the village to see if there was a water leak in underground water pipes, but no leak was found. Levels in the village water tank had been known to drop suddenly at certain times. Some villagers said there was a leak, others said that one or two villagers were getting up in the middle of the night and filling empty wine vats with water so they would have enough for cleaning during winemaking. When the local village gossip explained to me that, 'One chap was even forced to admit last time there was a water shortage four or five years ago that he'd been filling his empty vats up at 4 am. Someone had seen him opening a tap then at exactly the same time the water level in the village tank fell dramatically' I was incredulous. 'It's a small village, Monty, so that kind of thing is hard to get away with. The mayor dealt with it very well, just having a quiet word. No use pointing fingers in such a small community. It always backfires. But now, some people are accusing the lady with the newly built house at the top of the village,' my informant continued, 'of over-irrigating her lawn. It's on an automatic sprinkler system, you see, that comes on at 4 am...'

'But that's ridiculous,' I said. 'Her lawn is tiny. And, sprinkler systems are generally much more efficient than using a hose. If it is timed to come on during the night her lawn will assimilate water much more efficiently than during the heat of the day, obviously. However, there could be a leak between the water tank and her pump. If it is a new system there might well be a nut that has worked itself loose and just needs tightening.' I'd forgotten all about my idle piece of conjecture until the next day when I walked into the local *auberge* and someone at the bar, who I barely knew, said, 'Hello Monty. I knew the lady with the newly built house at the top of the village is using all our water. Well done for finding the leak in her pumping system. When are you going to report her to the mayor?' I spent the next half an hour inwardly cursing myself for falling into the trap of making any kind of comment to the village gossip, while explaining patiently to the person at the bar that I was as in the dark as anyone about why water was leaking, being lost or even being hoarded. I had never even met 'the lady with the newly built house at the top of the village' as everyone seemed to call her, but whoever she was she was the new kid on the block, as was I. It was quite easy to see why a rumour had got round that the new guy in the village (me) was accusing the new woman in the village of shenanigans with the water. It allowed the locals room for conjecture while keeping the new arrivals in the village at a politically convenient arm's length.

This was, after all, a very sensitive time in the village, and not just on the waterfront. Various factions were stepping up their campaigns for the following year's mayoral elections, albeit behind the scenes as no one had yet formally proposed themselves as a candidate. The two main candidates were canvassing support as subtly as possible bearing in mind the village had only around 40 people living there full time. No one would be foolish enough to put posters in their front window advertising their political allegiance as would happen in a big city neighbourhood where it was possible to lead a more anonymous life. Nailing your political colours to the mast was to take a huge risk. For instance, if you wanted some minor building work done on your house, such as putting in a new window, your neighbour could block it via a protest to the mayor. The reason given might be that the window overlooked the garden and would be an invasion of privacy. The mayor would have a duty to uphold the complaint, even if the garden was already in full view of the main public road running through the village, meaning the addition a new window could not, in fact, really be considered an invasion of privacy. This would then put the mayor in a spot, if the person making a complaint had voted for him and the people wanting the new window hadn't. It was universally agreed that the current mayor, André Foulquier, had run the village in an impeccably fair way during his 20-year tenure. No one had any complaints. In fact, when he announced his retirement the villagers had even convinced him to stay on for an extra year. This meant that when elections took place in the spring, votes were cast only for a French president rather than also for a new mayor, as would otherwise have been the case. Voting for this, however, took place in the *mairie* (mayoral building). Votes were cast into a clear-glass ballot box resembling a fish tank. The bottom was barely covered with ballot papers by the time the polls closed. Polling took place on two Sundays a fortnight apart: one for each of the two presidential rounds. Various members of the mayoral committee – Eric, Pascal, Christine, my next-door neighbour, Jacques, as well as others – did two-hour stints supervising the voting. The *mairie* looked out on to a clearing in the forest that mayor André had organised as a public space. There were children's climbing frames, slides and swings, a volleyball court, a parking area for camper vans, plus room for large-scale village barbecues with a covered barbecue area with mains water, gas and electricity.

During the final head-to-head run-off for President, voters had what appeared a simple choice. One candidate represented what seemed the typical French way of throwing as much money as possible at problems in the hope they'd go away. Around half of all French workers, a European record, *are* employed by the state, 'to fiddle with paperclips while waiting for a fat pension,' as one grumpy villager put it. The other candidate promised a break with the past by turning France into a more modern, market-oriented country, 'so we'll end up like the Anglo-Saxons, with lots of money but not so much soul,' as one hard-line, former state employee told me during the game of *pétanque* several groups of villagers were playing while waiting for the election to run its course. Initially this seemed to be a much more fiercely partisan contest than the election, but jokes about the game – which is very tactical – revealed an underlying tension about the big issue of the day: France's future.

'Don't forget the Anglo-Saxons contribute more money to the European Union than anyone else,' I said, tentatively, 'even after the rebate we get from Brussels.' This rebate had been negotiated by British Prime Minister Margaret Thatcher or 'La Dame de Fer' (French for 'the iron lady'), apparently simply by waving her handbag fiercely at the Eurocrats to get their chequebook out. 'And I know it seems like we don't want to be part of Europe, but whose currency would you rather have, the British Pound Sterling, or the euro?'

'Since we got the euro prices have shot up, it's true,' grumbled one chap, whose huge belly was perfectly shaped for the crouching-while-you're-throwing manoeuvre you need to adopt when you are throwing your large metal ball towards the 'pig': the small marker ball you have to get close to win the game. 'We should never have gone in with all those weaker countries,' he said, his belly rippling under his T-shirt as he launched his ball.

'And anyway,' I said, 'you Frenchies should be proud of us with our free market, strong economy, strong pound, low unemployment and so on.' There was the slightest pause, the shuffling of sandaled feet on gravel. 'After you bloody Normans invaded us in 1066, we're technically as much French as anything else. Okay, with a bit of Viking, Norse, Celt and Roman thrown in to the Anglo and Saxon mix. And, as statistically the number-one choice for Brits buying a second home abroad is France your country isn't doing so bad, is it? You've got bloody good roads, trains, hospitals, schools and food. Your football team's pretty good, too, even if I'm still not sure about your fascination with this ridiculous game of *pétanque!*'

When news came through that the modernist candidate was to be France's next president I went to the bar of the Auberge Taïchac to watch the Sunday evening news. I found a disconsolate group of traditionalists gathered in front of the television, who offered me a drink. 'From the outside looking in it seems to me everyone in France has sensed the need for change,' I offered, as delicately as I could, 'but up until now maybe no one has quite known how to achieve it. Maybe this new president seems a bit frightening to you tonight, but maybe it will turn out okay in the end.' This comment seemed to have the desired effect of brightening the mood, but I refused offers of another drink because I had to be up early the next day to de-sucker the vines with Silvana. She'd arrived the day before, after a gruelling overnight coach journey. 'It'll do me good to do some vineyard work after being stuck in a smelly coach all night,' she said, putting her arm in mine as we took Harry for his bedtime walk. The bright stars of the Milky Way were overhead in a sky clear enough to promise a fine morning.

Silvana and I arrived in the vineyard early the next morning with a pair of pruning scissors each. When she came to stay the routine was I'd take Harry out for a quick walk, dump him at home so Silvana could give him his breakfast while I went to feed and water the chickens, invariably stopping for an extended chat with René. I'd get back home to find some strong coffee, Silvana and Harry all waiting for me. We all arrived in the vineyard to see that the clear strip of recently and lightly furrowed ground running alongside the vine rows, left by Viviane and her horses, would make it easier for both Harry to burrow for imaginary hares and for Silvana and I to cut away shoots growing off vine trunks. These shoots are called suckers, as they don't normally produce grapes but simply take energy from the vine and so must be removed. They are also liable to attract disease because they grow below where the anti-mildew spray lands. I always felt that each time I cut a sucker away it was like I'd taken a great weight off the vine's feet, making their annual journey from skeletal stumps to grape-laden beings easier.

'Don't hurt your back Mont,' said Silvana, watching my first few bending and cutting movements like a lioness would watch her cub, although the effect of her sometimes ferociously protective concern for me would have been heightened had she been wearing battle fatigues or camouflage gear, rather than a well-worn pair of tracksuit bottoms.

'I'll be okay,' I said, making sure I stretched my back every so often in the opposite direction to the one I had to adopt for working.

'You really have to get right down, almost to where the vine trunk comes out of the ground,' said Silvana, who was so short she often appeared to be fully sat on the ground while trying to cut a particularly obdurate sucker. We'd both done this job to earn pocket money as teenagers, me in Bordeaux and Silvana in Tuscany, and at the end of the day your shoulders would be sore and the base of your back would be tight and aching. It was worth it however because you'd got to know each vine just a little bit more intimately. You could observe which vines were producing a canopy of shoots, leaves and grapes that was in balance and which were not. When Sil returned to France in a couple of weeks, we would need to make another visit to the vineyard, this time to twist off excess suckers growing within the canopy itself.

'The ones not cut last year are the worst,' I said, 'as you'll be cutting one-year old wood instead of new green shoots.' There weren't too many of these, thankfully, but they had to be cut all the same.

'They would produce grapes though, wouldn't they, if we left them?' asked Silvana, who had already found her first shoot containing a baby grape bunch. Grapes would only grow on the bendy, soft, green suckers that emerged from a sucker that had been missed last year, and which between last autumn and spring had hardened into a woody stem. Grapes grow on shoots emerging from one-year-old shoots. This is the same principle that is followed for winter pruning: leave enough of last year's wood to make this year's grapes.

'What's for lunch?' I asked, even though I could tell from the sun it was barely mid-morning.

'Rocket from your garden, with grated parmesan and pine nuts my mum told me to give you, and extra virgin olive oil. The oil will have sunk into the bread. So be careful when you're eating it otherwise you'll cover your T-shirt with oil.'

'And what else?' I asked, knowing that Silvana would never have made only a single thing for lunch. Italians liked to have a choice. Just think about how many different words they have for a simple cup of coffee.

'Sliced beetroot from your garden and hearts of wild artichoke I picked yesterday, marinated in olive oil and chopped wild mint. I found the mint growing near the chicken run. It'll fill you up without being too hard on your digestion. All this bending down in the vines is really bad for your stomach if it is still digesting and if it is bad for your stomach it means it'll be bad for your back, too.'

'You should have been a dietician, Silvana,' I said. 'Maybe I should hire you as my fitness coach.'

'Except you'd never listen to me,' she replied in Italian without pausing. 'You're not exactly Mr Sporty, are you? If you could get fit by watching football on television you'd be as fit as St-Martin's mayor.'

'I do listen to you,' I said, aware that St-Martin's mayor was 30 years older than me and regularly jogged up and down the mountain to St-Paul just for a coffee. 'Sometimes I listen. When I need to. I am a man after all, Sil. Just because men have big ears doesn't mean we always listen.'

'We should get some geese.'

'Er, sorry, you've lost me there.'

'You know your old neighbour in the allotments?'

'René?'

'No, the other one, with the plot on the other side. He's older than René. You know, he's always dressed very smartly. Jacket and cap. He walks around the village with a stick.' Gaston lived in a house just off the town square. He was a tall, elegant, well-spoken man, who on sunny days would walk around the village, no mean feat for a man of over 90 on far from flat terrain.

'Gaston? Why does he want geese?'

'Monty, he doesn't want geese. But he is worried about the weeds growing in his allotment. They look ugly, he said. Now that you've turned Eric's jungle of an allotment into something presentable Gaston's plot next door looks more of a mess. I'm worried he might give it a spot of weed-killer, to make it look nicer. Why don't you ask him if you can put some geese on there. They'll keep the grass down for you, and you can always eat them for Christmas.'

This was a great idea. My parents had kept geese in our back garden when I was small. I was terrified of them, especially since I was told if I didn't eat my dinner goosey goosey gander would gobble me up. I'm still not sure why we had geese. Partly, I suppose, to keep the grass down as geese can pretty much live off grass, especially if the grass is kept shortish and therefore tender for them. We got the geese just after my mum started running a business from home. Both my sister and I were nearing primary-school age, and with some spare time on her hands my mum had started selling carpets. Lots of new houses were being built in the area we lived in and people needed carpets. The business was a success, and mum stored her carpets in our huge garden shed. So, maybe we got the geese because they were good guard dogs. They make a terrible noise if disturbed and a couple of adult geese can even fight off most predators, including foxes, stoats or rats.

Silvana pestered me for a couple of days as she really wanted to get some goslings before her Easter visit came to an end when she'd have to return to Italy. I readied some tall cardboard boxes that had held air-conditioning machines and which someone had left uncrushed by the village recycling area, and we went to buy two goslings from a farm-supply business near Perpignan. We ended up with one grey goose (a Guinea) and a white one (a Toulouse), but as they were only a couple of months old they were too young to be sexed, so we didn't know if we had two geese, two ganders, or one of each. Silvana gave each gosling a foot massage when they arrived and gave them a swim in the stream at the bottom of the garden. The grey goose, which I called Marmaduke (hoping he'd be a gander), bolted off down the stream even though this was the first time he'd seen running water. It was a hell of job to fish him out from underneath the weeds and brambles growing there without hurting him. The white goose, which I had christened Petronella (even though she may well have been a he), was calmer, however. I made a small pen for them at the back of the chicken shed, to separate them from the chickens. I didn't want the newly arrived geese to be attacked by chickens keen to maintain their own superior position in the pecking order. However, when Silvana and I returned to the garden a couple of hours later Petronella's wing stumps – neither goose had any feathers yet, only down covered their squidgy, fatty flesh – were bloodied. Marmaduke had been pecking her, partly because he was a bit stressed and partly because he had assumed first place in their pecking order of two. Silvana was due to leave for Italy the next day, and I was unhappy about leaving the geese overnight in the chicken shed where it would be impossible to separate them from the chickens. I was pretty sure that there was no risk of any fighting at night, especially because chickens have pretty poor eyesight at the best of times and wouldn't see the new arrivals. But, if I was late down in the morning after sun up it could be carnage. So, we brought the geese up to the house to stay in our basement. Moving them again was stressful

for everyone, and having them in the house was a total
nightmare. They knocked their water bowl over half a dozen
times. They messed everywhere. Harry had to be locked at the
top of the house to make sure there were always two doors
between him and the geese. When we took Harry out of the
house for a walk we had to carry him, with eyes covered,
through the basement area. He rumbled what was going on
though, because he could smell and hear birds. So he was
stressed too. Not only had his house be opened up to uninvited
guests (Jack Russells are supremely territorial), worst of all he
was having to share space with his sworn enemies: birds.

'Can you imagine having kids?' Silvana said to me as we
crashed into bed that night, utterly spent. 'We get two ugly,
squawky little geese with stumpy beaks and we can't cope.'

'It's okay for you,' I said. 'You're off tomorrow. I am going
to have to build another pen for them in the chicken house and
then divide that pen into one place each for each goose
otherwise Marmie will attack Petronella. And, I'm going to have
to get some feed for them, as that's what they're used to eating,
which means I'll have to teach them to eat grass. They grew up
in a concrete pen for heaven's sake. I can't believe you talked
me into this. It's not as if I haven't got other stuff to get on with.'

We bickered ourselves to sleep, but woke up to find two
cute little balls of down waiting for us at the bottom of the
steps. By the end of the day I was able to call Silvana back home
in Italy to tell her that the geese were a real hit with the
villagers. When I'd asked Gaston if it would be okay to graze
geese on his land I also made sure to check with Gaston's
daughter and son-in-law. They lived half in Perpignan and half
in St-Martin. One old couple in the village had complained once

One of the 2,000-odd boar killed in
the St-Martin area every year.

Who will get this fresh boar's liver – the
hunter, or his dog?

'Scruffy-looking vineyards produce better wine than manicured vineyards.' Discuss.

My only fear now was a late summer hailstorm which would have wiped out the crop.

A half-ripenend bunch of Carignan. They took nearly five more weeks to ripen fully.

Squeezing grape juice onto a
refractometer for the last time
before harvest.

Look how many vine leaves are
needed to capture the sun's energy
to get just a few grapes ripe.

Eric above the stone fermentation vat he and I are about to renovate. The loose square hatch was replaced by a better fitting round one (seen in next photo).

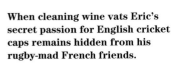

When cleaning wine vats Eric's secret passion for English cricket caps remains hidden from his rugby-mad French friends.

A rubber squeegee like the one I am holding won't damage the side of the cement vats I am cleaning.

Harvest day: Silvana's ploy of getting her mum to France on the pretext of a 'silly T-shirt' competition pays off.

Eric threatens reprisals with his scissors if Silvana continues to eat more grapes than she picks.

Monty and Andy try to locate Andy's black, pointy-eared dog Dinah on the day of the harvest.

Will Pascal have filled this grape bin up by the time he reaches the bottom of the row?

Shaded by a trailer full of freshly picked grapes, Pascal breaks for lunch.

Jacques' sunglasses are so dark he begins cutting the vineyard supporting wires instead of grapes.

It may not look like it but picking grapes really is a great way to relax.

Graham finally relaxes having found the perfect filling for his lunchtime sandwich.

Valène guards another precious trailerload of grapes as they arrive at the winery.

Into the vat they go...Graham and I carefully tip grapes in as whole bunches for a softer fermentation.

of having been bullied into selling a valuable plot of land for peanuts to a British family who'd then built an expensive (*ergo* characterless) house on it, and I didn't want any misunderstandings about the geese. Putting the word out also allowed anyone worried about the potential noise to voice their concerns, but everyone I spoke to said that it would be a real change to have not just chickens but geese on the allotments, too. Within a couple of days Eric had brought Paul and some of Paul's school friends to see them. Gaston's baby grandson was also a regular. René and his wife Adeline fussed over the geese, and Daniel made sure to throw any nice tender weeds their way. Plus, every time I went to the Auberge Taïchac for a coffee I was expected to give a full update on the geese, what they were eating – and when I'd be eating them (the latter question I fended off). As they couldn't stay with the chickens – there wasn't room and the geese would grow too tall to get through the hole in the chicken shed – I had another unwanted task on my hands. I'd have to build them their own goose house, and quickly.

Chapter 8

SOMETIMES I HAD AN UNEASY TIME GOING TO SEE THE GUY IN Caudiès-de-Fenouillet who supplied me with materials for DIY jobs, the former magician's assistant. The store he ran with his wife was shaded by the line of plane trees running eastwards just outside Caudiès along the main road towards St-Paul-de-Fenouillet. Going there made me anxious principally because the turn into the parking area out front was a tightish one for my longish van. I was always worried that I'd scrape some of the new machinery (such as ploughs and power generators) that was laid out for rental, or that I'd reverse into the sacks of cement, gravel and sand waiting obediently on wooden pallets for collection. I was also anxious because I considered myself a fairly incompetent fixer-upper. I had never built a goose house before, let alone in a foreign country, and not within a self-imposed deadline of a week. When I drew Mr Brico a rough design of the kind of goose house I wanted to build on the back of a till receipt he screwed it up. He then took me on a quick educational tour of the back of his warehouse, telling me I should think of it as a template for my goose house. He explained how first he'd cemented the vertical wooden struts into the ground, then positioned the wooden beams to support the roof and finally made the walls by nailing wooden planks horizontally, each plank overlapping the one below it in such a way as to keep the rain out.

'I'm not selling you the wood though,' Mr Brico said, lighting another filter-less cigarette from a soft pack kept in the top pocket of his overalls, 'because it'll cost you the earth.' I'd bought a few planks from him previously that I had used to make the raised beds in the garden. I remembered at the time thinking how expensive untreated, un-planed wood was.

'I'll take you to the sawmill in Caudiès if you like. It's where I bought those planks I sold you last time from. If your van works we'll go in that,' he said, flicking his cigarette towards a pile of metal fence posts before hauling his meagre frame onto the passenger's seat of the van. 'I used to have a van like this,' he said, 'when I first started my business. This one must be from 1975ish.'

'1976,' I said. 'It cost me one euro. The mayor of St-Martin sold it to me...'

'I knew I'd seen it somewhere before. Turn left out of the main gate, then right at the end of the village and I'll show you where the sawmill is.' We crossed Caudiès, driving across a pretty square with an iron fountain and Hansel and Gretel-style houses, then down a narrow side road that led to the wide, muddy yard of the sawmill. We negotiated our way around long lines of pine tree trunks – dark, grubby and newly stripped of their bark past pyramid-sized heaps of sawdust and newly cut, resin-scented planks laid in lines on small wooden chocks to air-dry. Near a mobile home that passed for the mill office Mr Brico showed me a large wire pen in which was an adult black boar, the size of a veal calf, calming eating hay. 'The mill owner who hunts caught it one day when it was a baby. I think he'd just shot its mother. Rather than let it go free he has kept it as a pet.' I guessed the mill owner would have had enough wood to have made the pen strong enough to keep the boar in should a nosey visitor like me get too close and panic it into escaping. But I didn't want to risk it and kept my distance. Mr Brico negotiated with the site foreman and soon I was driving away with the back of the van filled with planks cut with a large circular saw from the side of the pine trees when they first arrive at the mill.

'You can't use these off-cuts for building jobs,' said Mr Brico, 'because although the side from the inner part of the tree is pure pine and is flat, the outer side next to where the bark was is of course too curved to give the straight edge that house builders need. But, you can hammer these rough planks horizontally across your vertical supports to make the walls for your goose house. Make each wall separately, then hammer them together, then bang the roof on and you'll have a nice rustic-looking goose house. A bit like those log cabins you see in American westerns. You could use screws but it would take much longer, and the nails I'll sell you will be just as strong.' Even though the bill for the wood was way more than I thought I'd spend on housing the geese, I realised that had Mr Brico not taken me to his wholesaler I would have spent a frightening amount of money. I'd invited a friend from college called Graham and his wife, Charlotte, to stay for a long weekend. Graham was a big fan of France and had been to Perpignan a few times for European Cup rugby games involving London Wasps. Graham was the club secretary. Crucially, as far as the geese were concerned, when Graham and I were at college together he had studied estate management. This had modules covering building, planning, architecture and surveying. As well as being an all-round good bloke and rugby fan, Graham was now a chartered surveyor that meant he knew about construction.

'Let's get this straight, Mont,' said Graham when I'd told him he'd be singing for his supper during his weekend break in St-Martin. 'You want me to build a house for two geese?'

'Yup, that's right. It's like a chicken house, except for geese. Which are slightly bigger than chickens.'

'I know what a frigging goose looks like, mate,' said Graham, chuckling. He was a very good cook and had been on several of those 'how to cook game birds' cookery courses.

'It's not so much the bigger body, but the longer neck and bigger wingspan. So the doorway has to be substantial.'

'The doorway,' said Charlotte from my sofa, in the kind of serious voice you'd expect from someone working, as she did, as a lawyer for Britain's top national heritage preservation body when confronted with an historic building of aesthetic import. 'Right. Are we talking wall-to-wall carpets, air-conditioning and internet access for the residents of the goose house as well, or are you boys just going to go for the standard four walls, floor and roof option?'

'Listen, Lottie,' I pleaded. 'Silvana wanted the geese, not me. I'm up to my eyeballs with the vineyard, garden, chickens and dog – not to mention the van. If Graham can tell whether a City of London tower block is architecturally stable then I am sure he has the nous to help me bang a few bits of wood together to make something that'll resist our gale-force winds and protect the geese at night from Mr Fox.'

The goose house, which was supposed to be made of wood, ultimately contained more metal than a supersonic airliner, such were the number of nails and rivets it had banged into it. Graham had the genius idea of making a raised floor by trimming then nailing together two wooden pallets we had liberated from behind Eric's tractor hangar. 'The only geese I've ever come close to were on my kitchen chopping board,' said Graham, rolling several of the longest builder's nails I'd ever seen in his palm. 'It never occurred to me how frequently a goose can shit,' he said, curling his nose up as yet another moist, green pellet squished out of Marmaduke's fluffy white backside. 'The grass they eat looks pretty much the same coming out as it did when they ate it. Fast metabolism, I guess. Anyway, a raised floor will be a bit warmer for them and will make it easier to clean away the droppings.' When the goose house was finished I climbed in and covered the pallet-floor with some thick, plastic lino using some tacks left over from when John, Pete and I had felted the shed roof. I'd found a roll of old lino in the basement of my house that had apparently been Eric's mother's kitchen floor before she'd had a new one fitted. The lino covering would make it easy to sloosh out the goose droppings every morning with a bucket of water and prevent the floor from rotting as a result. As well as the wooden pallets, Graham and I had liberated a huge, not-quite-fully-bald tractor tyre from behind Eric's tractor hanger. Despite being unbelievably heavy and unwieldy, we rolled it around Eric's hangar and onto the van, then drove it down through the village, hauled it off the van and along the bumpy, narrow path leading to my vegetable garden. We then traced an outline on the ground around it and rolled it away before Graham banged some posts into the ground. Then, using a spirit level and string, we mapped out where we had to dig a round, level hole. The soil we dug out was used to make a new raised bed for vegetables by the long side of the chicken run. The tyre was rolled into the hole, and the rest of the lino was folded around the inside of the tyre and onto the bare patch of the earth at the centre where the wheel hub would normally be to stop the aquamarine plastic swimming pool liner I had bought from puncturing. Graham and I then laid this around the inside and over the tyre edge to make a watertight pool.

Before opening the irrigation sluice to fill the pool with water, Graham and I searched out an audience. Charlotte, Eric, Corinne and Paul appeared and duly applauded when the pool was filled. Marmaduke and Petronella immediately plopped in there of their own accord. Both geese flipped themselves under the water, circled underwater as best they could in the confined space, looking for non-existent weeds. At least, though, they now had a place where they could paddle and have a wash. A few days before the goose pool was ready, I'd carried Marmaduke past René's garden to the allotment area's water reservoir and placed him on the water thinking he'd be the happiest goose in the world. Here he'd have weeds to dive for, plenty of shade and frogs, birds and various forest creatures for company, plus the safety of being on water several feet deep. I left Marmie there to run back to get Petronella, but as I was on my way back to the reservoir with her under my right arm Marmie came charging at me along the path, honking terribly. Geese mate for life, and even if I was still unsure whether I really did have a male – female pair, it was clear that these two geese couldn't bear to be apart for more than a minute. Marmie chased Petronella and me back to the goose pen and strutted around Petronella protectively as soon as I had let her go free. This convinced me that I had to make a dedicated goose pool for them, and anyway I could recycle all the dirty water from the pool onto the vegetables and herbs I was growing, so nothing would get wasted.

Another good thing came out of Marmie's visit to the water reservoir, however. He pecked and gobbled up beakfuls of the fronds of a spiny green plant growing the length of the shady stream bank. The plant was common horsetail, also known simply as 'equisetum' after its Latin name *Equisetum arvense*. Although there are many different strains of horsetail, marsh horsetail, wood horsetail and tall horsetail being others, only common horsetail (sometimes also called field horsetail) is of interest to biodynamic farmers. This is because it is used to make one of the nine preparations needed for the farmer to be considered biodynamic.

'It looks like the kind of brush you'd clean the inside of a loo with,' said Silvana, as we gathered some by the water reservoir when she came to visit a couple of weekends after Graham and Charlotte had left. I told Silvana that some people call the plant 'bottle brush' because the wiry fronds growing off its long, thin central stem make the plant look like the kind of brush you'd clean the inside of a bottle with. 'Or like those rotating brushes that whir around the bodywork of your car at the car wash,' she said.

'Italian car washes are no fun,' I said, 'because you aren't allowed to stay in the car. In England you don't have to get out.

Mind you, the number of times I've stayed in and turned the car radio on only to see the aerial ripped off...'

'How are we going to make this horsetail tea, then?' asked Silvana. I had scrabbled across the bank above the reservoir to gather armfuls of horsetail that I was now handing to her. Silvana, typically, was laying them in neat piles: crowns at one end, the base of each stem at the other. 'Each one looks like a little Christmas tree, but with lots of branches missing,' she said. 'And there are no roots. Weird!'

'Common horsetail is a bit of a strange plant. It grows from spores, not roots. That's why collecting it is so easy. You kind of pull it off rather than out of the ground,' I said, nearly losing my footing on the soft, forest floor soil. 'And because it grows from spores it has a kind of power over the type of fungal-disease spores that attack plants – such as the kind of rot that can attack wine grapes turning them to vinegar.'

'Like a disinfectant, you mean?'

'No, Sil, it doesn't work quite like that. The idea is the horsetail pushes fungal spores off the plants, vines in my case, and back down to the soil where the disease spores usually live and so belong. If the fungal disease is on your vines it means your vines aren't healthy.'

'Er, well, hello Mr Wine Expert. Obviously if the vines have got the fungus then they're obviously not going to be healthy, are they?'

'Try and look at things from the other way around for a change, Sil. Shouldn't be too difficult for an Italian... The vines got the fungus because they were unhealthy. The vines are not unhealthy when they get the fungus – something was wrong before that and the arrival of the fungus merely tells you that there's a problem.'

'Such as?'

'Maybe you over-fertilised the vines, they grew too quickly, making the cells in their leaves or grape-skins too weak to resist the fungus disease. Like bricks in a wall when the mortar is not mixed properly and cracks form and the wall falls down. Basically, the vine's tiny cells are too weak because they are full of nitrogen. The vines might look nice and green on the outside, but they're dilute and full of water in the inside.'

'Mont, vines are trees, not fish.'

'Well, if you look inside a vine that's been fed with salt cubes which is what the chemical-fertiliser pellets are, then you'll see that the plant cells take up too much water too quickly when it rains because they are thirsty. This makes the cells swell and become weak. Like water retention in humans if you eat salty meat or crisps.'

'So, spraying the horsetail on acts like a kind of diuretic?'

'The horsetail puts more sun force into the vines because it is rich in silica. It has the highest concentration of silica of any plant. You know how you get those small packs of silica in the box when you buy a new camera, to stop condensation and humidity from fogging the lens? Silica does the same thing when you spray it on the vines or vineyard soil.'

'But you still have to use normal vineyard sprays like sulphur, right?'

'Yes of course. Biodynamics isn't some miracle sure. It's the icing on the cake, not an end in itself, at least as far as modern winegrowing is concerned.'

'In Italy we say cherry on the tart.'

'Cake, tart, currant bun, whatever. The point is you still have to get the nuts and bolts of winegrowing right, and adding the biodynamic cherry or icing to it just makes the cake that much easier to make and better to taste. So, making horsetail tea is one part of my anti-disease strategy. The other part is thinning the vine shoots.'

'And you'll be doing that after I've gone back to Italy?'

'Nope. Tomorrow morning, if it's fine. Which it will be because I've checked the forecast. You always say you hate being cramped in your office in Siena all week...'

'So, just like the last Sunday I was here you'll be getting me to work in the vines because, as you said last time, a bit of physical exertion will do me good, won't it?' I knew deep down that Silvana was happy to help, even if she was pretending to make me feel like I was imposing on her. We made a really good team, not just in the house or vegetable garden, or getting chores done, but in the vines too. We enjoyed each other's company, but didn't have to be nattering to each other constantly, and so would often end up hundreds of yards apart in the vines when the work was being done.

Perhaps only one van passed the vineyard during the long Sunday morning Silvana and I spent shoot thinning. The only noises Silvana and I heard were the usual ones: the wind on the vines and birds that flew so high overhead you were more likely to hear them rather than see them. Each vine had now produced shoots as long as my arm. These grew vertically, gripping onto the supporting wires strung horizontally across the vine posts. Four months earlier during winter the vineyard had looked like a cemetery: full of wooden gravestones, thin and oddly high. Now from afar it looked like someone had come along with a spray gun full of green paint and sprayed a single green hedge along the top of each row.

'What I'd like you to do is twist, flick or pluck off water shoots like this one,' I said, pointing one out to Silvana. I was tall enough to look down onto each vine, whereas Silvana's head reached about the same height as the top of the vine's green canopy of growth. 'Obviously, you know that each pruning spur has produced two shoots…' I began.

'Although a few of the shoots got knocked off by the horses when they did the soil work,' said Silvana, pulling at a shoot that instead of being vertical, soft and bearing bright green leaves along its length was hanging limply and at an angle to the ground, the leaves dry and brown.

'Well, that one's obviously taken a major hit. You can just pull those off and throw them on the ground, to stop them getting in the way. But, with the shoots that are left try to see where it looks like two leaves are growing from the same part of the shoot. Like this one,' I said, folding a shoot slightly towards me and away from the vine so Silvana could get a good look. She was wearing plimsoles with short socks and a pair of jeans that had been cut off above the knee. I knew from experience that that was the kind of apparel that would annoy you by the end of a hot working day. The jeans would be a bit too heavy, making you sweat uncomfortably, which is why I preferred a pair of loose, baggy shorts. The plimsoles were too flimsy for the terrain and would make your feet, and especially the ball under your big toe, ache unnecessarily. I was wearing heavy boots. My feet would be hot and sweaty at the end of the day, but they wouldn't ache. I was pretty sure that Silvana's feet would be hot, sweaty and achy, while the short socks would offer no protection from some of insects that would bite and cause annoying itches. There were even some weeds with sharpish spines on that would snap at your ankles. I hoped Sil was going to last the day, but wasn't convinced she would in what she was wearing.

'At least there's not much bending down to do today,' I said. 'Not like cutting off the suckers from the vine trunks. You'll find it easier if you work one shoot at a time. Take it somewhere near the top, and you'll see pretty clearly how the real leaves are a darker green than the water shoots or suckers. These are lighter in colour for a start. Plus, they are much softer to the touch, flimsier and more bendy. Once you get the hang of it you'll be able to pluck them off boom, boom, boom, like that,' I said, running my thumb and forefinger down the shoot and plucking off three water shoots, one after the other.

'Do I have to take every single one off?' asked Silvana, moving in close to me like she was cuddling me from behind. As Silvana's leg touched the back of mine I could feel that the backs of my knees had already begun to sweat, even though it was not yet 9 am.

'You can if you want, but really there's no point. Eric told me that you only want to remove the water shoots growing at the height the grapes are going to form. The idea is to get more air and light through the leaf canopy. That way we'll get riper grapes and less risk of disease. There'll be more airflow around the bunches. See how these water shoots are so soft? Basically they give off quite a bit of moisture when they respire at night. And during the day they don't really convert much sunlight into sugar in the grapes.'

'So, they are a bit like men then, just getting in the way of things,' said Silvana, curling both arms around my waist. At this point, while tiny flies buzzed with fantastically annoying persistence around my now sweating forehead, the option of going back to the house with Silvana for an extended morning siesta seemed the only option worth considering. We rarely saw each other now that we were living hundreds of miles apart and in different countries. And when we did see each other there was always something to do.

'They are, I grant you, a bit like men. But in Tuscany I've heard these water shoots or shoot suckers are called *femminèlle*...er, which implies they are female.'

'Well, that's what male vineyard workers in Tuscany may call them. But female workers there, like my mother, call them *bastardini*...er, which implies they are male.'

'Well, whatever they are, they've got to go,' I said. 'And *pronto*. Eric said I should wait another month to do this work.'

'So, why don't we go back to the house, take Harry out for a walk and relax?' Harry had been left at home because it was going to be a very hot day, and as we would be going home to lunch rather than picnicking in the vineyard we'd be able to let him out for a run while we stayed in the cool of the house.

'Well, Eric said if you take the water shoots out of the leaf canopy too soon in the season and it gets really hot you'll risk scorching the grapes.'

'Why don't we come back in a month, after mid-summer then?'

'Because by getting as much air through the vines as possible it stops the inside of the vines becoming humid and shady enough for grape moths to lay their eggs. The moth larvae are grape-worms and they burrow into the grapes as they ripen their sugars leaving a vinegary wine.'

'But, if it's too hot and the grapes burn...?'

'They won't. I have had a look at the biodynamic calendar. It looks like summer is going to be late this year. The planets are all in the wrong place apparently. In June the planet Venus is in the water constellation of Cancer, so if you cut hay it'll go mouldy in the barn. And in late July we can expect cooler nights apparently because Mars in the earth constellation of Taurus.'

'Aren't you taking a risk?' asked Silvana.

'Well, if we leave the water shoots on and get grapes that aren't burnt by the sun but are full of grape-worm the wine will be terrible because I'll have to pick the grapes far too early. And unripe Carignan is undrinkable. If we take the water shoots off, we should avoid the grape-worm. If it means the grapes are slightly too ripe because they've had a bit too much sun then so be it. Carignan needs more of the sun's heat and light than virtually any other vine to get ripe.' This was especially true of the vines at the bottom of the vineyard, where the soil was heavier and the vines were producing thicker, more hedge-like leaf canopies as a result. This meant that when I glanced across from the row I was in Silvana would almost have disappeared from view if I buried my head in the shoot I was divesting of excess leaves.

'It looks a lot better, anyway,' said Silvana at the end of the morning, as we re-grouped near the row of pine trees Eric had planted as a windbreak to get ready to head to the village for lunch and a siesta with Harry. 'I like the way the vines look. It really makes a difference thinning the shoots. You'd never have imagined. The little bunches have more space. You can see them more clearly. You can see where the grapes will be hanging at the end of the season and that there's all this life buzzing around because of the weeds.'

'That'll die down a bit if it gets really hot,' I said. 'The spindly weeds are well-adapted to the heat. They're tough and don't lose any water during the day. It's the lower-growing grasses that'll die off above ground, although the roots will keep going and be ready for when the rains come in autumn when the grass will turn green again. But let's not get ahead of ourselves about the grapes. Hail can strike at any time. I'm not counting my chickens, especially as every weather report I see is so up and down. Either we've really screwed up the climate, or our generation is the unluckiest weather-wise since the dinosaurs got wiped out by asteroid-induced climate change. Come on, if we're quick we'll catch the bread van in the square and we can have baguette sandwiches for lunch.'

It turned out the bread van that came to the village twice a week was due to come the following day. And the general supplies van that carried everything from well-cured salamis to feminine hygiene products had already been and gone too. We settled for some *fusilli* (pasta twists) with courgettes from the vegetable garden. Silvana sliced a clove of garlic and half a shallot into a bit of simmering extra virgin olive oil, then when everything was golden she added some thinly sliced courgette – which Silvana called zucchini. This was stirred into the pasta when it was cooked, then as a final touch she added some grated parmesan cheese pre-beaten with a couple of eggs. 'You should ideally only make this dish when the eggs are really fresh,' she said, 'as they only barely get cooked. It's a bit like *Spaghetti alla carbonara*, except instead of the bacon there's the zucchini.' I grated some pepper onto mine, but Sil preferred hers without.

I'd never been much of a fan of courgette, although growing it was easy enough, especially in a warm climate like St-Martin's. I'd raked up some compost into small mounds and stuck a couple of courgette seeds in each one, waiting to select the best-looking baby plant once the seeds had germinated and emerged from the ground. The plants produced huge, papery and slightly prickly leaves under which bright yellow flowers formed. These would grow into the courgettes, or huge marrows if you left them long enough. I'd spray mine regularly with biodynamic barrel compost mixed with stinging nettle manure because courgettes are greedy feeders (that's why you grow them in compost-rich soil). The only problem with them is they give so many courgettes. With plenty of sun and a good evening watering two or three times a week one of my courgette plants would give an average of one or two courgettes per day, far more than I'd normally eat on my own. That's why Silvana was educating me in how to make a filling (but not heavy) pasta meal from them. To reduce the potential crop she'd even lightly fry their yellow flowers in olive oil as an appetiser having first stuffed them with mozzarella cheese and anchovies, and dipped them in beaten eggs and flour.

Why weren't we ever taught these kinds of useful tips at primary school, I wondered? The first time I ever saw courgettes was during morning assembly during harvest festival when I was five. Various bright vegetables – red and green tomatoes, orange carrots and pumpkins, green-and-yellow-stripped marrows, purple and white beets and apples arranged to look like the red, amber and green of a traffic light – covered the high stage at the front of our assembly hall. The only free space left there was given to the piano my father was playing under the headmaster's direction so we could sing harvest-themed hymns in which the word 'manna' kept recurring. Then we'd trudge off around the town knocking on the homes of old people we didn't know to hand over vegetables we had neither grown nor had any idea of how to prepare. Wouldn't it just have been simpler for whoever had grown the food to give it straight to whoever needed it, I thought? Why can't the teachers see that? My rebellious, 'that-doesn't-make-sense' streak never left me. It's in my nature. It's perhaps why I found the unconventional approach organic and biodynamic winegrowers took to be so appealing. It went against the grain and not only that it worked. Why can't the conventional winegrowers who follow the herd and spray all these unnecessary chemicals see that, I thought?

However, my absolutely most depressing moment in wine occurred in a winery, rather than in a vineyard. I've seen some pretty depressing vineyards in my time. For instance an outstanding vineyard site in Bordeaux farmed for nearly 1,000 years with a topsoil that was literally sliding off the ground and onto the main road at the bottom of the hill because the wild grasses that had held the soil in place had been killed off by just ten years of weed-killer. But, even more depressing than that was the time I arrived to visit a top Bordeaux estate that had great vineyards but had fallen on hard times. When I arrived first thing one Monday morning for a visit I was met by two grey men in greyer suits rather than the overall-clad winemaker with whom I'd made the original appointment. The suits were from the insurance company that had just bought the vineyard and its characterful winery that was filled with two long lines of small, stone fermentation vats, ideal for the red wines the estate made. I congratulated the suits on having acquired the perfect winery.

'We'll knock it down and put some stainless-steel vats in which will look better,' one of the suits said. I couldn't persuade them that they'd be wasting their money, increasing their running costs and jeopardising the quality of the wine. For a wine fermented from red grapes to get its red colour you need to keep the fermenting grape juice and grapes-skins warm for potentially weeks on end. The best way to do this is by using vats made of a heat-retaining material, such as bricks or cement. 'It's easier for red wines to keep warm when fermenting in stone vats than in stainless steel,' I explained as we stood in the winery doorway. 'Ever heard of thermic transfer? How a stainless-steel kettle is too hot to touch when it's just boiled but is cool again minutes later, and how a fire brick warms up and down only very slowly. Stone vats change temperature very slowly and are energy efficient and environmentally friendly. With stainless-steel tanks you'll be constantly either having to warm them up or cool them down. You'll need a costly temperature control system.'

'We've already budgeted for that,' the friendlier of the two suits said. I said he should spend the money on renovating the old vineyard I'd seen by the driveway leading up to the winery that had many vines missing, but the suits wouldn't listen. I realised that for them acquiring a winery in France was a good tax- write-off, and the more money they spent the better, even if it was spent needlessly and with no thought for the wine or the environment. 'How can it make sense for a business to work like this?' I asked myself, the that-doesn't-make-sense indignation rising once again inside me.

I was determined to ferment my red wine in cement tanks. I had planned to rent tank space in St-Martin's wine cooperative. This, I'd assumed, was going to be pretty easy for two reasons. First, the cooperative had plenty of spare fermentation tank space, because the amount of wine being made there each year was much smaller than the cooperative's huge capacity. Second, because there was so much spare capacity I figured rental costs would be low, certainly much lower than in a privately owned winery. All I would need to do would be to keep an eye on the hygiene side, as the cooperative was far from pristine to put it mildly. This was not as difficult as it sounds. In the late 1980s, the 'flying winemaker' phenomenon emerged and the world of wine was transformed. The catalyst had been Australia. The bulk of its vineyards were churning out dreary, heavily alcoholic wines made in the style of port, sherry and even madeira. This made sense for wineries in hot climates using basic equipment. Then, it was discovered that using temperature control, winemakers could ferment their wines cooler and for longer. Heavy, oxidised, tongue-thrashing red and white wines suitable only for despised aunts with a drink problem were transformed into crisp, delicate, fruity (or 'fruit-driven' in wine lingo) wines good enough to take to a posh dinner party. Wine became trendy, no mean feat in a nation of beer drinkers. Soon Australian universities were churning out highly qualified young winemakers who, finding their own wine industry crammed to bursting point, were happy helping out for a harvest or two in Europe. Powerful wine merchants and supermarkets in the UK – which is the biggest wine drinking but (essentially) non-wine producing place in the world – started hiring flying winemaking teams to transform cheap and hitherto dreary wines from huge capacity wine cooperatives in places like Rioja and La Mancha (Spain), Mediterranean France, southern Italy and even Eastern Europe into the kind of cheap, fruit, clean, consistent wine people wanted to drink. The flying winemakers would rent a few vats in the corner of the cooperative, clean them up for next to nothing while buying a small amount of equipment like hoses, valves and the odd test tube so they could analyse the wine. They wouldn't (usually) spend money on big items like vats, or presses, though, they'd just manage to use them better than the locals: pressing the grapes less heavily to avoid bitterness and fermenting cooler to retain fruitiness. Result? Low overheads and quick turnover (white grapes picked in mid-August could easily end up as an off-dry white wine on a supermarket shelf in London for the pre-Christmas rush). In 1994, I'd been part of a flying winemaker team made up of one Kiwi, one German and two French guys in a massive winery in Chile, so I'd seen at first hand how the concept worked.

St-Martin's cooperative looked very similar to what I had encountered in Chile all those years before: dust and quite a bit of mould on the walls, outwardly grimy vats, but some sturdy cement vats that were perfectly clean and usable on the inside. And two decent presses (I'd only need one) to press the last bit of wine out of the red grapes once they had fermented. Several local winegrowers took their grapes to the cooperative, one of whom was Eric. Although he made wine under his own name of Domaine Laguerre and sold this wine as bottled, his excess grapes were fermented at the cooperative and the wine sold off in bulk. The wine that Eric and the other local growers made was of such good quality that the cooperative not only covered its costs but made a profit, a rarity in Roussillon where many cooperatives were in such dire financial difficulty they were having to merge, or pay-off grape-growers, or even declare a form of technical bankruptcy to keep operating. When I spoke to Eric about where I was going to ferment my grapes, just before my fortieth birthday party (a barbecue held in the village's municipal area in mid-July), Eric said I had to understand two things.

'Number one: you are not registered as a bona fide cooperative winegrower. There's a lot of paperwork to wade through and you have to be declared at the start of the season, you can't just become a cooperative grower halfway through. I could spend hours explaining it all and showing you all the documents but I'm not going to waste my time. Or yours.' This sounded pretty ominous, but before I had had time to digest this piece of news Eric started on his second point. 'Also, the cooperative isn't registered with the organic control people. So even if you could ferment your grapes there they would lose their organic certification.' I was holding a plastic glass of Eric's oak-aged, dry white wine. It was zippy and fresh and its salty tang was the perfect pick-me-up on what had been a day so stultifying hot that the French call it *canicule* (literally 'dog day').

'The wine in your hand is my oak-aged white, right?' said Eric. This wine was called 'Le Ciste', named after a flower commonly known in English as Sun Rose. 'The label shows the green *agriculture biologique* sticker on it from the French government to show the wine is made from organic grapes, right? I can only have that if the wine is fermented in my own cellar, the one behind your house. If I ferment the same wine in the cooperative and I put that green sticker on I'll get my balls cut off by the French fraud squad. And that's before every bottle with my name on it in St-Martin is impounded.' Inwardly I was kicking myself. How many books and articles had I written on organics. How many hundreds of emails had I responded to explaining to fellow journalists, wine merchants, consumers, friends, publishers and even would-be organic winemakers how the organic rules worked? And I'd fallen into the trap of thinking what happened in the vineyard was the main thing to worry about. The joy of getting away from my desk and into the vines had meant I'd taken my eye off the administrative ball leaving me as a winemaker without a winery.

'I thought you knew all that, Mont,' said Silvana, trying to cheer me up later that evening. She'd come over for my birthday, and I felt like my mistake would put a bit of a downer on things. The following day I had another chat with Eric in his cellar. 'I don't have any spare space, Monty,' he said. Eric's own winery was small but well equipped, and most important of all if I made my wine here I wouldn't lose the organic certification. He'd taken over his grandfather's house. The main fermentation area had some stainless-steel but mainly fibreglass tanks with lids that you could lower according to how high the level of the wine was. There was an inflatable rubber ring around the edge that could be pumped-up like a bicycle tyre to allow the tank to be sealed tight when the top was lowered to float almost on the top of the wine. This prevented leaving a gap of air above the wine. Air gaps are a green light to the bacteria that cause wine to go vinegary. Down a marbled staircase were the oak barrels in which Eric fermented some of his white wines and aged some of his red wines. 'What about these cement tanks? We could use these,' I said, pointing to a wall behind which were a bank of what looked like four tanks. There were four vertical metal trap doors along the bottom edge of the wall, four metal valves halfway up that could be opened to let a small amount of wine run out for tasting, and in the floor above us I'd noticed four horizontal metal trap doors into which a ladder could be lowered to gain access to the inside of each tank for cleaning (you could also slide in via the doors at the bottom, too).

'These tanks haven't been used for 30 years,' said Eric. 'All the trap doors need replacing. The cement walls inside might have holes in them. They're pretty filthy inside.'

'So, we clean them. Repaint them if needed. Patch up the cement if there are holes. I've never seen a hole in a cement tank before...'

'Yeah, but I bet you've never seen cement tanks in an earthquake zone. St-Martin is right on the edge of the geological fault-line pushing Spain up into France, you know. So the earth moves here, which means vats, and houses, can subside.'

'I have seen vats in an earthquake zone, in fact, in Patagonia, Argentina when I was writing that book on South American wines. Not a pretty sight. One tank looked like it had been lifted right off the ground. We can find a guy who works metal to make new doors and valves.' The two large valves used for pumping wine in and out of the vat that each tank had had seen better days. The threads around them onto which the hose ends were screwed were beaten up and warn. 'I'll pay my share of the doors, tops and valves for two vats. I'll need one vat to ferment in and one vat to rack the wine into once its fermented.'

'Monty, it's nearly August, and you may be picking in mid-September if this hot weather continues. No one, and I mean no one, works in France in the first two weeks of August. We'll never get the work done in time.'

'Yes we will,' I said, slapping the palms of my hands confidently against the tank walls like a racehorse owner on a prized yearling. 'We'll have to.'

Chapter 9

DURING MY TIME IN FRANCE THE SMALL METAL POST BOX ON MY front door was rarely disturbed by the postman. Apart from a few circulars re-directed to me from the UK, nothing much of interest arrived in the post. Generally, I tried to avoid the post office as there were always achingly slow queues – even minor transactions took a lifetime, not because the staff were inefficient but because customers spent so long chatting at the counter. I was also conscious of the fact that any vibration caused by the post-box flap being asked to creak into action meant a bit more of my front door's paint work would crumble away, so, trying to ambush the post van before it headed back to St-Paul at lunchtime had both aesthetic and practical benefits.

However, in late-July a succession of photocopied directives from St-Martin's mayor, André, began to arrive concerning water saving as reserves were so low. The village – its population now swelled by either city dwellers returning to their second homes for the summer holiday or by families who had rented empty houses – was using (according to the mayor's office) around 17m^3 of water per day. This was also roughly the amount that was arriving in the village reservoir each day from the natural water source in the mountains that fed it, and, by implication, us.

The problem was the reservoir was nearly empty, so any slight imbalance between the fixed amount that was arriving and the variable amount that was being used was a potentially serious problem. When André, his number two Jacques (my bushy-haired neighbour) and mayoral committee members (like Eric) measured the level in the stone water-tower, located between Jean-Luc the decorator's house and his donkey paddock, the possibility of a leak in the system had been ruled out. 'There is easily enough water arriving daily for all 100 residents' needs,' was the gist of a mayoral note sent on August 2, but as abnormally large amounts of water were continually being used at certain hours of the day it seemed someone really was stockpiling water, possibly in a wine vat – as had happened during the last water crisis several years before. Soon, there was a water ban and running water was only available from late evening to early morning. Bottled drinking water was provided on mayoral orders. 'The water that is being delivered by tanker is fine for drinking,' said André as he handed me six lots of six shrink-wrapped bottles from the back of the village's smart, new, post-Estafette van, 'but as we have not been able to test it officially it's best all residents drink this bottled water.' In other words, if someone picked up a tummy bug from the water being tankered in, then the village of St-Martin would be liable to pay any damages. Villagers were ordered to drink only bottled water from 8 am on Friday, August 10.

It was hard to believe we were short of water listening to

French organic wine growers I was talking to by 'phone (when my 'phone worked), which was three weeks out of every four on average. I had called them to get some winemaking tips but ended up listening to grim stories about how disastrous the recent excessive summer rainfall had been for them. 2007, like 1997, 1987 and 1977 (and even 1967), had been a black year for many winegrowers, especially in blue-chip wine regions like Bordeaux. Many, especially those newly converting to organics and biodynamics had had to revert to spraying products not approved under the organic rules to prevent mildew and rot infecting their vines. Reading between the lines, many had taken the decision to spray like this after it was too late and the crop was virtually lost anyway. They say the second year of organics is the hardest to manage. In year one the vines are still feeding off residues of chemical fertilisers left in the topsoil. In year two the vines get stressed when they realise that as the reserves of quick-fix chemical fertiliser begin to run low and the new regime of slow-release organic/biodynamic compost takes effect they'll have to start digging deeper into the soil to find most of the food they'll need. If really bad weather strikes (meaning wet and humid, essentially) in the second summer of converting to organics/biodynamics the vines can find it difficult to resist disease, as the stronger self-defence mechanism that organics/biodynamics is supposed to give the vines is not working fully. Most winegrowers are not financially strong enough to bear the financial pain of writing off their grape crop – especially when they are just getting used to paying fees to the organic inspectors in charge of organic certification.

When I worked in Bordeaux as a 'cellar rat' (winery dogsbody) in my teems, my boss was always very keen to use water for vat cleaning as efficiently as possible. Eric was the same, as the job began of cleaning out 30-years' worth of accumulated sludge and grime left since his grandfather's time in the cement vats we were renovating. The smell inside was distinctly mushroomy, but not exactly life threatening. Once the large amount of dirt at the bottom of each vat had been swept out, Eric rigged up a power hose to clean the vat ceilings and walls that were too high to reach directly by hand. Getting a thorough and cool soaking inside wine vats is no hardship when temperatures outside had regularly become almost unbearably hot not long after breakfast. The key thing was never to go directly from the cool, jungle-like humidity of the vat straight outside into the dry, desert-like heat of the village, if you wanted to avoid catching a chill. Eric recommended spending a couple of minutes in his cool, but not cold, barrel cellar to acclimatise before heading outside after my first soaking in the vats. I felt like a deep-sea diver going through a decompression chamber on my way to the surface, or more correctly outside and around the corner to go home for lunch and a clean up. The good news, apart from the fact that neither Eric, myself, nor Pascal who was also on vat-cleaning duty caught a cold, was that the vat walls were crack-free and in excellent condition. Eric and I had been worried that if the vat walls had been cracked they would have needed sealing with a glue-like liquid-lining called epoxy. This would have cost quite a bit extra in terms of time and money, and while painting it on we would have had to wear protective clothing because the paint gives off noxious fumes. We were both happy that Eric's grandfather had built these vats well enough to allow us to use them 50 years later, as originally intended, simply with bare walls albeit with some new doors and valves.

In the vineyard the absolutely overriding task in August was to make sure the grapes were protected from the wild boar. Everywhere you looked winegrowers were busy erecting temporary fencing to keep the boar out, and the Planels plateau, where my vines were, was no exception.

'Twenty years ago female boar would produce one or maybe two boarlets,' said Eric, as we drove to Perpignan to visit the hunting federation responsible for the eastern Pyrénées (Pyrénées-Orientales) *département* that covers the Roussillon wine region. 'Now they produce maybe five or even six boarlets. No one is really sure what happened, but it seems someone might have deliberately cross-bred the wild boar with either wild or even domesticated pigs so that the wild boar would produce bigger litters.'

'Why would anyone want to do that?', I asked, as Eric navigated his van through the centre of Perpignan and towards an industrial park on the south side of the city where a warehouse belonging to the Fédération des Chasseurs was located.

'I guess so that there were either more wild boar for the hunters to kill – it is a sport, after all, as far as they are concerned – or because artisans making wild-boar pâtés and wild boar sausages would have more raw material and so stayed in business.'

We were collecting a van-load of car batteries which the hunting federation loaned to farmers whose crops were threatened by wild boar or even deer. The batteries powered the temporary electric fencing designed to give an electric shock to any moist boar snout that touched it. The batteries were supplied in metal boxes to keep the rain and dust off and had two contact leads that had to be attached to the fence to make the electric circuit, plus what looked like a metal tent peg. 'You make an opening in the ground, then hammer that peg in, which acts as an earth,' Eric explained, as he signed the paperwork covering the 12 batteries that were needed to cover his dozen blocks of vines. 'You normally pour a bottle of water on the ground first, to make sure there's a good enough contact between the peg and the earth. For the Panels plateau we'll need just one battery,' he continued, 'as we'll fence off your part and my part in a single circuit.'

'Do you hunt?' I asked.

'I have a licence, but I don't hunt,' said Eric, adding, 'well, not anymore at least.' I guessed that after Eric and Corinne had got married she had put her foot down. Accidents happen and during a hunt they are often fatal. I remembered when working in Bordeaux as a teenager that someone from the neighbouring village died as the result of a bullet ricocheting off a tree. And, the previous year, one of the hunters in the St-Martin area died when a bullet passed through a deer via its ribcage and into him. Some hunters I had met who were also winegrowers seemed to be much more interested in and spent more time hunting than in their vineyards, and their wine suffered as a result. Eric was a clear exception. 'In the St-Martin area last year 2,000 boar were declared as killed by the hunt. And another 5,000 were killed in the rest of the Roussillon region,' said Eric. 'The number is probably a bit higher as not all kills are registered as they should be for one reason or another. With those kind of numbers and the fact that boar can still be hunted during the season without restriction suggests that the population is pretty much out of control.'

'There must be some kind of control,' I said. 'People can't just hunt.'

'Yes, of course it is controlled. You can only hunt on Wednesdays and weekends. And you can only hunt during the day, too.'

'Why? To avoid accidents?'

'Partly,' said Eric, easing past a roundabout very gently so the heavy batteries in the back didn't slide and crash against the sides of the van. 'Night hunting is seen as a bit unfair on the boar. If you drive around the vineyards after dusk when the boar come out of the forest you can easily see them with a spotlight on your car. They haven't got very good eyesight and they are blinded by the light.'

'What happens if you hunt at the wrong time, or on the wrong day, or without a licence?'

'Oooooh,' said Eric, smiling and flicking his wrist several times as if he had just touched something unexpectedly and blisteringly hot. 'First, if you're caught hunting in or from your car then the car is confiscated immediately as is everything in it. Apart from your documents, of course. They go with you to the prefect's office where your court appearance is arranged. You can plead innocent, but any paid-up member of an official hunt caught hunting at the wrong time can't exactly pretend to be unaware of the rules. Ignorance of the law is no defence. Second, you'll pay a massive fine, like tens of thousands of euros, which around here is the same as the value of an average house.'

'But, hang on. Boar are a recognised pest, right? So what about if you are a winegrower and you're out one night and you see boar eating your grapes?'

'I'll arrange for you to go out with the local hunt Monty and they'll explain how it works,' said Eric, 'but I go out almost every night as the grapes are ripening. From my Land Cruiser I often see wild boar in my vines, and let me tell you they're not there for the view. But only in really exceptional circumstances could I get away with shooting one. For instance, if there were 100 boar ransacking the vineyard, knocking support posts and wires over like a tornado. But boar don't go out in groups like that. They're not wildebeest or elephants. The bottom line is if boar have got into your vines then you need to check why your electric fence has short-circuited and is out of action rather than how many bullets are ready and loaded in your rifle. Maybe the boar have pushed some earth over the lowest wire when nosing for worms or roots causing a short circuit. Or a mother boar has seen her small boarlet jump between the wires to get into the vineyard. She'll just crash in there herself to get him back, leaving the way open for the rest of the group to come in. You just have to get out of your van and shout, scream, jump up and down and wave your arms around to scare them away. To make them remember that humans are around in that particular patch of vines. They won't come back there for a while at least, and hopefully will try their luck in your neighbour's vineyard instead. That's all you can do until you get the fence fixed. Even driving around with a rifle on the wrong day or at the wrong time will probably see you get into serious trouble with the law.' We made our way back across Perpignan, which was almost deserted, despite it being high summer, with most shops closed. 'I don't get it,' I said, as we cruised from one side of the city to the other, braking only for traffic lights, not for other traffic. 'It normally takes me 20–30 minutes to cross the city.'

'Yes, that's because your van was built only a few months after man invented the wheel,' said Eric, 'and because all the traders here are in Spain either on holiday or night-clubbing. France is on holiday and everyone goes south. If you live in the south of France (Perpignan) you go south, too, but to Spain. It's pretty simple.'

Putting the boar fencing up was also pretty simple, involving banging metal posts (rebar) into the ground at several-metre intervals and then twisting two insulating rings onto each post at various heights. The wire carrying the charge would run through the rings. 'I normally put two rings on each post, but the boar are becoming such a problem that next year I might go for three,' said Eric as we drove up to Planels one evening in his tractor, me sitting very uncomfortably on the near-side wheel arch. Eric explained that the bottom wire had to be just high enough off the ground to be exactly at boar snout height, but not so low that it could touch ground cover like grasses, weeds, or even stones because it would short the circuit leaving the fence with no electric charge. We got to a parcel of young vines that Eric had planted in the spring and I jumped out of the cab and stood behind the tractor while Eric passed me a spray nozzle. This was on the end of a very flexible rubber hose connected to a spray tank full of water. This was the same system Eric had used to spray my vines with liquid sulphur against mildew in spring, but this evening we were watering the young vines to stop them dying in the August heat. 'I can spray mature vines like yours from the tractor cab as they're at cab height and the spray hits the vines at a perfect right angle. But you waste a lot of water if you try spraying the ground around low-growing, baby vines like that. And the water jet is so strong it might rip the baby leaves off,' he explained.

When my phone had rung earlier that evening and Corinne had asked if I wanted to eat with her, Paul and Eric I guessed Eric had a job for me to do, although as it was so late in the day my mind was a blank as to exactly what. Corinne was worried about how hard Eric was working, especially with his fragile back, but she knew if he didn't water the vines soon they'd die, and several thousand euros would be lost. 'I love watering vines,' I said to Corinne. 'I did it as a kid in Bordeaux. It's good exercise: you have a nice walk and you feel good because you're helping a vine at the start of its long life.' It was true, I really did like watering vines, especially on a warm, balmy evening like this one was, with amazing visibility over the Pyrénées. 'My grandfather first planted this vineyard,' said Eric as we paused during the work, 'and he built the dry-stone walls around it using rocks he pulled out of the vineyard when planting.' It was a beautiful little plot, facing full south, with a bank of forest directly behind. It was a five-minute walk from my vineyard, but you'd never have known it existed unless Eric had taken you there. While all the vineyards on the Planels plateau were now protected by orange-coloured cord, this parcel of young vines needed no protection. 'Boar don't come in to eat vines, Monty,' said Eric, as we bumped off back to the village on the back road this time. 'They want the moisture from the grapes. These vines will only need fencing the year after next when they'll produce their first crop of grapes.'

Eric had taken the back road to the village as I had asked him to drop me off at the allotment so that I could close Marmaduke and Petronella up in their goose house for the night. On the way he stopped and got me to jump out of the cab so he could show me something.

'Notice anything weird about that tree?' he asked, pointing at an evergreen oak.

'Tree looks okay to me,' I said, admiring its perfect form, the finely textured bark and its brittle little canoe-shaped leaves which caught the sun's energy but gave no moisture back in return.

'What about under the tree?' asked Eric.

'Kind of looks like there's something wrong with the soil.' I remembered Eric had pointed out some truffle oaks to me once, but he'd never had time to explain to me how to tell under which oaks the truffles grew. Now was his chance.

'We call that *les brûlées*,' he said pointing directly under the tree, 'because it looks like the grass has been burnt. Truffles grow on the roots of oaks, but usually only where the soil is limestone. Your vineyard and the forests around it are on decomposed granite that is too acid for them. The mychorrizal fungi which colonise the tree roots and produce the truffle by feeding off the root need less acid soils, like limestone.' Mychorrizal fungi had recently become a buzz term among modern winegrowers, and organic and biodynamic winegrowers in particular. The fungi feed off the sugar that the leaves send down to the roots when trapping solar energy during photosynthesis. Suitably refreshed the fungi then push ultra-fine feelers (called *hyphae*) off from the roots and into the soil. This helps the vine roots digest certain hard-to-find soil nutrients, such as phosphorus for photosynthesis. And, because the mychorrizal fungi give the vine a much finer, more sensitive root system the vine should, in theory, be able to produce tastier, more interesting grapes.

'You can tell which oaks are truffle oaks because a certain

type of small fly lays its eggs among the ground cover above the soil where the truffles are,' continued Eric. 'The fly lays its eggs there because the presence of the truffle makes the area a good source of food for the fly larvae when they hatch. Nothing else grows there, though, which is why the soil looks almost like it has been hit by a flamethrower. If you're around from December to early February we can go truffling. They'd be delicious on some homemade tagliatelle pasta, which I am sure Silvana knows how to make. The truffles here are black by the way, so if you grate them finely enough onto the pasta the dish looks pretty good, too.'

Silvana didn't bring any pasta with her when she arrived in the middle of August for a few weeks' summer holiday. But, she did arrive with more transplants from her mother's garden (broccoli, brussels sprouts, cabbage and cauliflower), plus a couple of bags of human hair. These were provided by Silvana's sister, Emanuela, who owns a hairdressing business in Tuscany.

'Did you tell Emanuela what it was for, Sil?' I asked, as we began putting the hair to its intended use one late afternoon.

'Yes, and she said it was just another one of your crazy ideas. You know, she didn't want to give me any hair when I first asked her. She had to sweep it up and hide it in a bag without telling anyone else at work. Most of her clients are very traditional old ladies and the church still has quite a strong influence in the area where she works. Emanuela didn't want anyone thinking she was into black magic or something.'

'It's hardly black magic, is it? Dropping a few clumps of human hair around the vineyard to scare the boar away because they pick up on – and then are scared off by the human scent. The hunters Eric arranged for me to go out with said I could also try hanging clothes on the fence posts around the edge of the vineyard: T-shirts you'd worn for a couple of days which were soaked in human sweat would work. And, if we pee then we should do it in the areas we know the boar congregate.'

'If I'm having a pee *au naturel* in the middle of the night,' said Silvana firmly, 'the last thing I want is a boar coming to see what I am up to. You know some people are going to take issue with you for having an electric fence, even if it is a temporary one, around what is supposed to be a biodynamic vineyard.'

'Yeah, I know,' I said wearily, 'but if I opted for the purist biodynamic boar control solution I'm sure the very same people would give me an even harder time.'

'Why's that?'

'The best way of warding off the boar is to burn the hide of a boar, and then from the ash you make a spray by diluting the ash in water and stirring it in a special way to 'potentise' it. You spray that around the edge of the vineyard. It's called pest ashing or peppering. It works by driving a pest back to within its own natural geographical and population limits with its own burnt remains. It kind of brings the energy of the dead onto the land, acting as a repellent and sending a "don't come here" message to the boar.'

'Well, why don't you do that, then?'

'Because it is only said to work if you strip the skin from the boar when the planet Venus is standing in the constellation of Scorpio. And, as that won't happen until January next year I thought I would go for plan B, which was using some human hair and human pee as well as the more usual fence. I'm not saying the waves caused around the vineyard by the electric current are ideal, but at least I'm conscious of this potential problem. That's because I am trying to promote life in the vineyard, by stimulating the soil and plants with composts, teas and the biodynamic preparations. Boar aren't stupid. They invariably go for the organic rather than the conventionally farmed vineyards blasted with weed-killer first.'

'Because there are more worms and plant roots for them to eat,' said Silvana. 'Organic winegrowers I know in Tuscany have told me the same thing.'

Silvana said that in return for organising the human hair my part of the deal was to find some way that we could camp up at the vineyard, especially during the Perseid meteor showers in early August when the sky gives its own firework display. The perfect spot to view this was the vineyard plateau. The area was free of light pollution and the view was stupendously wide. With Eric's permission I'd asked Andy to do a bit of work on the stone cabin, repairing holes in the roof, fixing the broken side door and stabilising the chimney. The idea was partly to be able to use the cabin as a place to sleep nearer harvest to keep an eye on the wild boar, and also as a place to hang out in summer. Local fire regulations meant open-air barbecues were forbidden, but if the loose tile-work in the interior of the chimney was rendered, as Andy had advised, then we could have barbecues inside instead. Eric had plenty of old roof tiles that could be used to do this. Once the work was finished I would be able to use the cabin as a focal point for visitors, journalists or trade wine-buyers. If they weren't blown away by my wine maybe they'd be blown away by the view from the cabin.

Silvana had, in any case, bought me a tent for my fortieth birthday. 'I am not sure about sleeping in the cabin,' she said as she watched me erect the tent just in front of the stone water trough. 'Whenever Harry comes up here he spends his whole time looking for mice and rats in the walls and roof. I'd rather sleep in a tent to be honest. It's a three-man tent: you, me and Harry.' It didn't take long, however, for Harry's capacity to be a major pest to come to the fore. When Sil and I were eating our picnic dinner, using the stone water trough as an improvised buffet table Harry would try and steal food on his way via the trough onto the roof. If we put him in the tent with us while we were sleeping off the effects of a glass or two or Marinette's nut liqueur he would try to rip his way out by clawing at the canvas. In the end we just let him run free, and laid ourselves face-up on the water trough so we had a 180° view of the night sky. Silvana and I had always been ultra-competitive when it came to spotting shooting stars during our walks around the village with Harry after sunset. As darkness fell we'd normally see one or two shooting stars every half an hour or so, but during the Perseid meteor shower you could see three or four every couple of minutes.

'The meteor showers are supposed to be especially good this year,' I said, my head strangely comfortable as it rested on the cool stone. 'That's because they fall around a new moon, so without a bright and distracting full moon the sky will be nice and dark, making it easier to see the meteor traces. The peak will be around 4 am, apparently, because the constellation Perseus (from which the meteors come) will be directly above our heads. It's only just coming over the horizon now, so we've got some free time for a nap, or a walk around the vineyard to check the boar fence is okay, or...'

'I can see Orion,' said Silvana, 'and the Great Bear and the pole star in the Little Bear.'

'Go back to the Great Bear, or Big Dipper as they call it in America. In England we call it the Plough. Follow the end of the plough (or bear's tail) and it points to a really big bright star – that's Arcturus. The next bright star you see if you continue to follow roughly the same straight line is Spica. That one lies on the ecliptic and is roughly at the centre of the constellation of Virgo. Star constellations lying on the ecliptic are the ones biodynamic growers are interested in. This is because the sun, moon and planets all pass along the same path – called the ecliptic because that's the only place where eclipses happen. And the sun, moon and planets always pass in front of the same 12 constellations, Cancer, Aries, Sagittarius, Virgo and so on. It takes the sun one year to pass in front of all 12, but it takes the moon only just over 27 days to make the same journey.'

'Even if you can't see the moon?' asked Silvana.

'We can't see the moon tonight because it's between the earth and sun and we can only see the moon when sunlight is reflecting off it. The point is if you're biodynamic you see the moon as having influence on different parts of plants depending on which constellation it's in front of.'

'Such as?'

'Biodynamic growers see plants as being made up of four organs: roots, leaves, flowers and fruit or seeds. Each organ relates to one group of star constellations. Roots grow in the earth and so are linked to earth constellations: Taurus, Virgo and Capricorn. Fruit, like wine grapes or grain crops, need heat or fire to ripen the seeds inside, so they are linked to fire constellations: Sagittarius, Leo and Aries.'

'This sounds a bit like the hocus-pocus astrologers write in their daily newspaper star-sign columns.'

'I'm talking about astronomy, the physical position of what we can see in the sky right now. We can't see the moon but it is out there, and in front of the constellation of Cancer. Your newspaper astrologer is still partially working from star charts that were last relevant when the ancient Greeks were stargazing.'

I then explained to Silvana what I had already explained to her mother about the precession of the equinoxes. I didn't mention the fact that Silvana's mum had crashed the car not long after I had finished talking. 'Whenever you use biodynamic techniques to heal the soil, such as spreading solid compost, or spraying biodynamic barrel compost, or the horn manure sprays, the theory goes it is best done when the moon is in front of an earth constellation. It seems to make whatever benefit you're trying to bring to the soil more powerful. I'll try and pick the grapes and bottle the wine when the moon is in front of either a fire/fruit or earth constellation. Even a flower constellation would do: Libra, Gemini, Aquarius. The ones to avoid are the water constellations: Pisces, Cancer and Scorpio. They exaggerate the moon's own strong relationship with water. I don't want the grapes or wine taking on any dilute characters.'

'What's that constellation, Monty?' said Silvana, pointing eastwards, over the top of the tent and across the Planels plateau to some bright lights moving on the horizon. 'Massey Fergusonius Minorus, or Fordus Tractorius?'

'I forgot to tell you that Eric is sulphur dusting tonight. I've done some sulphur dusting by hand during the day, but he said it was too hot and I risked burning the vine leaves, which is why he's doing it at night. I've been helping him water his young vines by hand in return for him sulphur dusting mine.'

When Eric pulled up in his tractor Silvana and I offered him a glass of nut liqueur that he refused because he was driving. I asked him how everything was going vineyard-wise. 'It's looking good,' he said, flipping the goggles he wore to protect his eyes from the sulphur dust onto his forehead with his right hand as Silvana succeeded in forcing a small salad sandwich into his left one. 'Ripening is on schedule, at least as far as anything around here is ever on schedule. The grapes are starting to change colour and ripen so this is the last sulphur treatment they'll need. You normally reckon on five or six weeks with Carignan from the moment the grapes start to change colour until harvest. That means you'll be picking end of September, or early October at the latest. Just keep an eye on the boar fence.'

The next day at sunrise, and after making sure our early morning pees were strategically directed at two rows at the top of the vineyard where the boar always seemed to like to pass along, Silvana and I were able to take a more detailed look at the vineyard. The Carignan grape bunches were a peculiar sight. Just over half the visible berries on each bunch had the kind of milky-green colour, size and texture of freshly podded peas. The other grapes, however, were various shades of red anywhere between a dilute pink and deep purple. I got Silvana to taste a green grape from a Carignan bunch and then another one that was darkish purple in colour.

'Pah,' she said, as she spat out the first one. 'That's so acid tasting. My tongue is like sandpaper. This one's sweeter, but still acid,' she said as she spat the pip of the riper looking one out. The riper looking grapes were still acid tasting and therefore not fully ripe, but at least nature was doing her job. The final stage of ripening had begun. In the summer heat, acid inside each grape was evaporating, making the grapes taste less sharp. Also, sugar was being moved into the grapes from the leaves, making the grapes taste sweeter and riper. The grapes were also swelling notably in size and changing colour. Ever since the baby berries had first formed after flowering each one had been coloured green because they were so rich in chlorophyll. Now, colouring pigments were forming in the grapes as they changed colour – to golden-yellow for the white grape Maccabeu, or purple for the red grapes like Carignan, Grenache Noir and Syrah.

'It won't be easy to see if or by how much the bottom half of the vineyard is further behind compared with the warmer, upper part,' I said. 'We'll have to wait until every grape on every bunch has changed colour, and for the sugar levels to build up. Then I can get the refractometer out.' The refractometer I used was a pocket one. It looked like a thick marker pen, with an eye-piece at one end to look through and an angled pane of glass at the other. To measure how much sugar was in the grapes you squeezed some grape juice on the glass, pointed it at the sun and looked through the other end (by being angled you weren't looking directly at the sun, otherwise you'd damage your eyes). The way the waves of sunlight refracted through the grape juice told you how concentrated or sugary the juice was. A numbered scale behind the glass allowed you to see how alcoholic your wine would be if the grape juice you were measuring was fermented. One of the reasons modern wines are increasingly strong in alcohol is that winegrowers can measure more accurately than ever how sweet, in other words how potentially alcoholic, their grapes are and can time the date of picking accordingly. Another reason is that many modern winemakers can now use strains of yeasts that are super-efficient at converting sugar into alcohol. Yeasts start slowing down the more alcoholic the grape-juice-come-wine becomes, eventually stopping completely around 15–16% alcohol. As yeasts also only work at their best at certain temperatures, wineries that have temperature control can control how quickly or slowly the yeast can work at converting sugar into alcohol. I led Silvana down to the bottom of the vineyard. 'Right,' I said. 'We're going to do what's called a "quick and dirty".'

'Sounds interesting. I'm listening.'

'Before you get any ideas it's an expression I picked up when I worked on the vineyard in California. We're going to pull off any water shoots/suckers that we missed last time, especially those that are stopping direct sunlight getting on the bunches, or any big leaves that are causing too much shading.'

'So the bunches will ripen quicker,' said Silvana, who had already started rifling through the shoots on a bushy-looking vine to pluck off any excess vegetation.

'It's not just the bunches that need to ripen, but the main-grape-bearing shoots do too. They should get browner in colour and harder. It's called lignification. If the shoots don't lignify they won't be able to withstand winter. They need to do that to produce the kind of strong spurs you want to be able to leave at pruning for next year's crop. Quick and dirty means we're not trying to make the vines look beautiful or pluck off every single water shoot that's getting in the way. We're just going to take off as much as we can as quickly as we can, without being obsessive. As long as we leave each vine looking like there's a balance between grapes and leaves, it'll be okay.' It only took an hour or so spot-checking the few vines right at the bottom of the slope. These were the ones that had benefited most from summer rain and sun, and had grown biggest of all. I knew I didn't have to warn Silvana to be gentle. We didn't want to cause the softening berries to bang and bruise themselves against vine posts, supporting wires, or hardening shoots. If the grapes-skins were damaged in any way the grapes would either rot if it rained, or was foggy; or would raisin badly if it got really hot.

It took more than a couple of weeks for all the grapes to have changed colour. And, of course, the boar began to take a real interest in my ripening crop. Every morning I could see fresh hoof prints and topsoil that had been disturbed overnight as the boar nosed for worms and roots. If they were scavenging for worms then at least the compost was doing its job of making the soil more alive, I reflected. But it was a worrying sight to find whole bunches that had had every grape sucked off as if by a powerful vacuum cleaner. I remembered what Eric has said, that they were after the moisture the grapes contained, and considered for one mad moment putting some water troughs out for them as a decoy before the rational side of my brain told me that if I did that I'd have every boar south of Paris camped around the vineyard. The boar didn't really seem to attack every vine row right across the vineyard, just the same couple of rows on either edge of the vineyard that they passed through to get from the forest at the top of the vineyard to scrubland at the bottom. All I could do was keep checking the electric fence and scream and shout every evening at nightfall into the forest. It was a good way of letting off nervous energy even if it scared the wits out of Harry who barked madly as I screamed. 'This kind of behaviour would get us locked up in England,' I told him. 'But, if the boar are coming for the grapes, at least it means harvest is not far off now.'

I waited another couple of weeks and then began checking the sugar levels, spot checking individual grapes using the refractometer. The local press was full of reports of how wine-growers nearer the coast had started harvesting from the first week in August. They began with the white grapes (Maccabeu, Bourboulenc, Vermentino, Viognier, Grenache Blanc and Grenache Gris) for their dry white wines. When Eric asked me to take his van down through the Maury valley to collect things he needed for his own harvest (spare tyres for vans and trailers, grease guns to prevent various bits of machinery from seizing, extra pairs of grape scissors for the harvesters), I could see Muscat and Grenache Noir vineyards being picked for sweeter, port-style wines. Ripening was later and slower away from the coast and up on the plateau where we were. When Eric began his white-grape harvest at the end of August he explained how to check the sugars in my grapes more thoroughly. 'Walk up and down two rows of vines, one each on either side of the vineyard. Pick single grapes off both sides of each row. This way you'll get grapes exposed mainly to the morning sun on the one side and grapes exposed mainly to the evening sun on the other. When you pick a grape from a ripening bunch, always vary your approach. Pick one grape from the very bottom of the bunch, then as you continue walking make sure the next one comes from the very top of the bunch which gets more sun, then one from the middle of the bunch, one from the inside and the outside and so on, as you walk up and down. When you've got about 100 berries in your bag bring it to the winery, we'll crush the grapes in the bag by hand, make a hole in the bag and sample the juice trickling out. This way you should get a much more accurate picture or how ripe your vineyard is than if you just check the odd berry here and there.'

I ran checks on the top and bottom half the vineyard. I tasted the grapes and chewed the skins to see if the flavours were becoming ripe. I spat the pips into my palm to see if they were changing from unripe green to a riper, darker brown. By the end of the second week in September grapes in the top half of the vineyard were capable of making a wine with just over 12% alcohol, while those in the bottom half would have made a wine with only around 11.5% alcohol. I knew that for Carignan to taste ripe enough for the kind of wine I wanted I'd need a level of around 12.5–13% potential alcohol. I was also keen for the grapes in the lower part of the vineyard to catch up with those at the top, so I sprayed them with biodynamic horn silica. I stirred by hand a few grams of horn silica in water for one hour, then sprayed this over the tops of the vine shoots. Horn silica is made in the same way as horn manure, but instead of packing manure into cow horns you put finely ground silica (quartz) in instead. The horns are buried in the ground over the summer months. During this time, the silica is said to become especially rich in the light-giving qualities that plants like vines need to ripen their grapes. Horn silica is also said to improve taste qualities and to maintain the health and fertility of plants. When I told Eric, who was pressing his white-wine grapes, what I had done, he said, 'Don't worry too much about there being a tiny imbalance between the top and bottom parts of the vineyard. If anything it'll add a bit of complexity.'

'Maybe I should pick my white grapes separately and not ferment them with the red grapes? That would make my red wine a bit stronger tasting, and I'd have a white wine to sell.' Seeing Eric running juice from his white grapes out of the press and into barrels for fermentation had made me reconsider the possibility of making a white wine. 'Monty, number one: you don't have enough white grapes to fill up the press to make pressing worthwhile. Second: you don't have any vats to ferment the juice in. Remember? Third: are you really going to get your crew of people to go up to your vineyard to pick it twice, once to pick a few Maccabeu vines, then again to pick the red grapes? It makes no sense.' It was exactly what Pascal had told me months ago, during pruning. 'Here, taste this,' Eric said, proffering me a glass of fresh grape juice. 'The stress of your first harvest is clearly getting to you old man! You're not thinking straight. This is full of sugar, vitamins and minerals. Drink it, take a siesta and focus on the satellite weather reports on your laptop.' This was more good advice. The excitement of getting involved with Eric's harvest and the stress of my own was starting to take its toll. A combination of the way the grapes were ripening and the satellite photos had allowed me to select the ideal date for picking as Monday, September 24. Silvana,

Francesca and Graham all arrived in St-Martin ready for the harvest on the Saturday, allowing Graham to prepare Francesca her first-ever full English breakfast of fried bread and scrambled eggs on the Sunday morning. I put John, Peter and Andy, as well as Eric's usual picking crew, on standby. The weather started to close in on the Saturday and Sunday, and I was far from confident Monday would be any different. 'The satellite pictures show there'll be a window of fine, windless and sunny weather tomorrow,' I said as I helped Eric load the grape-picking bins onto his tractor-trailer as dusk fell on the Sunday evening. 'Prepare for the worst and hope for the best,' said Eric, as I handed him stacks of picking bins half-a-dozen high over the trailer's tailgate.

'That's not the easiest thing in the world to do,' I said, feeling my whole body tense with expectation. The last time I had got stressed and lifted something, in June, I had put my back out for three weeks and I was petrified of doing the same thing the night before the harvest of my first ever wine. 'I've got people who've flown in from London and Tuscany hoping we'll pick tomorrow.'

'Well, if you can't pick tomorrow you'll have to wait another week, as the long-term forecast looks bad. Rain is on the way. Then you'll have to wait a couple of days for the vines and grapes, plus the vineyard soil, to dry out which will take you into October...'

I handed Eric the last of the picking bins and returned home for a light dinner. Usually Harry had one pre-bedtime walk, but tonight I took him out no less than three times to burn off my nervous energy. In the morning, the skies were the kind of bright grey that usually means it is drizzling and will continue to do so all day long. So many thoughts buzzed through my head. Do I wait and hope it clears? Do I call it off now? Who do I call first to say, 'don't bother coming today, it's raining'. Do I need to see Eric or will he have done the sensible thing and gone back to bed? If I wait until it is dry will the grapes have rotted by then? What am I going to do? Instead of putting my steel-tipped work boots on I put my Wellingtons on as a precaution against the rain. It was the first time I had worn them since compost spreading. As I was getting Harry ready for his walk I kicked the wall so hard in frustration the big toe on my right foot almost bent completely backwards. Graham sprang down the stairs, arriving just as I was limping out of the door. 'It's nice and dry and brightening up already. What would we do without satellite photos, eh?' It wasn't raining. In fact it was warm and dry, and the sky was hazy, rather than properly cloudy. As soon as Harry, Graham and I returned from the walk we called upstairs to Silvana and Francesca to get some flasks of the strongest coffee they could manage prepared, then rendezvous with us around the corner by Eric's winery.

'You've picked a good day for it,' said Eric, firing up his tractor and forcing Graham, who was checking out the picking bins, to dodge a dark cloud of exhaust fumes. 'You'll have taken those jumpers you're all wearing off by 9.30 am. It's going to be a hot one.' Conscious of my bruised toe I resisted the urge to jump up and down in elation, but tried to focus on what I needed to do: make sure everyone had their own supply of water to drink to prevent dehydration, plus a pair of picking scissors. Inside the winery the fermentation vats were clean and waiting to be filled with grapes. The picking bins were on the back of Eric's tractor, its glass cab now reflecting the morning sun, which was making me sweat already. The boar had been allowed to take only a tiny amount of grapes over the last few weeks. So, all we had to do now was to pick the ones that remained. 'This is it,' I said to Silvana as I dumped Harry on her lap as we clambered into my van; Graham and Francesca following in Graham's hire car. 'All that scrabbling around on hands and knees pulling weeds and shoots off is over now, thankfully. We've done the hard part, getting the grapes to grow and ripen. Now comes the hard part. Making sure I make a wine as good as the grapes I've got. I'd never forgive myself if the wine ends up tasting really boring because I got the winemaking side of things wrong!'

Chapter 10

B Y THE TIME SILVANA, HARRY AND I CLAMBERED OUT OF THE truck the vineyard was swamped by vehicles and an encouraging number of people: Eric's French crew, of course, Andy, who was soon deep in conversation with Graham and other ex-pats including John and Pete. The only person missing was René. The night before he'd very kindly offered to feed the chickens and get the geese out of bed, 'whatever the weather brings, so it'll be one less thing for you to worry about'. I had sent him on his way with a huge jam tart that Francesca had baked for René's wife Adeline.

René said he'd come up to see the vineyard being picked around mid-morning, along with mayor André. Both men had said they were keen to taste their first (almost) grapes from biodynamically farmed vines. The Carignan grape's dark skin certainly looked pretty tempting in the early morning light, each grape like a ripe, dark plum in miniature. The grapes made a satisfying pop when you pushed one against the roof of your mouth, leaving your teeth and tongue to deal with the thick, crunchy skins and cool, sweet juice. I think I'd already eaten the best part of a bunch when I finally managed to gather everyone together at the top of the vineyard to outline some sort of plan. I felt like a general about to lead his troops into battle, although I've never been much of a public speaker. At least I knew my words, a mix of French, Italian and English, would carry, as for the first time in days there was very little wind.

'I know many of you have done this before,' I began rather nervously, looking particularly at Eric's six-strong crew, as well as Silvana and Francesca. They'd all picked grapes before and had no doubt already heard something along the lines of what I was about to say. 'But, for those of you who haven't it's pretty simple. Please place the bunches you cut in the picking bins as carefully as you can. It's going to be hot today. If the grape-skins get broken after being thrown around, then grape juice will leak out and oxidise in the heat. The wine will end up tasting dull and vinegary. Cut any bunches that are obviously unripe and leave them on the ground.' I pointed out an example of an unripe and undersized bunch. These are the size of small fir cones and grow from secondary flowers at the very top of some vine shoots, but are never ripe or flavoured enough for top wine (although some people distill wine from such grapes into illicit, home-made brandy). 'And when you cut, please make sure to hold the bunch in your hand like this,' I said, bending somewhat inelegantly down towards a normal-sized bunch of grapes. 'If you cup the bunch in your hand it won't fall to the ground and get bruised and dirty.'

'It'll also help prevent you cutting your fingers off,' said Graham in English, with his typical eye for life's practicalities, then adding to me as an aside, 'worth bearing in mind if this winemaking lark doesn't work out for you, Mont, and you need a full set of fingers to return to the somehow glamorously bohemian life of a struggling wine writer...'

'In case anyone's fingers need sewing back on there's a first-aid kit in the back of that grey van,' I said out loud in French, pointing to the van Pascal, Jacques and the rest of Eric's crew had arrived in. 'Graham has surgical training.'

'Was that something about me?' asked Graham, scratching his chin with the end of his scissors.

'I told Eric's crew that you were here to pick grapes and not get distracted by trying to practise your schoolboy French by talking to them about rugby. Eric, Jacques and Pascal are huge rugby fans in case you hadn't guessed. They were admiring the rugby shirt you were wearing first thing this morning.'

'Either that or they were impressed by my generously proportioned midriff,' said Graham, admiring his middle.

I knew I'd forgotten something important, but then Eric, who had been unloading picking bins with Pascal and Jacques, stepped in to make a suggestion about logistics. 'Make sure that you pick from this side of the vines,' he said, pointing to the western, or cabin-facing side of a row. 'You'll be able to pick more quickly because you'll get a clearer view of what you're picking. This is because the wind normally comes over the mountains from the west and pushes the shoots eastwards, towards the ocean but away from you if you remain on this side.' I remembered when Silvana and I had removed the shoots and leaves from the ripening vines over the summer how we had worked only on the opposite side to where we were now about to pick. This was because you always remove shoots and leaves from the side of the vine row exposed to where the cooler morning sun rises (the east). Removing too much greenery from the side where the hotter evening sun sets (the west) would almost certainly have meant the grapes getting sunburnt.

Everyone was organised to start picking in teams so that four vine rows would be picked at once. Eric's crew – Dominique, Pascal, Jacques, Valène (Pascal's niece) and another young woman called Sylvaine – took a couple of rows, while Silvana, Francesca, Graham, Andy, John and Pete took another couple adjacent. I helped Eric place bins next to the vines, spacing them up and down the rows according to how heavy the crop was. Helping Eric with his own harvest had given me a fairly good eye for how far apart to place the bins. The idea was that the pickers wouldn't have to stop and wait for an empty bin because all the bins were completely full. If you left too many bins in a zone where there were only a few grapes it meant bins would be only half filled or worse, left empty. Then you'd waste time hopping over or clambering under the vineyard supporting wires to collect the still empty bins for use elsewhere. Of all the pickers Sylvaine and Valène were the best prepared. They had each attached a belt around their waist. Clipped to this was another belt that was then clipped onto a picking bin. This meant they could use their bodies instead of bending down with their hands to drag partially filled bins down the rows in search of more grapes. When four rows of vines had been picked, the filled bins along the two outer rows of each group of four were regrouped along the middle two rows. Like this the tractor trailer would need to make only a single pass for every four rows harvested when collecting the filled bins.

It didn't take long for everyone to settle into their own rhythm while picking, with Sylvaine and Valène, Jacques and Pascal, Graham and me, Silvana and Francesca and Andy, John and Pete chatting as they cut. Every so often a grape would fly my way thrown by Eric when he needed to get my attention, to put more bins out, or to point out a vine that someone had missed and was still clinging to its precious grapes. We worked our way from the far side of the vineyard where the longest rows were westwards and back to the shorter rows closest to the cabin. We stopped mid-morning for coffee, then for lunch. Most people had peeled off at least one layer of clothing by then. As soon as I had picked my first couple of bunches my adrenalin levels just dropped off the radar. I had a real sense of contentment: scuffing around the vineyard in my boots feeling the long grass stroking my knees, eating handfuls of grapes until my chin was stained with juice and watching bin after bin be filled with perfect-looking grapes. It was such a change to hear the noisy background hum of conversation after spending so many hours here either on my own or with Silvana when we only had the wind, birds and Harry for company. The noise was only broken by the sound of an accordion player from Perpignan who I'd hired for the morning. One of Silvana's vineyard-owning friends called Giancarlo played classical and even rap music to his vines in Tuscany. This was part of a scientific research project with the university of Florence. The aim was to see whether the sound of music, or rather the sound waves the music made, helped vines resist pests and diseases. Initial results seemed very positive. Giancarlo told me how he remembered playing the accordion to his pickers when he was younger and how it had helped keep their spirits up during long, hot days of gruelling work. The music helped people maintain a good speed and meant they still worked with the necessary care and attention. He advised me to do the same. If René and mayor André thought this was a crazy idea they didn't say anything when they finally arrived. It was hard not to feel humbled by the energy of this old man who had lost part of his fingers and who walked with a pronounced arthritic stoop, yet was so excited and got so carried away that André and I even had to restrain him from trying to load the heavy grape bins onto Eric's trailer. But, we did let René clip a few bunches with a pair of scissors he had brought and which I knew he had been sharpening daily for nearly a week in anticipation of my harvest.

The picking bins were coloured red on one side and grey on the other. This was to make stacking them safer and easier. When empty you would stack a pile of bins so the same colour was always on the same side. However, when the bins were full of grapes you always stacked them alternately because there was an inner lip on the red side of the bin. This buffered the grey bottom of the tray you were stacking on top and meant that neither the grapes, nor your fingers, would get crushed. By mid-afternoon my entire vineyard had been picked. 'They've done well, your crew,' said Eric. 'Silvana and Francesca are really quick pickers. If ever they need a job…And the English guys were good, too. I thought it would take one, maybe even two days to pick your vines. *C'est du bon boulot, ça,*' which means 'great job'.

I followed Eric's crew as they went off to pick Eric's neighbouring vineyard. This was also planted with Carignan that he used for his easiest drinking wine. This was a red wine called 'Eclipse'. Graham, Andy, John and Pete stayed on to help Eric's crew pick some more grapes. They all said how much better my vines looked in comparison and how my vines produced noticeably more grapes per vine. 'It must be the biodynamics,' someone said, without a hint of irony. 'Not so fast,' I had to counter. I was always wary when people seemed to see biodynamics as some sort of quick fix, miracle cure. 'First: it takes several years for the full biodynamic effect to be felt, so I won't be making any miracle claims for it in my vineyard in just my first year. Second: part of my vineyard is on top of some kind of underground stream which is not the case in Eric's vineyard,' I said pointing out a diagonal strip of extra-green vines which lay directly above the underground water source. 'This extra water means my vines benefit from a more humid soil and it's only normal that they'll not only look a bit greener but produce more grapes and won't suffer from heat stress. Third: the vineyards were planted at different times and so are different ages. It makes a big difference on which day the vines actually went into the ground. Maybe some of my vines were planted when the moon and Saturn were in opposition, for example. That's always a good time to plant. I planted the toma- toes in my vegetable garden during moon – Saturn opposition, and René says he can't believe how well my tomatoes how ripened compared to his.' Graham, inevitably, wanted more detail as we both walked back in the direction of my van.

'You're a surveyor, Graham. So you know that no matter how well you design a building, if you build it in the wrong place...'

'Yeah, but that's only the location, isn't it? It doesn't make any difference *when* you build a house.'

'Okay, you're right, in the sense that buildings are inert objects. But, ask any cottage thatcher if the straw or reeds they use to thatch a roof with is cut from the fields on just any old day. They'll say "no". If my vines were planted when the moon was in the right place and the neighbouring vineyard was planted when the moon was in the wrong place then I am convinced that there will always be a huge difference between them throughout the life of both vineyards. A moon – Saturn opposition is a good time to plant, or sow, crops.' What biodynamic growers mean by a moon – Saturn opposition is the moment once a month when the moon is on one side of the earth and Saturn is on the opposite side. A moon – sun opposition produces a full moon, because the earth is in the middle of the sun and the moon which is why the moon is bright, reflecting the light of the sun. A moon – Saturn opposition is said to have a balancing effect because the moon apparently helps plants to grow and produce crops, while Saturn enhances the warmth forces that plants need to ripen.

'Think about it this way,' I said. 'Humans needs healthy bones and healthy flesh to grow in the right way. Mums produce milk for their newborn babies, calves, lambs, or sows partly for the calcium it contains. This calcium helps good bone formation. The moon is supposed to influence calcium, which is maybe why some people will only get their fingernails (that contain calcium) manicured only at certain times of the month. Your skin or flesh on the other hand is full of silica. Your skin has a strong relationship to the bright objects in the sky. This could be the sun – think of sunburn – or Saturn, which is like a mini-sun. It's

a giant planet, far bigger than then earth, remember?' Maybe the
fact that Graham spent most days stuck in an office and the
shorts he was wearing revealed legs that weren't showing many
signs of sunburn meant he let me continue talking, unchal-
lenged. 'Anyway, biodynamic growers say that if the balance of
lime and silica is right on your farm then your crops will grow in
the right way. It's like the biodynamic horn manure and horn
silica sprays. The horn manure works on the plant's bones – the
root system. The horn silica works on the plant's skin – its
leaves. You can't use one without the other otherwise you'd have
plants with too many roots and not enough leaves, or vice versa.
It's all about balance. And things that are in balance, be it a
plant, body, or even psyche of a human being, or in your case
Graham an office block, work best.' When we had reached my
van it struck me that I had got so used to seeing the vineyard
laden with fruit I was almost sad that its last bunch had been
picked. However, this was no moment for sentiment. Eric's
trailer was laden with filled picking bins and he told me he
needed me to empty these as quickly as possible so that he'd
have enough for his own on-going harvest. Pascal was already on
his way to St-Martin with the tractor and as he saw me in his
mirror he let me pass in my van so that I could be at the winery
ready to help him back it into the tight winery courtyard.

The light-blue paint on the double wooden doors of Eric's
winery was in much better condition than that of my front door
I noted, as Pascal pulled the tractor's handbrake tight. Graham
and I flipped the heavy metal flap on the back of the trailer to

open it. On board were around 130 full bins of grapes, with another 130 or so more still in the vineyard.

'I'm pretty sure we're not going to put them in that press, are we?' asked Graham, pointing to the large silver cylinder behind us – a pneumatic press. This was one of the most modern presses available. Grapes were tipped inside it via a hatch. When the hatch was shut tight, the press was turned on and a bag inside the press was gradually inflated with compressed air. Pressing could be a noisy business, as air would be let out of the press periodically so the press could be turned so that the grapes inside could tumble freely, allowing for more homogeneous pressing when the bag was re-inflated. When inflated, the bag would press the grapes inside against the side of the cylinder. This was perforated with holes big enough to allow the juice, but not the skins or pips, through. The juice fell down via gravity onto a metal collecting tray directly under the press cylinder. From there it could run by gravity or be pumped into a tank or barrel for fermentation.

'I will use that press, but not until my wine has fermented,' I told Graham. 'If I was making a white wine then yes the grapes would go straight in there. For white wine you press the grapes first and collect the juice to ferment it. And you chuck the skins, pips and stems away as they don't get fermented. You only need the juice for white wine. For red wine it's different. You need to ferment the juice and grapes together to get the colour out of the skins. It's called extraction. Whatever the skin colour, the juice inside a grape is always clear. There are a couple of weird grapes called *teinturiers* that have red-flesh but don't worry about them. All you need to know is that if I put my red grapes in that press and fermented the juice that came out, then I would end up making a white wine.' We began humping the crates off the trailer and dragging them to a round, stainless steel-lined hole in the winery floor just beyond where the press was. This was the opening to the top of the vat in which my wine would ferment. 'We're going to tip the grapes in there, as whole bunches,' I said to Graham. During picking I'd asked everyone to try to cut as close to the top of the bunch as possible so as to keep the stems at the top of the bunches as short as possible.

'At the risk of stating the obvious aren't you going to thresh the grapes first like they do in Bordeaux?' asked Graham, 'to get rid of the stems?' When I had worked in a Bordeaux winery ten or so years before, Graham had come to visit me and had seen how winemaking was done in Bordeaux.

'I would do if I wanted to make a wine like Bordeaux, or just about any other red you care to name. Except Beaujolais.'

'Beaujolais? Isn't Beaujolais Nouveau one of the naffest wines around?' asked Graham.

'There are some very good Beaujolais reds,' I said, 'but most of it is dross because the producers there got greedy, over-produced and made too much thin-tasting wine. But, the way they make their fruitiest wines (Beaujolais Nouveau) is by allowing whole, uncrushed bunches to ferment. That's why we're tipping these grapes in the tank like this, without crushing them. The idea is that each grape ferments from within and you get a wine with lots of colour and fruit, but very little tannin. So, the wine can be drunk young which means I get paid earlier rather than later.'

'It looks like some grapes are getting crushed anyway as we're tipping them in the vat. This vat looks to be nearly twice my height, so they have a long way to fall.'

'It's okay if a few grapes get crushed. In fact it's all part of the plan. A bit of juice will leak out of the crushed grapes right at the bottom of the vat. If the first grapes into the vat don't get crushed falling, they'll get crushed by the weight of the grapes above. The grape juice that is squeezed out will be targeted by the wild yeasts present on the grape-skins.' I scraped the pad of my right forefinger against a grape-skin, showing Graham how the greyish white waxy layer on it could be rubbed off. This waxy layer or bloom was full of yeasts.

'Those yeasts will start eating the sugar in the juice and the fermentation will begin. When we eat two things happen.'

'Er, we stop feeling hungry and get fatter?'

'Okay, three things. We grow, plus we produce gas so we belch or fart, and we need to shit. Yeast are no different when they eat. In their case they shit the alcohol that makes the wine. Plus, they'll fart out carbon dioxide gas. When we have put all the grapes in the tank I'll seal the top of the vat tight with this lid,' I said, pointing to a round stainless-steel lid with a thick rubber washer in its inner rim for a tight seal.

'The carbon dioxide gas will protect the grapes at the top of the vat because they won't start fermenting immediately as they might oxidise. But, the main reason for closing the vat is because it will force the yeast to work in a different way than if we were doing a Bordeaux-style (or classic) fermentation.'

'In a different way meaning what?' said Graham, whose feet were now surrounded by what looked like a thin layer of mainly black, but sometimes yellow marbles, but which were grapes that had fallen shy of the vat as we were emptying the boxes in.

'Well, yeast work quickest when there's plenty of oxygen. If there's no oxygen in this wine vat because we have sealed it tight then the grapes will still ferment. But, they will ferment in a different way because enzymes in the pulp will do some of the work, rather than the yeast. It's called intra-cellular fermentation if you want the technical term. Basically, the cells in the grapes get broken to release the sugar that then ferments. It's also called carbonic maceration, carbonic because another name for carbon dioxide is carbonic acid.'

'But, if the grapes are going in as whole bunches, it means the grape stems are going in, too.'

'Right. And you want to know why I was getting so uppity in the vineyard asking the pickers to leave as short a bunch-stem as possible?'

'Yeah, mate, I was. Isn't the wine going to taste of the stems?'

'The stems adsorb some of the red-wine colour and they can make the wine taste harder and more tannic. But, as the juice in each grape is fermenting within the grape it means the juice shouldn't pick up any flavours from the stems. Putting whole bunches in the vats means by definition that stems will go in as well. But, the aim is to get the biggest ratio of grapes to stems as possible. So, cutting stems as close to the bunch as possible makes sense, to maximise fruit flavours and minimise the tannic ones, especially because towards the end of the fermentation the grapes will start to implode and the juice will start soaking with the stems. Carignan is potentially one of the most tannic grapes. So is the Cabernet Sauvignon grape, that makes red wines in Bordeaux, California, Chile and so on – and that can age for decades. The difference is that a young Cabernet Sauvignon can be very tannic, but a good one will also be classy. If you make a Carignan red wine in a deliberately tannic style, it'll just be tannic and not very elegant.'

When the second trailer-load of grapes was safely in the vats, I took Graham downstairs so we could stand in front of my fermentation vat, the smallest one in a group of four. One vat contained Eric's Syrah that was fermenting. The vat next to mine was empty. This was the vat my fermented wine would be put into to. Another empty vat on the other side hadn't been renovated in time for harvest. 'Just to confuse you even more Graham, what I am trying to do with my red wine is make something that has the fruity appeal of a Beaujolais but with the slightly more serious side of a good red Bordeaux.' I explained how Beaujolais Nouveau could be ready for sale within six weeks of the grapes being picked and wouldn't usually survive much beyond one year in bottle, but that I wasn't expecting my wine to be ready for sale and possible drinking until six months after the harvest. 'My wine will be drinkable from between six months and three years after harvest.'

'And here was I thinking wine was simple,' said Graham, heavy on the irony. 'I've done those wine-tasting courses, but, unless you're actually in a winery seeing it happen, a lot of it just doesn't make sense.'

'To use a film analogy, I want to make a wine somewhere in between a quick, easy-to-follow cartoon and a feature film. I've drunk some of the most expensive bottles of wine ever made, but the wine that gives me most pleasure is a good everyday quaffer. It's wine you can afford to drink with every meal, and if you drop the bottle you won't feel tempted to jump off the nearest cliff. That's what I want to make. A wine I'd pay money for myself.' I put my right arm in the air and stretched my fingers as high as I could to touch the wall of the tank. 'At the moment, wherever I put my hand on the wall of the fermentation tank there will be grapes directly behind, but no juice. After the first few days of fermentation, as the berries start to release their juice this part of the tank will be juice,' I said touching an area the same height as my knees, 'while everything above will be grapes. They'll start to float upwards because carbon dioxide bubbles given off by the yeast will attach themselves to the skins. The fermenting action of the yeast warms the juice, too. It'll reach around 28–30°C compared with about 14°C right now. The extra heat helps extract colour. In white wines, there's no colour to extract so they ferment much cooler than reds, at 15–20°C. Any hotter and the white-wine flavours turn boiled.'

'At that stage,' I continued to Graham, 'the juice will be a reddish liquid that contains as much alcohol as a strong beer and as much sugar as a fizzy drink. In other words, the wine will be half made. It should have softish, fruity flavours, but will lack a bit of colour. It'll be grapefruit pink, rather than blood-orange red.'

'Now you're going to say something like "now comes the difficult bit". Am I right?' said Graham, rocking gently on the balls of his feet and smiling.

'Then what I am going to do is switch from making a soft, fruity Beaujolais style red. I'll open the top of the vat. Then I'll attach a hose and a pump to this valve,' I said, gripping a large, tap-like piece of stainless steel. 'That's the exit valve for the tank. If I open it the wine-come-juice will flow out. You put a tub underneath for it to fall into. This allows the wine to get frothy, showing how the yeast are filling up with the air they need to carry on the job the enzymes were doing.'

'The job of converting the sugar that's still left into wine,' said Graham, who was now clearly getting the hang of what was going on.

'You can then pump this juice-come-wine over the grapes in the tank. It's called a "pump-over", funnily enough. That's the Bordeaux-part. You have to be careful not to over-do it because the juice now contains some alcohol. The alcohol is useful because it's what helps extract the red-wine colour from the skins, and the tannins that will help the wine age a bit in bottle. But, as alcohol is a solvent you also need to be careful not to extract too much bitterness from the pips.'

'Er, and the stems too, I guess,' said Graham, wandering off to examine the bungs on Eric's barrels while I held a wine glass next to a valve at the very bottom of the tank that I opened by a whisker to fill the glass with cool, pink grape juice. It tasted sweet, but crisp, with really clear flavours of red fruits such as raspberry, strawberry and red plum. 'It's amazing to taste a whole vat-full of grapes rather than just eating one or two at a time during picking,' said Graham. 'And, it doesn't have any of those horrid green or banana-like flavours you said an unripe Carignan would show, either.'

Silvana's initial verdict on sampling the grape juice was, 'it tastes better than I thought you'd manage', which in Silvana-speak was actually a pretty big compliment. 'You would have got distracted from the winegrowing and spent all your money had I let you keep that herd of cows you'd set your heart on.' One year on and Silvana was still having to guide me when it came to my finances. Before leaving for Italy Silvana sat me down to crunch some numbers. I'd been struggling to guess exactly how much wine I would actually end up producing. That was pretty critical information when it came to budgeting for the number of bottles, corks, labels and cardboard boxes I would eventually have to buy. When I'd asked Eric the week before the harvest how much wine my grapes would give me he looked at me blankly and then across the vineyard and said, 'I've been doing this for years, Monty, and I can honestly say that not once have I got my pre-harvest estimate right. Whatever you get would have been even more if that north African wind hadn't blown in.'

At the end of August and beginning of September temperatures in St-Martin and the rest of the Roussillon region had risen ferociously. As Eric said, a hot, blustery wind had blown up from Africa, even bringing a bit of Saharan sand with it. Up until then Roussillon had boasted probably France's happiest winegrowers. While many other areas of France suffered wet weather bringing all sorts of disease problems Roussillon's vineyards promised both above-average yields and very high quality. That equates to winegrowing paradise. However, the wind's heat had made the grapes shrivel slightly, as they dehydrated. This meant that each grape would produce less juice that ultimately meant less wine.

'I'd guess you lost around 20 per cent of your potential crop,' said Eric, chewing a grape, and pointing out how the grape-skins were more deeply coloured and spicier tasting than before. 'But if it is any consolation, you're not the only one. Every other winegrower around here has suffered a similar loss. The good thing is your wine will be extra concentrated.' This was because there would now be proportionately less juice to grape-skins, and it was the skins that contained the colour, flavour and tannins. 'You're going to have to be careful of not going overboard when it comes to extracting colour and tannin from the grape-skins. If you extract too much you'll still make a good wine, but not one for fairly early drinking which is what you said you wanted.'

But it was one thing getting the winemaking right, to make a wine that people would want to buy, and quite another trying to work out how much I could sell the wine for. Realistically no one was going to pay top dollar for the kind of fairly simple, but smooth, fruity red I had planned to make. But to work out my selling price, I had to know exactly how much wine my grapes would produce.

'Lucky for you,' said Silvana, wearing the justifiably worn look of a teacher with a particularly slow pupil, 'the spreadsheet programme I devised for you will save your little brain a lot of work. What you need to do is add in the number of picking bins we filled and the average weight per bin and it'll tell you how much wine will come out the other end.' Silvana had devised a formula based on ten years working in a Tuscan winery making red wine. While Silvana tapped the keyboard, I stayed absolutely silent. 'Right,' she said, leaning forward in her chair and pushing the laptop in my direction, 'you have approximately 6,500 kg of grapes. Around 15 per cent of that is stems, another four per cent is skins and pips. All of that you'll throw away of course when the fermentation is over and you press the wine.' What Silvana was saying was that as well as losing a fifth of my potential crop to the late-summer heat, another fifth of what was left had to be thrown away. At least that part was normal – you can't bottle a red wine that has skins, pips and stems still floating in it. So, when the fermentation was finished the wine would be run out of the bottom of the tank and pumped into a clean one. This was called the free-run wine. Then the oblong hatch on the bottom side of the vat would be opened. As the top hatch was already opened this would allow fresh air to circulate. I'd then be able to crawl into the tank without risking potentially fatal carbon dioxide poisoning. With a plastic shovel (a metal one would scratch the vat walls) I would then shovel out the slush of grape-skins, pips and stems into large bins placed under the bottom of the tank's hatch. This slush would then be emptied into Eric's shiny pneumatic press. The small amount of wine still trapped inside the now largely shrivelled grapes would be pressed out and collected. This was called the press wine. I would have to taste what was coming out of the press regularly over a period of two to three hours as the press was turning (slow, gradual pressing like this was the best way to get the biggest amount and best-quality press wine). Towards the end of the press cycle only harsh, bitter wine would be coming out. That would be sent to the distillery, rather than be combined with the free-run wine.

'Bear in mind that the numbers in my formula are mathematical,' said Silvana. 'Mathematics is a science unlike nature, which has a habit of surprising you. But, these numbers will give you a pretty good idea of how much wine you'll get. Bear in mind that after pressing you'll lose another two or three per cent of the finished wine in the lees.' The lees was the thin layer of sludge that would form naturally after a few days at the bottom of the tank the wine was being stored in. For red wine it had a pinkish colour and a yoghurt-like consistency. This sludge was made up of the wine yeast that had died having done their job of fermentation. The lees would also go to the distillery. Under French law, and for every bottle of wine I declared I had made, a small percentage of the total volume would have to go to be distilled into industrial alcohol. It was a form of tax that you could pay by sending press wine, and sludge. Both contained some alcohol after all. Even the pressed skins and stems that came out of the press had to go to the distillery as they still contained traces of alcohol too. When Silvana had made her calculations she said I would have over 4,500 litres of wine, or between 6–6,500 bottles of wine. Under French law I was allowed to produce four times that much for the surface area of vineyard I had. But, a combination of having an old-vine vineyard on dry, very windy mountain terrain with no chance (legally or practically) of irrigating meant I knew from the outset I'd never get anywhere near that. The late drying wind had lost me potential bottles but had increased quality. Had I lost those potential bottles to a hailstorm I would have struggled to make a wine of even moderate quality, because the vines, leaves and grapes would have suffered so much bruising, disease and other collateral damage.

'You can either up the price you had planned to sell the wine at to make a decent profit,' said Silvana, 'or keep the price as you had always planned it. You can't economise on the corks, or the cardboard boxes. You'll increase your profit margin if you forget your idea of putting the wine in clear glass bottles and go for green ones instead.' My wine was going to be sold in the UK where the market for recycled green glass is much smaller than the huge amount imported every year as wine bottles. There was a demand for clear recycled glass, however. 'Monty, a red wine bottled in a clear glass won't look nice. Besides, it takes more energy to make a clear glass bottle than a green glass one.

And the price is usually higher for the kind of bottle you want.'
Silvana also told me I'd could make savings by designing a
simple wine label with as few colours as possible and scaling
down my plans for a dedicated website. 'Then you can stick to
your plan to sell each bottle for around £2.50.' I was not
registered in the UK as a wine importer so I would have sell to
a company who was. They would collect the wine from France
and pay to insure it and transport it into the UK (adding 5–15p
per bottle depending on how efficiently this was done). Once it
crossed the English Channel excise duty (payable on all
alcoholic drinks) of around £1.50 would be levied. Then they
would sell it either directly to the public via mail order or their
own wine shops, or to someone with their own wine shops,
restaurants or wine bars. Value added tax (17.5%) would be
payable on every bottle sold. 'In a wine shop your wine will sell
for £6–7.99,' said Silvana, 'depending if the importer is looking
for a 20 or 30 per cent margin. In a restaurant where mark-ups
are much bigger it might sell for £20–35.' At my kind of price
level I knew that I'd make less money per bottle than anyone
else in the sales chain, but I'd known that from the start. And I
was happy with my, albeit small, margin, I told Silvana. 'The
numbers are all academic of course,' said Silvana, clicking my
laptop shut and coming to sit on my lap, 'and only make sense
if the wine tastes good enough for someone to want to buy it.'

Bill Baker said he would come to taste my wine. He was due to
make a wine-tasting trip to south west France, but said he had
no problem driving further south to see me if I could organize

a place to stay. This was the same Bill Baker who had said that trying to make organic wine was akin to throwing one's money away. When I drove Bill up to the vineyard it was cold, blustery and drizzling with rain. As a wine writer I had been used to being driven around by winegrowers keen to get me to taste their wine. Now I was behind the steering wheel as Bill squeezed into my van, with Harry on his lap. I remembered how once I had trekked into the middle of Uruguay to find what I supposed would be one of the world's most out-of-the-way organic vineyards. Its owner had proudly shown me his huge flock of egg-laying chickens. 'As organic growers we appreciate the manure the birds give us, and the income we get from their eggs is vital, too,' he said. I realised just how vital when I tasted the red wine. It came from some of the oldest vines in South America, but had the colour of a pathetically pale rosé. It turned out the guy was slinging the chicken droppings on to the vineyard soil as fertiliser, but without composting them first. Raw chicken shit is like nuclear fuel as far as vines are concerned. No wonder his wines were producing such thin, colourless grapes. They were burning up. Bill made it clear he was not here to listen to me waffle on about compost spreading, ploughing weeds by horse instead of weed-killing them, or pruning and picking by the moon. Even when I got down on my knees to show him how healthy the soil and wild grasses growing in my vineyard were he just shrugged. 'Wine is wine, and at the end of the day a wine only interests me if I think it's the kind of wine the clients I deal with want to spend money on.' Bill was far too modest to say that actually he sold wine to some of Britain's finest restaurants and most demanding private collectors.

Once we got out of the cold and into the relatively warm surroundings of the winery I told Bill that I had tried to make my wine in a fruity, but not too simple, style and that it was mainly Carignan, with the other grapes like Syrah, Grenache and Maccabeu that also grow in the vineyard thrown in.

'It's still on skins, is it?' asked Bill, meaning the wine was still fermenting and in contact with the skins. 'So malo hasn't started yet then, I presume,' he added to himself. These were the kind of comments and questions I'd have made as a wine writer. Malo meant the malolactic fermentation, which all red wines (and some whites) undergo. It's a natural process that usually happens when the yeast have done their work. Malo is more a transformation than a fermentation as no alcohol is produced, although the wine does bubble a bit. This is because bacteria are softening appley-tasting acid (malic acid) into softer, more buttery-tasting lactic acid. If this natural process didn't happen all red wines would taste really harsh.

'What about bottling?' Bill asked

'I'll bottle it next March,' I said. 'Unfiltered, of course, and under the right lunar constellation.'

'I wouldn't expect anything else from you, dear boy,' said Bill, politely containing his impatience.

This was the moment of truth. I very gently opened the bottom valve on the tank to fill two glasses, knowing that if I opened the valve even a fraction too much the pressure of the wine would send me flying across the winery floor as if I had been hit by a water cannon. As Bill took the glass, notebook in hand, I suddenly realised just how powerless I was as a winemaker, despite the effort and often physical pain of managing the vineyard for the last year, the constant stress about what the weather would bring, and whether the boar would leave me any grapes to pick. It made me understand how powerful I had been leading the easier life of a critic. Bill was free to judge my wine in any way he wanted, to make some notes, and go back to England to pass the word around that my wine was either a hopeless non-starter or a promising commercial proposition.

First he gave the glass a swirl up to the light to check the redness of its colour. Was it deep enough, or too light because my part-Beaujolais, part-Bordeaux winemaking strategy had failed? Then, Bill stuck his nose into the glass and grimaced. This wasn't going well, until I realised he was wiping a stray wisp of hair away that had been getting in his way all morning. Then, he tasted, slurping the wine around his mouth briefly before spitting it out on the floor. Was that the spit of a man angry at yet another wine selling itself only on its green credentials or was that the spit of a man confident he'd tasted a potential winner? As Bill scribbled a note, time stood still. Then, finally, he spoke.

'In my opinion,' he said, because wine is about opinions more often than facts, 'you're absolutely on the right track with this wine. It's got good fruit and should soften up after malo,' he said, 'without losing that gutsy, southern French character that'll make it very popular in restaurants.'

It took me a moment for what Bill had said to sink in. On the right track? Gutsy, southern French character? Very popular in restaurants? I couldn't stop a smile spreading across my face. It took all my English reserve not to let out a whoop of joy, down my glass in celebration and think about attempting the physically impossible task of giving Bill's generous frame a hug. I had done it. Bill, who had been so firm but fair when judging a mostly dull set of bio wines with me all those years ago, had judged my wine. He didn't care whether it was biodynamic or not, just that it was good. And to Bill it seemed that it was. As I took a sip of wine – my wine – with Bill nodding his approval and Harry patrolling around my feet, it was one of those crystalline moments that you want to go on forever. Bill, however, had other ideas.

'Right then,' he said 'where are we going for lunch?'

MONTY'S

FRENCH RED

Vin de Pays des Côtes Catalanes

2007

I made this smooth, ripe, fresh-tasting southern French red for everyday drinking, not for wine snobs. Vine pruning, weed ploughing (by horse), grape picking (by hand) and wine bottling (spring 2008) were all timed according to various beneficial lunar cycles. I believe working with natural forces strengthens all that is good in the soil, the vines, the grapes and the wine. It also helps keep costs down, both for wine drinkers and our planet. Monty Waldin

CERTIFIE
AB
AGRICULTURE BIOLOGIQUE

VIN ISSU DE RAISINS DE L'AGRICULTURE BIOLOGIQUE CERTIFIÉ ECOCERT SAS F32600 L'ISLE JOURDAIN.

L01/2008

12.5%vol

750ml

Mis en Bouteille à la Propriété par EARL Les Planels pour Monty Waldin 66220 St Martin de Fenouillet. Product of France. Produit de France

Contains sulfites - Contient des sulfites

Epilogue

SIX MONTHS LATER, I'M STOOD IN A PRIVATE UPSTAIRS ROOM IN A north London pub, trying to remember the words of the speech I'm about to make.

I'd rank speech-making somewhere between bomb disposal and bungee-jumping in the list of things I enjoy doing. Public speaking has always paralysed me with fear. At least this time I had the consolation of knowing that with any luck tonight's audience would have been loosened up by a glass or two of wine – more specifically, my wine. For at long last, after all the hard work, this was the official launch party for Monty's Organic Red.

Two figures immediately stood out as I scanned the room, Eric and mayor André. They'd arrived that afternoon direct from France, Eric looking tanned and relaxed and wearing a collared shirt rather than a T-shirt for possibly the first time since I'd met him, while André and his wife Marie-Thérèse looked like chic teenagers, rather than late-sixtysomethings. All three were, in fact, walking advertisements for the Mediterranean diet.

The pub, the Cock Tavern on Kilburn High Road, had been lent to me for the evening by Cliff Roberson. Working in his upmarket wine shop in London's Kensington all those years ago had helped me make the kind of wine trade contacts that ultimately had led to me make my own wine in St-Martin-de-Fenouillet.

'It's not always what you know, it's who you know,' Cliff had never tired of telling me, as we watched his wife Helga check all the wine glasses were clean and the food for the evening was perfectly presented and – in the case of the French cheese – at the right temperature. Cliff speaks like a barrow boy but is one of the most cultured men I have ever met. He succeeded like no one has before in selling bucket-loads of cheap and cheerful wines to the supermarkets while also punting rare collectible bottles to toffs.

Cliff was also one of those people that always has new ideas; he introduced Chilean wine to the UK, 'and Peruvian wines,' he'll admit too. 'Though that one wasn't quite such a success!' His latest ruse was taking over a dowdy north London pub 'that by midday was full of the drunkest people you've ever seen', and transforming it into a classy pub-restaurant and venue for live music, stand-up comics and other live events.

'So you went for a green coloured bottle in the end, I see,' said Cliff, cradling a bottle of my wine in his palm. I'd asked Cliff's advice about whether to go for a clear glass bottle or a green one. I had been worried about the recycling question: the market for recycled green glass in the UK is minimal because the UK's own wine industry is so small, whereas clear glass can be turned into bottles for home-grown products like Scotch whisky.

'The problem with putting red wine in a clear glass bottle is it can make the wine look cheap, especially when the bottle is half full,' Cliff noted. 'It'd be OK on a picnic, for example, but might not look so good in a restaurant, or during a dinner party. Worth bearing in mind as the style of wine you've made is food-friendly. And if you are worried about energy use you need to be sure it doesn't actually take more energy to produce, or clarify, the glass for a clear bottle than for a green one.'

I'd never realised just how important the 'look' of the bottle was, until I saw several people stroking – yes, stroking – the label. Very few people in the now crowded room would have known that Neil Tully, the guy that had designed the label, and who had told me exactly which type of paper stock to use, was present.

His Bath-based company, Amphora Design – an amphora being the Roman name for a wine jug – was one of the UK's leading designers for wine labels, and one of several firms I'd asked to come up with possible designs for my wine. I'd given several different designers a pretty basic brief for the kind of label I envisaged – just words, no pictures.

Some of the designers had come back with labels showing the medicinal plants used in biodynamics – stinging nettle, chamomile and so on; others had used images of the moon, and even of compost and soil in their designs. These designs were brilliant but perhaps too far ahead of their time: I was worried many normal wine drinkers just wouldn't be ready for a wine with that kind of label.

Although Neil and his team had also come up with several *avant-garde* label designs – one of which was so modern and sexy it might only have worked had my wine been destined for a lap-dancing club – he had also come up with one design that stuck to my basic outline. Neil had then transformed this into something much more textured, by using a simple colour scheme of black lettering with red – as it was a red wine – for key words.

'Everything on the front label was drawn by hand,' said Neil, looking at the label for the first time on a wine bottle. 'It's so tempting as a designer to do everything using a computer, which can spit letters out all day long. But drawing the lettering by hand gives your label the kind of look a wine farmed as far as possible by hand merits. The amount of space between the letters on the label is a bit random, as it should be when you write by hand. Computers make sure every letter is always exactly the same space apart from its neighbour.'

All of which felt appropriate somehow. Modern vineyards are planted using laser beams but before the advent of the tractor the rows would have been lined up using two posts, a piece of string and someone riding up and down on a bicycle to make a straight-ish line in the earth before planting began. Neil's haphazard lettering made me think of my rented vines, and echoed how approximately they were spaced on their mountainside.

Across the room, I spotted someone else I hadn't seen for a while: Hilary Lumsden, my former book publisher, whom I'd had that initial heart to heart with all those months before. The last time I had seen Hilary both of us were single. She was running the wine department for the world's biggest publisher of wine books, whilst I was writing some of them. Now she was a mother and, something she didn't know, I was about to become a father.

Silvana's bump was only noticeable under a loose-fitting jacket if you knew you were looking at a pregnant woman, and we had tried to keep the news quiet, at least until the first trimester was over. Most people's reaction on hearing the news was incredulity before they blurted out the question 'was it planned?'

Hils was much more tactiful, of course, and just said 'I knew you'd get there one day, Mont.'

The baby thing had kind of happened organically, if you'll pardon the pun, as neither Silvana nor I are the kind of people to sit down and discuss parenthood for months on end before taking the plunge. We'd simply arrived at the stage where if it happened, all well and good, and if not, then we'd have accepted what nature did, or did not, intend.

Hilary knew Silvana and I weren't married, but didn't start giving me chapter and verse about 'doing the decent thing'. This was in marked contrast to my school friend Andrew and his wife Emma who, having first complimented me on my wine, then began extolling the virtues of marriage. Andrew even reminded me of the summer after leaving school that we went travelling (around Europe) together.

'We were driving around Europe and I remember vividly being in some grimy bar with you, Mont, in some tourist beach resort hell-hole like Rimini and you said you'd never have kids and never get married.' Andrew smiled. 'Well, you've changed your mind on the kids part, so might as well think about the marriage bit as well. If something happened to you it would be much better for both Silvana and your baby if you were married. Think about it, anyway.'

Andrew asked where he could get a crate of my wine, and I pointed him in the direction of the generously framed Alastair Marshall, the wine buyer for the wine merchant part of a well-known brewery called Adnams.

Adnams is based in Southwold, a seaside town in Suffolk that seemed stuck in the 1950s, a plus point in my book. When my grapes were picked and had safely fermented into wine I had finally felt ready to begin the business of actually trying to sell the stuff. I had contacted a number of British wine merchants to see if any of them were interested, of which Adnams were one.

Some of the merchants wanted me to send samples of the wine. I said I would only do this when the wine was bottled – I didn't want to send wine that was still unfinished as such wine does not travel well. You end up paying lots of money for couriers and the wine never tastes great – like a cake straight out of the oven. You have to let it rest first for it to taste right. But waiting to start the sales process until the wine was bottled meant several more months of having all my capital tied up.

Alastair was different, though. He simply said straight off the bat he would come to St-Martin in January to taste my wine from the tank. 'I love the sound of what you are doing,' he told me down the phone, adding that 'besides we have lots of people on our mailing list who love Carignan-based red wines. We in the buying department like that style of wine too, and our enthusiasm seems to have rubbed off on our customers.'

As Carignan is often misunderstood and considered to be

a pretty weird grape – potentially tannic, unforgiving, and rasping in the wrong hands – what Alastair was saying was massively encouraging. Even better was that Alastair was looking to buy wines for Adnams' brand new range of wine shops – previously Adnams had just sold wine either by mail order, or via their own chain of pubs.

The wine shops were located in traditional market towns in the east of England and had been given the name 'Cellar & Kitchen'. This reflected the fact that as well as wine, beer and all the other types of drinks you'd expect to find in a normal wine shop, the Cellar & Kitchen shops also sold everything you'd need for your kitchen: pots, pans, plates, cutlery, and wine glasses, plus condiments like olive oil. This was a bonus as I didn't want my wine to end up in a traditional – meaning excruciatingly dull – wine shop with nothing but bottles to look at.

There was even a Cellar & Kitchen shop in my adopted home of Stamford, Lincolnshire. I quite liked the idea of popping down to my local wine shop and seeing my own wine in there. That's a vain thought, I know, but if you've ever worked 12-hour shifts humping heavy wine boxes in a wine shop for a meagre salary as I had maybe it's excusable.

Alastair liked my wine enough to offer to buy every last bottle. He said the price I was hoping to sell it for was a fair one, and would allow him to sell the wine to the public at a price they would also find fair. Alastair also said he hoped that if it all went well that in the future I'd rent more vineyards from Eric and make more wine.

'The only thing I'd like you to do,' he said as he tasted the wine on one of those freezing cold January days which made our noses turn runny, making wine tasting especially tricky, not to say messy, 'is to give it a light filtration at bottling. That'll just soften up some of those edgy tannins the Carignan grape brings to the wine.'

I could have softened the wine in another way – by fining it with egg white, milk powder (casein) or gelatin, but this would have meant vegetarian and vegan wine drinkers wouldn't buy it. I didn't want to fine my wine with anything foreign but was happy to follow Alastair's filtering suggestion. He, after all, knew his customers better than I did.

So when the bottling day came I asked the bottling crew to place a filter between the vat the wine was being pumped from and the bottling machine. The machinery arrived on the back of a lorry, complete with a three-man crew, who travelled around the south of France bottling wines for those – like me – who couldn't afford their own bottling machine. You simply pay a fraction of a few pence for each bottle that is filled by the machine – 6,547 to be precise in my case.

At the start of the day the chief of the bottling team had taken the temperature of the wine. He then calibrated the bottling machine to fill the bottles to a certain level.

'Wine, like any liquid, expands when it warms up,' he had explained, as he ran a few bottles through the machine as a trial run. 'Your wine is cold, so if we filled the bottles to the level you'd normally see for a 75cl bottle in a wine shop on an averagely warm day, you'd end up losing money. You'd have put around 78cl of wine in each one, instead of 75cl. It doesn't matter for a few bottles. But for a few thousand...'

I'd chosen to bottle into round shouldered, Burgundy-shaped bottles appropriate for a southern French red, not the narrow, straight-shouldered Bordeaux ones. Empty ones were placed on a conveyor at one end of the machine. Then, as they arrived underneath a series of nozzles each one was filled. A cork was punched into the bottle neck, a foil capsule was dropped and squeezed tight above this, and then the wine labels – both a front label with my name on and a back label with a short description of the wine I had written were stuck on. Finally, the filled and labelled bottles were then placed by hand into cardboard boxes holding 12 bottles. These were then stacked fifty to a pallet, leaving me with just short of eleven full pallets at the end of the day.

Back at the party, Eric asked me what I thought of the cork, as we opened another bottle and raised a glass to each other, Silvana electing for a soft drink. I said I was happy with the cork, called a DIAM, which Eric had recommended.

Cork taint can be a real problem for wine – plastic corks, foil corks and natural corks all have their problems. I'd tasted plenty of Eric's wines and had never had a 'corky' bottle. The cork he – and now I – used was made by grinding bark from the cork oak tree, then cleaning it of the impurities that make for 'corky' wine. Such wines smell like hamster cages. The cleaned cork dust is compressed back together using a food-grade polymer to make it cork-shaped.

This was a bit of a compromise as obviously a man-made polymer is not 100% 'organic' (although as it is part of the packaging and not the wine this doesn't stop the wine being considered organic or biodynamic). But, as Silvana said, with her economist's hat on, 'it makes no sense to spend all that time, effort and money making a wine that gets spoiled by choosing the wrong bottle cork.'

Eric, meanwhile, was re-filling his glass for at least the third time. He drinks very little wine normally, spending most of his time spitting wine out during professional wine tastings, but he was clearly enjoying himself – and my wine. As he gulped down another mouthful he said to Silvana, while grinning at me, 'Not bad for a beginner. I'm going to have to keep my eye on Monty, you know!'

My speech was a predictably garbled, nervy affair which, to my relief, turned out OK in the end. The one person who wasn't there to hear it, sadly, was Bill Baker.

The night after Alastair had tasted my wine in France in January we bumped into each other in a restaurant in Perpignan – there was a big organic wine fair on in the town we'd both been attending. Bill had died of a suspected heart attack the night before.

'He was wine tasting with us up at Southwold only last week for an Adnams fine wine do,' said Alastair.

Silvana and I had squeezed – along with several hundred other mourners – into Wells cathedral for Bill's send-off less than a fortnight later. His coffin was so tall and wide the pall bearers had trouble getting it into the cathedral – you could almost hear Bill roaring with laughter at their plight.

Bill had certainly seemed to get the most out of life, valuing what was important: good food, good wine, good company, his family.

Simple really, but so hard to stick to in our helter-skelter century. Bill had even told me he was hoping that once he had got his kids through school he'd be able to run a little farm in a forest – he loved trees and the wood they gave – in Italy, with his wife and children.

We all have a dream, and that was Bill's. I don't know what my future holds, or even what my dream is, but I do know I am renting enough vineyards from Eric to make some white and rosé wine, as well as more red wine next year.

I also know now something I have suspected for a long time: that the best place to write about wine is on the back label of bottles of wine you grew and made yourself.

Acknowledgements

I HAD THOUGHT THAT BECOMING A WINEMAKER WOULD ALLOW ME TO abandon my writing desk at least semi-permanently, but Gordon Wise of Curtis Brown was persistent enough to convince me that writing a book about my experiences really was a good idea while Tom Bromley and his team of publishers at Anova agreed not just to publish it but to go the extra mile by commissioning both Lotte Oldfield to produce the original artwork, and Hilary Lumsden, my favourite wine editor, to keep the text on track.

If you are considering moving to France your life there will be a lot easier if you end up in a village with a mayor as dynamic, practical and well-organised as André Foulquier of St-Martin-de-Fenouillet. I was fortunate enough to have been given a hands-on view of what life as a winegrower there would be like by Roy Richards, Mark Walford and Gérard Gauby of the Le Soula winery. Tom and Nathalie Lubbe of Domaine Matassa, Richard Case of Domaine de la Pertuisane in Maury, Jean Pla of Fenouillèdes Séléction in Maury and Philippe Mario of Stratégie Conseils in Perpignan all in varying ways helped render more manageable France's potentially overmighty bureaucratic burden.

As for day-to-day life Brigitte Benet and Houccine Amar Amghari of the Auberge Taïchac in St-Martin-de-Fenouillet proved an irresistible social focus. Martine Bozec of the local mayor's office had the knack of finding me whatever official form I needed for my 'phone, van, or even bath. Patrick da Silva of the Peugeot garage in St-Paul somehow kept my van from seizing up. Osteopaths Rupert Elverson in Tuscany, and Frédéric Py in France consistently kept my back from doing the same. Andy Green, John Holms and Peter Opie rose to every building challenge, despite as ex-pats being heavily involved in their own life-changing projects in France.

Francis and José del Bano, Jean-Pierre and Lucette Betrand, Claudie Beylal, Viviane and Arnaud Dautas, Joep Graler, Jacques and Josiane Larroche, Genévieve Pla, Jean-Luc, Eric and Sylvie Rochette, Daniel Salinas, the Sire family (Christine, Marinette and André in St-Martin and Serge and Marie-Anne in Fosse), Veronica and Nicolaas van Lawich, Gaston Foulquier, and above all the ageless René and Adeline Pastoret, all generously provided food, tools or advice to make my social life, allotment, house or vineyard run smoothly.

Eric and Corinne Laguerre's decision to rent me not only a vineyard with organic certification in a prime site but one with the status of a cherished family heirloom was an act of both extreme recklessless and kindness. Eric's vineyard crew, especially Pascal Bozec, Dominique Bernard, and Jacques Bozec made me realise just how far removed from the day-to-day practicalities of winegrowing wine writers like me who spend most days in ivory towers of our own construction are. Thanks to them all and to everyone else who helped pick the grapes at a moment's notice, ensuring my first harvest was a healthy and happy one.

Beverley Blanning MW and her husband Geoff, Emma Bowman and James Cameron, and Graham and Charlotte Wynde were generous hosts during trips to the UK, as were Francesca Fiore and Savino Carlone during trips to Italy.

John Atkinson MW, Bill Baker of Reid Wines near Bristol, Justin Howard-Sneyd MW of Waitrose, Jem Gardener of organic wine specialists Vinceremos in Leeds, Alastair Marshall of Adnams in Southwold, Jane Masters MW, Tim Atkin MW, Neil Palmer and Lance Pigott of organic wine specialists Vintage Roots in Berkshire, Cliff Roberson of Roberson Wine Merchant in Kensington, Neil Tully of wine label designers Amphora Design in Bath and Olivia Mailhes of Oeneo Bouchage in Céret, France were all unstinting in their efforts to help me bottle, market and sell the wine.

Ant Palmer, Hugh Fairs, Sharon Stansfield, Gemma lys Cooper, Elaine Foster, Jenny Spearing, Sarah Sapper, Luc Tremoulet, Dominique Margot, Alex Jean Pierre, David Lawrence, Shelia Humphreys, Nigel Farrell, Jamie Munro and Paul Sommers of Tiger Aspect Productions all helped make a necessarily relentless filming schedule as enjoyable and unintrusive as possible, as did Cat Jeffcock, Lynda Regnier and Linzie Bisset.

Harry, my adopted dog, justified his tag as man's (if not necessarily either a goose or a chicken's) best friend. Finally, my partner Silvana was the intellectual, practical and emotional rock upon which this project was built.

For more about organic and biodynamic wines in general, visit
www.montywaldin.com

Photography

Front cover photography by René Pastoret
Back cover photography by Toby Merritt © Tiger Aspect
Productions Ltd 2007
Monty biography photo by Jonathan Glynn-Smith
(www.jonathanglynnsmith.com)

Plate section photography

All photographs of Monty by Silvana Carlone except;
Section Two; Photos 2 & 5 by Ant Palmer
Section Three; Photo 6 by Ant Palmer
Section Two; Photo 4 by Alex Jean Pierre
Section Three; Photo 10 by Gemma Lys Cooper
Section Three; Photo 13 by Graham Wynde
Section Three; Photos 17 & 20 by Toby Merritt © Tiger Aspect
Productions Ltd 2007

All other photography taken by Monty Waldin

All Photography © Monty Waldin 2007 except where indicated above.

Label designed by Neil Tully MW and his team at
Amphora Design, Bath, UK.

Chateau Monty logo designed by Tony Bannister
Illustrations by Lotte Oldfield
(www.lotteoldfield.com)